Two of the contributors to this volume have died since the Institutes were held: Rev. William J. Devlin, S.J., and Dr. Gregory Zilboorg. It is to the memory of these two distinguished men that this book is dedicated in gratitude and appreciation. The papers do not pretend to provide minute and magical techniques, the application of which will automatically bring about cures. They do attempt to provide a genuine *understanding* of the psychological implications of some spiritual problems and of the means that are to hand, in the combined and devoted labors of theologians and behavioral scientists for achievement of balanced, mental health.

PERSONALITY AND SEXUAL PROBLEMS

THE PASTORAL PSYCHOLOGY SERIES,
NUMBER 1

PERSONALITY AND SEXUAL PROBLEMS

IN
PASTORAL PSYCHOLOGY

Edited by

WILLIAM C. BIER, S.J.

FORDHAM UNIVERSITY PRESS • NEW YORK

Table of Contents

Preface

In 1955 the Psychology Department at Fordham University inaugurated a series of Pastoral Psychology Institutes intended to acquaint members of the clergy with the findings of psychology, psychiatry, sociology, and allied disciplines in the belief that the insights provided by these relatively new and fast developing behavioral sciences would prove helpful to clergymen in their pastoral work. The Institutes have been continued on an alternate year basis since that time, the 1963 Institute having been the fifth and the most recent in the series.

The Institutes have all followed the same general pattern, being conducted for five days, Monday through Friday, of a single week toward the end of June. Although they were designed primarily to provide psychological insight into pastoral problems for the clergy attending, it is evident that these Institutes provide much more than mere information. They are a living experience in which the give-and-take of interchange during discussion, and the day-by-day association with people of other professional specialties, brings about significant changes in feelings and attitudes. A better mutual understanding among psychiatrists, psychologists, and the clergy may be accounted one of the principal gains of the Institute series. This is an experience which no amount of reading can provide, one which comes only through personal contact and living experience. Through the kind of inter-professional contact provided in the Institutes comes a clarification of role and an increase in mutual respect. The clergyman sees clearly that there are some pastoral problems which are beyond his resources and which require handling by a professional psychologist or psychiatrist. Members of the latter professions in their turn are enabled, through experiences provided by the Institutes, to appreciate more fully the role of religion and religious values in the lives of their patients. Mental health is a large and indeed a common problem calling for the combined resources of religion no less than those of psychiatry.

The papers presented in the present volume are derived from the 1955 and 1957 Institutes. This is the reason why the current volume is number 1 in the Pastoral Psychology Series being published by the Fordham University Press, even though it has been preceded in print by two other volumes in the series. Volume 2, containing the proceedings of the 1959 Institute under the title: *Problems in Addiction: Alcohol and Drug Addiction,* was the first to be published. It was followed by Volume 3, *The Adolescent: His Search for Understanding,* the outcome of the 1961 Institute. The 1963 Institute which concerned "The Priest and Marriage Problems" will provide the material for volume 4 in the series and will be published shortly.

The proceedings of the 1955 and 1957 Institutes had originally been issued in limited, paper-covered editions, and hence they were temporarily by-passed in publication in favor of the two more recent Institutes. Despite the fact that copies of these earlier volumes have long been out of print, there has been a continuing demand for some of their materials which are available nowhere else. It also became evident that these topics were of interest to a considerably wider group of persons than the clergymen for whom they were originally intended. For these reasons, a permanent place was reserved for them as volume 1 in the Pastoral Psychology Series. This place is now filled by the present volume.

Not all of the materials published in the original two volumes have been reproduced in the present one. Timeliness of the material in fast-moving and rapidly changing fields, availability elsewhere, and treatment in subsequent volumes of the series were some of the criteria employed in determining the materials which have been included.

The authors of all the principal papers were contacted and given an opportunity to up-date the material in whatever way seemed appropriate to them in view of the projected reissue after seven and nine years respectively. Some of the contributors found little which needed to be changed, others made limited changes, while one author rewrote his paper entirely. All bibliographical references and biographical notes about the contributors have been brought up to date. The present volume is, therefore, a selective reissue of the earlier two volumes with appropriate up-dating of the material presented.

The three most recent Institutes have each been built around a single topic, as the titles given above will indicate. However, the first two Institutes, those represented in the present volume, treated a variety of topics judged important in pastoral work. Anxiety, guilt, scrupulosity, personal and sexual development, homosexuality, masturbation, and sex education—these will at once be recognized as genuine pastoral problems and equally as areas where the behavioral disciplines represented by the Institute faculty have something to contribute to the clergyman who is confronted by such problems in his pastoral work. It is felt, therefore, that the present volume, to which has been given the somewhat general title: *Personality and Sexual Problems in Pastoral Psychology,* serves as a good introduction to the Pastoral Psychology series as a whole, presenting as it does an over-view of a number of typical pastoral problems, and leaving to subsequent volumes in the series the more detailed treatment of more specific topics.

The first three topics treated in the current volume, namely, anxiety, guilt, and scrupulosity came from the 1955 Institute, the others from 1957. In the 1955 Institute a formal discussant was appointed for each of the principal papers and a summary of each topic was provided on the final day of the Institute. This practice was not continued in subsequent Institutes because it appeared to involve too much repetition and because it seemed that the time involved could be more constructively used in other ways. It accounts, however, for the fact that the first three papers in the present volume are followed by a discussion and by a summary at the end, a feature not found in the case of the remaining topics derived as they were from the 1957 Institute. It has been our experience in conducting the Institutes that the informal discussion after the formal papers constitutes one of the most valuable features of the Institute for those who are present, but that almost nothing of this kind of discussion can be captured for presentation in published form. This interchange between members and faculty of the Institute is a living experience which cannot be reproduced in printed form. It is one of the genuine advantages accruing to those who attend an Institute in contrast to those who are able merely to read the proceedings.

In the time which has elapsed since the presentation of the papers included in this volume, death has overtaken two of our most distinguished contributors, actually those whose contributions occupy the first two places in the book. Father William J. Devlin, S.J. who contributed the paper on anxiety and abnormal fears died of a heart attack on January 7, 1961 at the premature age of 55. Dr. Gregory Zilboorg, well known psychoanalyst and prolific author, who wrote the paper on guilt, died on September 17, 1959 after a brief illness. He was 69. It is to the memory of these two distinguished men that the current volume is dedicated in gratitude and appreciation.

In a more happy vein, it is a pleasure to report that it was the initial meeting at the time of the 1957 Institute of two additional contributors, Father George Hagmaier, C.S.P. and Father Robert W. Gleason, S.J. which led to their subsequent collaboration in the volume which has become so well known: *Counseling the Catholic* (Sheed and Ward, 1959). Both of these writers used the contributions which they had initially made to the Institute in the section on homosexuality as chapters in the above-mentioned book. Similarly, Father John C. Ford, S.J. first presented at the Institute in his paper on the moral aspects of autosexuality material which subsequently appeared in *Contemporary Moral Problems,* Volume I: *Questions in Fundamental Moral Theology* (Newman, 1958), which he published in collaboration with Father Gerald Kelly, S.J.

The late Father Devlin in his paper on anxiety had a caution for the Institute members which bears repeating for the benefit of the larger group who will read these pages. "There is no question here," he wrote "of such things (so often asked for by the untrained) of minute, specific, magical techniques for handling problems, as if the patient were a mechanical robot who recovers miraculously when you produce the proper technique." The reader will not find in the pages which follow any ready-made, antecedently-elaborated formulae for the treatment of psychological problems, for the all-sufficient reason that any such proposed solutions are pseudo rather than real, illusory rather than genuine. What the book does attempt to provide is a genuine *understanding* of these conditions, which is the first step toward any helpful approach. Father Mailloux says much the same thing in a slightly different context when he writes ". . . the dialogue (between confessor and penitent) is pursued at different levels of communication and, sadly enough, oftentimes without the slightest realization of the fact that neither one is actually comprehending what the other is talking about." The priest who reads the pages of this book will, we think, be helped in his dialogue with his psychologically troubled penitents.

The Pastoral Psychology Institutes are arranged by a Committee formed for that purpose. Dr. Alexander A. Schneiders, Rev. Joseph G. Keegan, S.J., and this writer served on the Committees for both the 1955 and the 1957 Institutes. In both instances Dr. Schneiders was Committee Chairman. In the first Institute we were aided by Rev. Vincent de P. Lee, S.J., and Rev. Victor R. Yanitelli, S.J., and in the second Institute by Rev. Robert W. Gleason, S.J., and Rev.

William G. Lawlor, S.J. I gladly take the opportunity available to me as editor of the proceedings to thank these men for their generous donation of time and to gratefully acknowledge their contribution to the planning and conduct of the Institutes. Genuine gratitude is expressed also to the New York State Department of Mental Hygiene whose partial support of these two Institutes enabled the Department of Psychology to launch the series.

It is a pleasure finally to acknowledge the contribution of the Fordham University Press and particularly that of its Director, Rev. Edwin A. Quain, S.J. whose interest, initiative, and resourcefulness have been indispensable in transforming the Pastoral Institutes into a published series in Pastoral Psychology.

December, 1963 William C. Bier, S.J.

PERSONALITY AND SEXUAL PROBLEMS

Anxiety and Abnormal Fears

WILLIAM J. DEVLIN, S.J.

Father William J. Devlin, S.J. was a man of exceptionally broad attainments as indicated by the degrees which he held: Licentiate in Philosophy (St. Louis University, 1933), and in Theology (St. Louis University, 1937), Master of Social Work (Catholic University, 1940), Ph.D. in Psychology (Catholic University, 1942), and M.D. (Loyola University, 1947). After a series of residences and fellowships in psychiatry, Father Devlin assumed the post of Clinical Instructor of Psychiatry and Neurology at Loyola University, Chicago, in 1953. In his work at the University, and in his frequent lectures to the public, and before learned societies, he dedicated himself principally to promoting rapport and understanding between psychiatry and religion. Father Devlin died of a heart attack on January 8, 1961, at the age of 55, when he was at the height of his career.

The footsteps of modern man have been dogged by a nameless, formless, psychic uneasiness; a diffuse apprehension of mind that is unspecific, vague, objectless, painful, accompanied by feelings of uncertainty, helplessness, menacing expectation, panic. This experience is called anxiety—a reaction on the part of man in the face of danger, danger which threatens some value which the individual holds essential to his existence as a personality.

1

Anxiety differs from fear because fear is a reaction to a specific danger which can be located spatially and to which an adjustment can, at least in theory, be made. An individual experiences various fears on the basis of a security pattern he has developed; but in anxiety it is this security pattern itself which is threatened. In fear the relation of the personality to a given object is threatened, and, if that object can be removed, either by reassurance or appropriate flight, the apprehension disappears. But, since anxiety attacks the foundation, core or essence of the personality, the individual cannot "stand outside" the threat, cannot objectify it, and thereby is powerless to take steps to meet it. He feels caught, or, if the anxiety is severe, overwhelmed; he is afraid but uncertain of what he fears.

Anxiety is objectless because it strikes at the basis of the psychological structure on which the perception of one's self as distinct from the world of objects occurs. Mounting anxiety reduces self-awareness. In proportion to the increase in anxiety, the awareness of one's self as subject related to objects in the external world is confused. In anxiety the individual is less able to see himself in relation to stimuli and hence less able to make adequate evaluation of the stimuli. In severe cases anxiety is often experienced as a "dissolution of the self." The objectless nature of anxiety arises from the fact that the security base of the individual is threatened, and since it is in terms of this security base that the individual has been able to experience himself as a self in relation to objects, the distinction between subject and object also breaks down.

The neurological concomitants of anxiety are manifested by an overstimulation of the autonomic nervous system. The person suffers from a rapid heart, palpitation, precardial discomfort, nausea, diarrhea, desire to urinate, dyspnea, and a feeling of choking or suffocation. The pupils are dilated, the face is flushed, the skin perspires; the person suffers from paresthesias and tremulousness, feels dizzy or faint, and often has a sense of weakness and impending death. Restlessness is acute; the person may express beseeching and apprehensive appeals for help. If one pays attention exclusively to somatic symptoms, one may easily be led astray; thus it happens that the general practitioner sometimes treats such conditions as cases of indigestion, ulcers, functional heart disease, suspected tuberculosis, thyrotoxicosis, neurocirculatory asthenia, hyperinsulinism or dysinsulinism.

If the anxiety attack becomes chronic the person may experience difficulty in falling asleep, may be disturbed by fearful dreams, suffers from coarse tremors or trembling, complains of a "band around the head" or of a "quivering in the stomach." He is absent-minded and seems worried without knowing about what or why. He complains that his mind is in a constant daze and that he is unable to control his thoughts. He is apprehensive, is afraid to be alone, and yet does not desire conversation. He feels too tired to attempt anything constructive and continually seeks a physical explanation for his distressing mental state.

Because anxiety is the common psychic denominator underlying all mental upset, emotional disorder, and behavioral maladjustment, it will be most profitable to speak about the various types of anxiety, its varied manifestations, so that we can obtain a clear-cut picture of this important psychic phenomenon, leaving to the later period a discussion of some of the practical problems relating to anxiety and pastoral work.

NORMAL ANXIETY

The phenomenological description of anxiety given above is applicable to different kinds of anxiety, especially to normal, neurotic, and pseudo or defensive anxiety. *Normal* anxiety is, like any anxiety, a reaction to threats to values the individual holds essential to his existence as a personality; but normal anxiety is not disproportionate to the objective threat, does not involve mechanisms of intra-psychic conflict like repression and dissociation, and hence does not require neurotic defense mechanisms for its management. Thus, it can be confronted constructively on the level of conscious awareness, or can be relieved if the objective situation is altered. The undifferentiated and diffuse reactions of very young infants to threats such as falling or not being fed, fall into the category of normal anxiety, as do the seried experiences undergone by a child as he progresses through the development process.

Another common form of normal anxiety is that inhering in man's contingency, that is, his vulnerability to the powers of nature, to sickness, and to eventual death. Another is that related to the development of each human being as an individual in a social matrix, a world of other individuals. As seen most clearly in the development of the child, this growth as an individual in a context of social relationships involves a progressive breaking of emotionally dependent ties with parents, which in turn involves greater or lesser crises and clashes with parents. Otto Rank (1929) has emphasized that normal anxiety inheres in all experiences of "separation" throughout the individual's life. If these potentially anxiety-creating experiences are negotiated successfully, if they are met by constructive development and increasing employment of the person's own courage and powers, they lead not only to greater independence on the part of the child, but also to re-establishment of relations with the parents and other persons on newer levels of daily functioning.

The origins of normal or objective anxiety are simple. Normal anxiety is an expression of the capacity of the organism to react to threat; this capacity is innate and has an inherited neurophysiological *modus operandi*. Freud remarks that the "tendency toward objective anxiety" is inherent in the child, his belief being that it is an expression of the self-preservative instinct, and has an obvious biological utility. There is no inheritance of specific anxieties, but simply the general capacity to react to threat. Nor is the capacity for anxiety learned, although the quantities and forms of anxiety in a given individual are learned. This means that normal anxiety is a function of the organism *qua* organism; every human being will experience anxiety in situations of threat to its vital values. But what the individual regards as a situation of threat to vital values is largely due to learning or experience.

Particular foci of anxiety are the expression of patterns which develop out of the interrelation of the individual's capacities for reacting to threat with this environment and conditioning. The matrix in which these patterns develop, i.e., in which the conditioning occurs, is the family situation in particular, which in turn is part of the larger general culture in which the individual lives. The kinds of anxiety experienced by a given individual are culturally conditioned in the sense that the values or goals held by an individual to be essential to his existence as a personality are products specified largely by the culture; while the quantities of anxiety experienced by a given individual are conditioned by the degree of unity and stability in his culture. If the culture is relatively unified and stable the individual will be able to orient himself (whether he is in accord with the cultural mores or not), and his experiences of anxiety will be relatively less frequent and less tense.

POSITIVE AND CONSTRUCTIVE USE OF NORMAL ANXIETY

It is through the positive use of normal anxiety, by the confronting and moving through anxiety-creating experiences, that self-actualization—that is, the expression and creative use of the individual's capacities—can occur. The capacity to bear anxiety is one measure of self-hood. In fine, all the positive aspects of self-hood—inner-freedom, self-direction, enlarged self-awareness, responsibility, creativity—develop as the individual confronts, moves through, and overcomes anxiety, in other words, as he uses normal anxiety positively and constructively.

And how do we use normal anxiety positively and constructively? Kurt Goldstein (1939, 1940) has stated that every human being encounters frequent anxiety shocks in the course of his normal development, and that his capacities can be actualized only through an affirmative response to these threats to his existence. Goldstein gives as a simple illustration the healthy child's learning to walk despite the fact that he falls and gets hurt many times in the process. When we try to understand the constructive use of normal anxiety from the objective side, we note that it is characterized by the individual's confronting the anxiety-creating situation directly, admitting his apprehensions, but moving ahead despite the anxiety. In other words, it consists of moving through anxiety-creating experiences rather than moving around them or retrenching in the face of them.

These ways of meeting anxiety were described countless times in studies of anxiety and fear among soldiers in combat during World War II. The most constructive attitude consisted in the soldier's frankly admitting his fear or anxiety about going into battle, but being subjectively prepared to act despite his apprehension. It was frequently pointed out in these studies of soldiers that courage did not consist in the absence of fear and anxiety but in the capacity to move ahead even though one is afraid. This constructive confronting of normal anxiety in daily life and in crises which require moral rather than physical courage (such as the crises in self-development often attended with profound anxiety, which occur during psychotherapy), is sometimes accompanied by the affect of "adventure." At other times, however, when the anxiety-creating experience is more severe, confronting it may entail no pleasurable affect whatever, but is accomplished only by the sheerest kind of dogged determination.

When we view the process subjectively—that is, when we ask what is going on within an individual that enables him to confront the danger directly whereas others in the same situation may flee— we discover some very significant data. To draw an illustration again from the studies of soldiers, it has been pointed out that often the subjective motivation which enabled soldiers to confront dangers was their conviction that the threat connected with backing out was greater than the threat faced in battle. Expressed positively, the values achieved in confronting the danger were greater than the values of flight. For many a soldier the common value was probably the expectation of his fellow soldiers; he must not let the group down; he must not appear "yellow" to his buddies. So a person is subjectively prepared to confront unavoidable anxiety constructively when he is convinced (consciously or unconsciously) that the values to be gained in moving ahead are greater than those to be gained by escape. Just as anxiety arises when the values the individual identifies with his existence are threatened, so the individual confronts anxiety-creating experiences and moves ahead without succumbing to them when the values he identifies with his existence are stronger than the threat.

If one pictures anxiety as resulting from conflict between the threat and the values the person identifies with his existence, one can say that neurosis and emotional morbidity mean that the struggle is won by the threat. The constructive approach to anxiety, on the other hand, means that the struggle is won by the individual's values which of course vary with each person. Most people are motivated by elemental values which they may never articulate, such as the need to preserve life itself, or some elemental trend toward health. On other levels social prestige may be a very important value. Another is the satisfaction to be achieved by the expansion and wider use of one's powers. They may be the classical, hedonistic, stoic, humanistic values; they may be the values centering around what someone described as the "frames of orientation and devotion" given in classical religions, whose ultimate constructive effect consists of the individual's intensive love of God.

NEUROTIC ANXIETY

Besides normal anxiety, there is neurotic anxiety, an anxiety difficult to understand and to find solution for because of the neurotic element present. Essentially, it is the reaction of a person inordinately vulnerable to threat that is disproportionate to the objective danger. It involves repression and other forms of intrapsychic conflict, and hence, as a result, is managed by various forms of retrenchment of activity and awareness such as inhibition, the development of symptoms, and the outbreak of varied neurotic mechanisms. It cannot be confronted constructively on the level of conscious awareness, and cannot be relieved if the objective situation is altered because it will attach itself to another objective situation.

These characteristics are related to each other; for example, the reaction is disproportionate to the objective danger because some intrapsychic conflict is involved, which explains the vulnerability to relatively minor objective threats. Thus the reaction is never disproportionate to the subjective threat. It will likewise be seen that each one of the above characteristics involves a subjective reference. The definition of neurotic anxiety can be made only when the subjective approach to the problem—that is, the approach based on the question of what is going on intrapsychically in the individual—is included.

People with neurotic anxiety are those who are inordinately vulnerable to threat, and their incapacity for coping adequately with threat is not objective but subjective, that is, their age and objective capacities fit them to cope adequately with threat so that their incapacity is due not to objective weakness but rather to inner psychological patterns and conflicts. This includes fear of their own impulse claims (Freud), or fear of their own hostile or excessively dependent feelings, and the expression of these feelings because it would result in a real danger to them. This danger includes punishment or disapproval of others upon whom they are essentially dependent or at least on whom they deeply depend, this dependency preventing them from using their coping capacity.

As a general statement we can say that these conflictual patterns usually have their genesis in those situations in early childhood in which the child was not able objectively to meet the problems of a threatening interpersonal situation, and when at the same time he could not admit consciously the source of the threat (as, for example, parental rejection). Hence repression of the object of the anxiety is a central feature of neurotic anxiety. Although the repression generally begins in the child's relation with his parents, it continues in the form of repression of similar threats as they occur throughout life. Repression of fear of the threat results in the individual's being unaware of the sources of his apprehension; thus in neurotic anxiety there is a specific reason why the affect is "objectless" in addition to the general source mentioned earlier of the objectless nature of all anxiety.

The repression itself (or dissociation or blocking off of awareness) which occurs in neurotic anxiety renders the individual more vulnerable to threat and thus increases his anxiety. First, repression sets up inner contradictions within the personality, thus making for a shaky psychological equilibrium bound to be easily threatened in the course of everyday life. Secondly, because of the repression the individual is less able to distinguish and fight against real dangers as they occur. For example, the person who represses a good deal of aggression and hostility may at the same time assume a compliant and passive attitude toward others, which in turn increases the likelihood that he will be exploited by others. Finally, repression increases the individual's feeling of helplessness in that it involves a curtailing of his own autonomy, an inner retrenchment and shelving of his own power.

INTRAPSYCHIC CONFLICT IN NEUROTIC ANXIETY

But what is the nature of this intrapsychic conflict present in neurotic and not in normal anxiety? What are its origins, and what are the various theories of conflict? It is easy to see that conflict is opposition, and intrapsychic conflict is opposition between the psychological elements within an individual himself; he is like a house divided against itself, a house that is not strong, and hence he will not be able to withstand the threatening situations of life at all as well as one not so divided.

With regard to the specific origins of neurotic anxiety, Freud centers his attention chiefly on the birth trauma and the fear of castration. At first he treated both as literal sources of anxiety, but later he employed them more symbolically—the birth experience stood for separation from the mother, and castration for the loss of a prized object of value. Present Freudian analysts have added another use to the term "castration," making it the equivalent of punishment. But if separation from the mother is seen as the origin of anxiety (or rather conflict with consequent experience of anxiety), the crucial issue is the meaning of this separation, that is, what is the nature of the relation between the child and its mother that the child should feel threatened by separation, and what particular values significant for the child are threatened?

Since anxiety is a reaction to a threat to values held essential to the existence of the personality, and since the human organism owes its existence to its relation to certain significant persons in its infancy, the essential values are originally the security patterns existing between the infant and these significant persons. Hence there is considerable agreement that the relation between the child and its parents is crucial for the origins of anxiety. In Sullivan's concept of neurotic anxiety, the mother occupies the significant position. The mother is not only the source of satisfaction of the infant's physical needs; she is the source of its over-all emotional security as well, and whatever endangers that relationship is a threat to the infant's total status in his interpersonal world. Hence Sullivan (1953) holds that anxiety has its origin in the infant's apprehension of disapproval by its mother. This apprehension occurs via empathy between infant and mother long before the infant is sufficiently mature to be consciously aware of approval or disapproval. For Horney (1937, 1939) basic anxiety has its origin in the child's conflict between his dependency on his parents and his hostility toward them because of this dependency. Others hold that anxiety has its origin in the conflicts centering around the developing individuality of the child and the need to relate to other persons in the community.

It will be noted that the term "conflict" emerges in the last two statements. Neurotic anxiety always involves inner conflict. There is often a reciprocal relation between the two: the state of persistent, unresolved conflict may lead eventually to the person's repressing one side of the conflict which then produces neurotic anxiety; and anxiety, in turn, brings in its train feelings of helplessness, impotence, and a paralysis of action which tend to cause or increase psychological conflict. Freud (1926) felt that the conflict underlying anxiety is between instinctual needs within the individual and social prohibitions. His topological description is that the ego is caught between the id (instinctual urges, chiefly of libidinous character) on the one hand and superego (cultural requirements) on the other. The threat which brings on anxiety is seen by Freud as the threat of frustration of libido or, what amounts to the same thing, the threat of punishment if the libido is gratified. Others state that frustration of itself does not cause conflict. The basic question is, rather, what essential value is threatened by the frustration?

Some persons have a great deal of sexual expression (that is, suffer no frustration) and still have much anxiety. Others bear considerable sexual privation and are not prey to excessive anxiety. Thus something more than the need for mere sexual gratification is occurring. The problem is not the frustration in itself, but whether the frustration threatens some mode of interpersonal relationship which the individual holds vital to his security and self-esteem. In our culture, sexual activity is often identified by the individual with his sense of power, esteem and prestige; in such a person the threat of sexual frustration is very likely to cause conflict and anxiety.

Many do not disagree with Freud's (1926) phenomenological description of the frequent relation between sexual repression and anxiety in his Victorian culture (as well as in our own culture to a large extent). But this relation is due to the fact that sexual prohibitions are very frequently the means in our culture of authoritative constraint of the child by his parents, and later by society through moral and religious codes. These constraints result in a suppression of the child's development and expansion. Sexual impulses will then involve a conflict with these authorities (usually parents) and will arouse the prospect of punishment by and alienation from the authorities; and this conflict will in many cases certainly produce anxiety. But this does not mean that libidinal frustration itself causes conflict and anxiety.

The threat of frustration of a biological urge does not cause conflict and anxiety unless that urge is identified with some value essential to the existence of the personality. When Sullivan (1947) states that the activities directed toward the pursuit of security are ordinarily of much more importance to the human being than those directed toward physical satisfactions like hunger and sex, he does not mean to discount the biological (in its limited sense) aspect of behavior, but to indicate that the physical needs are subsumed under the more comprehensive need of the organism to maintain and extend its total security and power.

For Horney (1937) the early conflict in the child between his dependency on his parents and his hostility toward them sets the basis for the contradictory trends in the adult personality which underlie later anxiety. Anxiety and hostility are interrelated: anxiety gives rise to hostility and hostility in anxious persons is always related to basic anxiety. The anxious child is excessively dependent upon his parents, but at the same time hostile toward them in proportion to his dependence. In adult patterns this interrelationship between anxiety and hostility often takes the form of the anxious individual's being very closely attached to some other person, for example, a wife or husband (due not only to excessive dependence but because of guilt over the hostile feelings), but simultaneously feeling hostile toward this other person because the attachment not only symbolizes the individual's own helplessness but also increases his feelings of weakness.

In both the child and adult the hostility will be repressed in proportion to the dependence, for fear of arousing counter-hostility or alienating the very persons on whom one is so dependent. Repressed hostility generates more anxiety in several ways, among them being: (1) the repressed hostility is often projected on other persons, and thus the feeling that one lives in a hostile and threatening world is increased; (2) the individual who is struggling against repressed hostility is less able to distinguish and protect himself against real threats and exploitation, and hence he is rendered more helpless. Repressed hostility is thus a specific source of anxiety. The effect of anxiety is more basic because the hostility would not have to be repressed in the first place except that the individual is anxious and fears counter-hostility or alienation. Neurotic strategies are devices for preserving security despite the presence of underlying conflicts. Whenever these neurotic strategies are threatened, the conflicts are re-activated and neurotic anxiety results.

However, the more positive expression of the conflict may lie in the deeper groundwork of man's two-fold need for dependence and independence, or in man's two-fold relationship to himself (as an individual) and to others and God (as a social being). Rollo May (1950) hints at this when he suggests that there is a common denominator in these conflicts that underlie anxiety, namely, the inter-mutual relationship of the individual and his community. On the one hand the human being develops as an individual, unique and, to an extent, discrete from other individuals. Actions, no matter how much conditioned by social factors, are still actions of an individual. At the point in development at which self-awareness emerges, there also emerges a measure of freedom and responsibility in each individual action. But, on the other hand, this individual develops at every moment as a member of a social group upon which he is dependent not only for the early satisfaction of his biological needs but also for his emotional security. It is only in interaction with other individuals in a social nexus that the development of a "self" and the development of personality are understandable. Personality is essentially an interpersonal phenomenon.

The infant's and child's existence consists of a progressive differentiation of himself from his parents. When he is viewed from the individual aspect of the interpersonal relationship, his growth consists of decreasing dependence on parents and increasing reliance upon and use of his own powers. When he is viewed from the social aspect of the interpersonal relationship, the child's growth consists of his progressive relating to the parents on new levels (dependence of a new type on a higher level). Blocking of development at either pole of this relationship engenders psychological conflict, the end result of which is anxiety. Where there is "freedom from dependence" without corresponding interrelationship, there is the anxiety of the defiant and isolated individual, hostile toward those whom he believes to be the occasion of his isolation. Where there is dependence without freedom (symbiosis), there will be a lack of capacity to act on the basis of one's own powers and therefore a readiness to be threatened by every new situation which requires autonomous action, and a hostility toward those whom one regards as instrumental in the suppression of his capacities and freedom. In each case the hostility increases the conflict and the neurotic anxiety.

Another mechanism will also be present, namely, repression. The utilized capacities and the unfulfilled needs are not lost but repressed (or better still, tied up in the conflict). The phenomenon is often observed clinically that the defiantly independent, isolated individual is repressing considerable need and desire to make affirmative relationships with other people, and the symbiotically dependent person is repressing the need and desire to act independently. The mechanism of repression itself decreases autonomy and increases helplessness and conflict. In the last analysis, therefore, the source of conflict and neurotic anxiety lies in the interpersonal relationship between the infant and its mother or mother surrogate, and different types of mothers answer the dependent needs of their children differently.

HANDLING OF NEUROTIC ANXIETY

How does a person handle neurotic anxiety, that is, the anxiety of the conflict which is the primary etiological phenomenon in all neurotic patterns, and the common psychic denominator in all mental and emotional disturbances and behavioral maladjustments, including the special group called psychosomatic or psychophysiological illnesses?

The negative methods of dealing with neurotic anxiety are really methods of allaying or avoiding the anxiety without solving the conflict which causes it. In other terms, this means evading the conflict situation rather than resolving it. These negative methods range all the way from behavior traits like shyness, tenseness, timidity, apprehensiveness, sensitivity to the opinion of others, getting embarrassed easily, to personality traits like a tendency to worry, inferiority feelings, experiencing difficulties in making decisions and being afraid of making mistakes, overconscientiousness, ambitiousness, and the feeling that one must live up to self-imposed and extremely high standards.

When anxiety becomes more disturbing it may be expressed in such symptoms as depression, irritability, sleeplessness, restlessness, paralyzing indecision, attacks of weeping, feelings of inadequacy and inferiority, accompanied in some instances by a paranoid attitude, chronic fatigue, and inability to concentrate. Besides such behavior traits, the negative methods of dealing with neurotic anxiety can run the gamut of neuroses and psychosomatic illnesses to the extreme of psychosis and, in very severe conflict situations, even death (Cannon, 1942).

In such instances, there is first of all the episodic attack of neurotic anxiety. In this attack, along with many neurological symptoms already mentioned, there can be considerable tension which may be tolerated by the voluntary and involuntary musculature and relieved in various ways. This may include using normal functions such as laughter and speech excessively, alcoholism, or frantic activity such as generalized restlessness, or compulsive activity such as compulsive sex behavior or compulsive work. It should be noted that frantic activity is generally neither productive nor directed toward solving the problem which causes the tension. It is an expression of the tension experienced in anxiety, and an effort to relieve the tension, but it is activity of only a pseudo-productive nature. Since the activity does not resolve the conflict, and the conflict remains, the activity tends to become compulsive. This type of neurotic anxiety is one example of "free-floating anxiety," since it is not attached to any specific object, situation, thought, or action, nor to the voluntary musculature or organ system. Normal anxiety could show the same picture, but the difference lies in the quantitative variations in the anxiety manifestation, the more severe type being neurotic anxiety which is the product of inner conflict. It is this neurotic anxiety which must be relieved before any attempt can be made to help the person with his problem.

When persistent neurotic anxiety is either too severe to be admitted to conscious awareness, or becomes too great to be tolerated in conscious awareness, the neurotic methods of avoiding anxiety occur. Neurotic patterns have their origin in the individual's need to protect himself from anxiety or, more accurately, from the anxiety-creating inner situation or conflict-involving threat. We say that the neurotic behavioral patterns and symptoms are defenses against the anxiety-creating situation, the threat, or in neurotic cases, the conflict-involving threat, in contrast to the usual statement in psychoanalytic writings that these patterns are "defenses against anxiety." Accurately speaking, the defenses are not against anxiety but against the situation which creates anxiety.

Sometimes the phrase "defense against anxiety" is used simply for stylistic purposes as a shortened form for the accurate but more complex statement. However, at other times it is mistakenly used to mean what it says, namely, that the individual carries a certain quantity of anxiety in the form of unrelieved excitation, and this is what he needs to defend himself against. Freud expressed this view explicitly in his last theory of anxiety as undischarged libido. The inaccuracy of this notion of carrying a certain amount of anxiety as unrelieved excitation can be demonstrated in many therapeutic sessions when severe anxiety may be relieved without any pronounced expression or abreaction of affect, perhaps with no more affect than quiet relief. The relief occurs when the threat is removed or, in neurotic anxiety, when the conflict is clarified. It is important for clarity of thinking to emphasize that there would be no anxiety unless the individual were confronted with the same threat; the anxiety continues, not because a certain amount has been generated but because the threat continues.

People who exhibit inordinate amounts of anxiety are not to be accurately described as carrying a considerable amount of excitation, but rather as persons who are inordinately vulnerable to threat and therefore are often and perhaps even continually in situations of threat.

Thus, a neurosis is an intra-psychic compensatory pattern by which security can be preserved despite conflict. It involves some form of repression of tendencies which are associated with the conflict situation (Freud), or in Sullivan's term, dissociation, a demarcation of awareness. It also involves inhibition of those activities which would place the individual in a situation of danger. The psychological symptoms in neurosis are various forms of compromise which facilitate the avoidance of the danger situation.

PSEUDO-ANXIETY

The first type of neurotic pattern is the anxiety neurosis, a chronic persistent state of anxiety which is diffuse and not restricted to any definite object or situation. Although many authors state that there is no specific psychological mechanism used as a defense against the inner conflict and the consequent anxiety, others more insightfully see the psychological mechanism of anxiety itself used as a defense against the inner conflict and consequent anxiety. Such people have not effective defenses against anxiety except to be continually cautious and alert, in other words, to behave anxiously and to show others that they are anxious. This behavior may be summed up as a method of saying to others: "See how anxious I am—do not make me more anxious."

In cases in which being anxious and showing anxiety is the defense against more anxiety, the individual often seeks to avoid conflict by assuming an appearance of weakness, as though he believes that others would not attack him, nor forsake him, nor expect too much of him if they saw he was anxious. We call this anxiety which is employed as a defense in this manner defensive or pseudo-anxiety. It is again a "free-floating" type of anxiety, not restricted to definite situations or objects, and distinguished from normal anxiety by its intensity, and from neurotic anxiety attacks by its chronicity. One of the common manifestations of this pattern is seen in the chronic worrier whose day and night are characterized by persistent fretting and worrying about a multiplicity of things. It is highly doubtful whether such a defensive use of anxiety would have developed unless the subject was considerably vulnerable to genuine neurotic anxiety on a deeper level.

Many authors state that the anxiety neurosis is the easiest neurosis to treat. Experience proves the contrary; it is among the most difficult. It is somewhat confusing to hear these authors recommend such adjunct treatments as electroshock therapy and prefrontal lobotomy for the condition. It is important in psychotherapy to distinguish this pseudo-anxiety which is used as a defense against normal as well as neurotic anxiety, because this defensive pseudo-anxiety constitutes an exception to the generally accepted principle that "anxiety must be relieved before the defenses against it can be relinquished by the patient." When pseudo-anxiety is honored or taken at its face value in psychotherapy, the underlying conflict is not and cannot be clarified because the pseudo-anxiety being a defense, it, like any other defense, serves to cover up the conflict. From this, it is easy to see that a therapist or counselor would quite differently approach persons with normal anxiety, neurotic anxiety, and pseudo-anxiety, and therefore the one doing therapy must be able to distinguish clearly among these three forms of anxiety.

OTHER NEUROTIC ANXIETY PATTERNS

Other types of neurotic patterns handle the conflict situation and the consequent neurotic anxiety by various forms of compromise which facilitate the avoidance of the danger situation. In such neurotic patterns which, for the sake of brevity, we will refer to simply as anxiety, the anxiety can be (1) *fixed,* that is, not free floating, as in the various phobias; (2) *dissociated* or discharged by some gross personality disorganization such as aimless running or "freezing," depersonalization, dissociated personality, stupor, dream state, somnambulism, or fugue, reactions that must be differentiated from schizoid personality and from schizophrenic reaction; (3) *converted* into functional symptoms appearing in organs or in parts of the body, usually those that are for the most part under voluntary control. The symptoms occur in the main on the sensory-motor level of activity, and thus include various types of anesthesia or loss of sensation, such as blindness, deafness, anosmia or loss of smell, and lack of sensation in certain areas of the body; also various types of motor dysfunction such as paralysis of one extremity, of one side of the body, inability to walk, convulsions, tics, tremors, posturing, and catalepsy; and all the time of course, there is nothing organically wrong with the nervous system or the musculature; (4) *automatically controlled* by some repetitive thought or act as seen in the obsessive-compulsive reaction where there is a persistence of unwanted ideas and of repetitive impulses to perform such acts as touching, counting, ceremonials, rituals, and hand washing.

In addition, there are several other anxiety states or conditions, including (5) *allayed anxiety,* which is partially relieved by depression and self-depreciation, the reaction itself having been precipitated by a current situation, frequently involving some loss to the patient, and often associated with a feeling of guilt for past failures and deeds, the degree of the depression being dependent upon the intensity of the patient's ambivalent, conflictual feelings toward the loss and dependent also on the realistic circumstances of the loss; (6) *anxiety converted into psychosomatic forms of illness* either through "somatization reactions" involving varying types of somatic complaints or psychophysiological reactions often referred to as "organ neuroses" with a predominant, persistent involvement of a single organ system such as the neurodermatoses, bronchial asthma, essential hypertension, migraine headache, peptic ulcers, and dysmenorrhea. Here one sees the inverse relation between conscious anxiety and the existence of somatic symptoms. In proportion to the degree that anxiety can be tolerated consciously, somatic symptoms do not appear; but when the anxiety related to the conflict becomes too great to be dealt with, symptoms may appear and then the anxiety disappears from consciousness. The symptom or symptom formation is thus a method of coping with the conflict situation by means of alleviating the anxiety without resolving the problem. Finally, in situations of severest conflict, the individual may be powerless to cope with the threat by means of any of the above-mentioned compromises and is thus forced to renounce a large area of activity or reality (for example, psychosis), or even to renounce existence itself (for example, voodoo death).

ABNORMAL FEARS OR PHOBIAS

Of all the ways mentioned above of handling anxiety negatively we will spend further time only on the abnormal fears or phobias. We have seen that there is such an entity as normal anxiety, a response to danger which threatens the very core of the personality; so also is there normal fear, a response to a specific, *de facto* danger which can be located spatially, and is proportionate to the fear experienced. Normal anxiety is the generic capacity, whereas normal fear is the expression of the same capacity in its specific, objective form.

Abnormal fears or phobias are different. They are reality situations wholly out of proportion to the fear they engender. They are objects or situations to which neurotic anxiety has been attached in an effort to avoid experiencing the anxiety and, more basically, in an effort to avoid the real dangers centering around the person's intrapsychic conflict. A phobic reaction is a defensive one in which the person attempts to deal with his anxiety by detaching it from a specific idea, object, or situation in his daily life, and displacing it to some symbolic idea (obsession), object or situation (phobias as such) in the form of a specific neurotic fear.

Although the patient consciously recognizes no actual danger to exist, still when exposed to the specific phobia-stimulating symbolic object or situation, he is powerless to prevent experiencing an intense sense of fear. The intensely distressing sense of apprehension associated with the consciously feared object or situation is actually derived from other sources—the intrapsychic conflict—sources of which the patient is unaware. A defense against the anxiety and the conflict arising from this unrecognized source is provided through the mechanisms of displacement and symbolization. By these means the anxiety is kept from rising from its real source—unconscious, forbidden tendencies and impulses, for example—by concentrating on some situation or object which is usually symbolic of the threatening tendency or wish.

A great variety of phobias has been described. Among them are fear of dirt, of bacteria, of germs, of syphilis, of certain animals, of travel by a certain type of vehicle, etc. Many of them have Greek names attached to them as agoraphobia, a fear of open places; claustrophobia, a fear of confined or closed spaces; phobophobia, a fear of fear. A claustrophobia might, for example, prevent the occupancy of a Pullman berth or attending Mass on a Sunday because the church is so crowded. A Catholic with a fear of germs refuses to use the public holy water font at the church and carries his own private supply. When exposed to the specific situation which evokes his fear the phobic patient experiences faintness, fatigue, palpitation, perspiration, nausea and tremor. He may be unable to continue with the duty at hand and be overwhelmed with panic. He can control his anxiety if he avoids the phobic object or situation.

If the patient were to carry out a phobic activity, it would unconsciously mean to him that he was performing the forbidden activity which arouses the dreaded anxiety. He also constantly punishes himself for his unconscious tendencies and impulses by the distressing restrictions and sufferings imposed by his phobia. Many cases of obsessional neurosis develop a well-marked depression, secondary to their obsessional illness. Phobias are twice as common among women as among men. Of special concern are the monophobics who have one pervasive phobia; this phobia may represent the last shred of reality that such people are holding on to. If it is removed, they will erupt into a full-blown psychosis.

The common denominator of the negative methods of avoiding anxiety is a shrinking of the area of awareness and activity, thus obviating the conflict which causes the anxiety. The same is seen in brain-injured patients who are not neurotic but whose capacities for coping with environmental threats have been greatly curtailed; they seek to limit their environment (for example, by writing in the extreme corner of the paper), or to avoid change in environment or in their behavior (for example, by fanatical orderliness in their rooms). The demarcation of awareness and limitation of activity as methods of avoiding anxiety-creating situations amounts to the curtailing of the freedom of the individual, involves some sacrifice of the possibility for self-development and self-realization, and limits communication with others and interrelation with one's community. The neurotic is in a state of "shut-upness" with all his abilities entirely bound up with his intrapsychic conflict.

Can neurotic anxiety be used constructively? In regard to neurotic anxiety all agree that it indicates the presence of a problem which needs to be solved. Neurotic anxiety can be treated constructively as a warning, a danger signal that something is amiss within the personality and in the person's interpersonal relationships. The anxiety can be accepted as a challenge to clarify and resolve the underlying problem and thus overcome the anxiety. Anxiety indicates that a conflict is ensuing, and as long as there is a conflict a positive solution is within the realm of possibility. In this respect anxiety has been likened to the prognostic value of fever—it is a sign of struggle within the personality and an indication, speaking in psychopathological terms, that serious disintegration has not yet occurred.

ROLE OF THE PRIEST

How can these people suffering from neurotic anxiety or from the various negative ways of handling this anxiety be helped? And how can the priest, untrained in the diagnosis and treatment of such people, be of help to them? It is quite evident, I hope, that if such a patient is to be helped, the underlying problem or conflict must be clarified and resolved, with the consequent overcoming of the neurotic anxiety, and help provided to move forward through the adoption of practical, realizable goals. Two treatment processes are agreed upon by the various schools of psychotherapy: (1) an expansion of awareness, by which the individual sees what value or goal is threatened, and becomes aware of the conflict between his goals and how this conflict developed; this is the laborious process of making the unconscious conscious, which must be done by a process of analysis, but analysis that is dynamic and attuned to the irrational, because all of these conflicts have their origin in the preconceptual stages of the patient's existence; (2) re-education, by which the individual restructures and resynthesizes his goals, makes a conscious choice of values, and proceeds toward the attainment of these values responsibly and realistically, unhampered by the bondage of the distressing intrapsychic conflict, and with a true feeling of internal freedom. In summary, the process of therapy is an analytico-synthetic one.

This is a brief summary of the psychotherapeutic process, a bare skeletonized outline of what happens when two human beings, with no instrumentality on hand other than the interpersonal relationship existing between them, slowly bring to the light of consciousness the intrapsychic conflict that is keeping the patient from realizing the full growth of development which is his God-given right. This summary in no way indicates the subtle interchange of feelings, the delicacy of timing, the dynamic understanding, the slow but progressive movement, the emotional communication that takes place in this unique interpersonal relationship. There is no question here of such things (so often asked by the untrained) of minute, specific, magical techniques for handling problems as if the patient were a mechanical robot who recovers miraculously when you produce the proper technique. Each patient is unique and he brings his particular problem bedecked in the unicity of himself; he will progress through therapy in his own unique way.

The relationship is unique from another angle: it centers around sick people, psychically sick people with an illness that has its roots in the preconceptual stages of the individual's life before the intellect was active and in full bloom. This sickness centers around irrational processes, and thus appeals to reason or any type of intellectual approach is a waste of time. It is only through the analytico-synthetic method that these people can be helped; and it should be quite evident that no untrained priest should attempt to use these methods, proficiency in which requires months of supervised therapy experience, and even a personal analysis, plus a working knowledge of dynamic principles. Moreover, there are dangers in treating patients by hit or miss methods: (1) the phobics may be forced into counterphobic types of reaction, or thrown into acute panic; (2) monophobics may be thrown into psychosis; (3) symptoms may be removed too fast and the patient exposed to severe anxiety; (4) the symptoms of the patient with an anxiety neurosis may be coddled and supported with the result that he becomes worse.

Can the untrained priest then do anything for these people? First of all, he could treat these people under the supervision of a trained person (usually a psychiatrist, although a trained clinical psychologist or psychiatric social worker could supervise) provided the priest had some understanding of personality dynamics and some understanding of the therapeutic process. Or, he could work collaboratively with the trained person in the event that the patient was having moral or religious problems, supporting the patient during the two stages of therapy, and taking over the patient after therapy was finished for positive guidance and direction in the religious and moral areas.

DIAGNOSIS OF ANXIETY

Is there any other way the untrained priest can help such people? We come here to the question of diagnosis. It looks as if we have placed the cart before the horse in speaking about treatment before diagnosis. However, it was only because the trend of the paper led naturally into the question of treatment that this question was taken up first. I hope it in no way indicates that diagnosis is not important; on the contrary, as we shall see, it is most important.

In reference to diagnosis we shall confine ourselves to the two main topics of our paper, anxiety and abnormal fears or phobias. With reference to anxiety we have seen that there are four types of anxiety to be considered: normal anxieties; neurotic anxiety (more severe ordinarily than normal) and manifested in panic or in the episodic anxiety attacks; the defensive or pseudo-anxiety of anxiety neurosis, which is a defense against the intrapsychic conflict and the consequent neurotic anxieties; and finally, fixed anxiety (with anxiety as such absent from consciousness) as seen in phobias, obsessive ideas, compulsive acts, conversion symptoms, dissociative reactions, depressive reactions, somatization reactions, and psychophysiological reactions.

1. *Diagnosis of anxiety.* Let us consider first of all the three types of anxiety that are conscious—normal, the neurotic, and the defensive or pseudo-anxiety of the anxiety neurosis.

A. There is a general principle in psychotherapy that neurotic anxiety must be relieved before the defenses can be relinquished by the patient. On the contrary, for different reasons, normal anxieties and defensive or pseudo-anxiety should not be relieved; to do so would not help the patient, in fact, it might hurt him.

a. *Neurotic anxiety.* This type of anxiety is the result of unfortunate learning in the sense that the individual was forced to deal with threatening situations at a period, usually in early childhood, when he was incapable of coping directly or constructively with his experiences. In this respect, neurotic anxiety is the result of the failure to cope with previous anxiety situations in one's experience.

b. *Normal anxiety,* on the other hand, is not the result of unfortunate learning; it arises rather from a realistic appraisal of a dangerous situation. To the extent that a person can succeed in constructively meeting the normal day-to-day anxiety experiences as they arise, he avoids the repression and retrenchment which set the pattern for later neurotic anxiety. Thus a patient with normal anxiety should be encouraged and helped to meet and to move through the anxiety-creating experiences rather than to move around them or to retrench in the face of them. This can be done by subjectively preparing him to confront unavoidable anxiety constructively through the conviction (conscious or unconscious) that the values to be gained in moving ahead are greater than those to be gained by escape.

c. *Defensive or pseudo-anxiety.* This type of anxiety is a defense against the intrapsychic conflict and its consequent neurotic anxiety. If we attempt to relieve this type of anxiety, that is, honor it and take it at its face value, we strengthen it and the defensive system. With this strengthening of the defense which covers up the conflict, the underlying conflict is neither clarified nor resolved.

B. There is a need in diagnosis not only for expert evaluation of the type of anxiety but also for its *depth,* by which we mean its correlation with specific personality types. This is done by evaluating or determining where along the developmental scale this anxiety was first experienced. More and more we are finding a correlation between the traumatizations of the personality at various stages of development and the variant pathological personality types that grow out of such trauma.

It is evident that severe anxiety experienced during the early stages of personality development will be more traumatizing to the personality than if it were experienced at a later stage of growth when the personality was stronger and more mature. For this reason, pseudo-neurotic schizophrenia and agitated depression, the former more than the latter, must often enter into the question of the differential diagnosis of anxiety. Pseudo-neurotic schizophrenia would have to be ruled out in the case of episodic anxiety attacks (aped by a schizophrenic catatonic excited outburst through pseudo-neurotic symptoms), but more often in the case of anxiety neurosis. Its manifestations are usually more severe than those of anxiety neurosis (because a more primitive type of anxiety is appearing) plus the fact that other symptoms, more appropriate to schizophrenia, are usually present. Agitated depression would also have to be ruled out in the case of anxiety neurosis, the help in this case coming from the depressed features of the patient.

2. *Diagnosis of Phobias.* With reference to phobias, usually the diagnosis as such is not difficult because it is easy to recognize the disproportion between the fear and the object or situation causing it. Of more importance is the evaluation of a monophobic, especially one who has a single, all-consuming, all-pervasive phobia. A monophobia, aside from the possibility of its being a fixation of neurotic conflict and anxiety, often is the last straw of reality grimly held on to by a psychotic. To remove this symptom-defense too fast would throw the

patient into a psychosis. Thus it would be more comfortable to know whether you are dealing with the phobia of a neurotic or a psychotic.

SUMMARY

In summary, we might briefly describe a general *modus agendi* for an untrained priest in helping anxious parishioners. It would be impractical to send every parishioner with anxiety complaints to a psychiatrist. Some of these parishioners may be experiencing the normal, day-to-day anxiety centering around the normal, conflictual problems of living (domestic, social, financial, moral, and religious). On the other hand, other parishioners may be manifesting rather severe symptoms of anxiety or may be harassed by a phobia. The severely anxious ones (as were described) and the phobics should be referred to a psychiatrist for diagnosis, the less severely anxious (on the basis that theirs is a normal anxiety and general knowledge of their background gives evidence of no big upsets) should be helped to meet constructively the anxiety-creating situation. If after a period of trial these latter do not meet the situation constructively, they should be referred for psychiatric diagnosis.

In regard to those referred to the psychiatrist for diagnosis, the priest, if he is interested, can ask the psychiatrist whether he could carry on the therapy with the patient. If the case is quite complicated and the anxiety severe, and the priest quite inexperienced, the psychiatrist may take over the treatment of the case himself but ask the priest's collaborative support in regard to the religious and moral problems of the patient. The priest should assume this task and should expect, since he is collaborating, to know from the psychiatrist what he is doing as well as the shifting current status of the patient, and the relation of the patient's particular problem to his difficulties in the fields of religion and morals. The priest can then deftly handle the religious and moral problems of the patient in terms of the patient's particular conflict and can also support the psychiatrist by encouragement of the patient and maintenance of interest in working on the problem. If the case is not too complicated the psychiatrist will ordinarily give his permission but then the treatment should be done under the supervision of the psychiatrist. The experience will be of inestimable value to the priest.

These simple rules will be of great protection and help to the parishioner as well as to the untrained priest, and will insure a harmonious working relationship between the psychiatrist and the priest. Also it will result in new experiences for the priest which will be of invaluable aid to him in his relationships with other parishioners and in his work in the confessional.

REFERENCES

Cannon, W. N. "Voodoo" death. *Amer. Anthropologist,* 1942, *44,* 169-181.
Freud, S. *The problem of anxiety* (1926). New York: Norton, 1936.
Goldstein, K. *The organism: a holistic approach to biology.* New York: American Book, 1939.
Goldstein, K. *Human nature in the light of psychopathology.* Cambridge: Harvard Univer., 1940.
Horney, Karen. *The neurotic personality of our time.* New York: Norton, 1937.
Horney, Karen. *New ways in psychoanalysis.* New York: Norton, 1939.
May, R. *The meaning of anxiety.* New York: Ronald, 1950.
Rank, O. *The trauma of birth.* New York: Harcourt, Brace, 1929.
Sullivan, H. S. *Conceptions of modern psychiatry.* Washington, D. C.: William Alanson White Foundation, 1947.
Sullivan, H. S. *The interpersonal theory of psychiatry.* New York: Norton, 1953.

DISCUSSION

Richard D'Isernia, M.D.
Medical Director, St. Vincent's Hospital, Harrison, New York

Father Devlin's paper presents ample evidence of his profound and extensive knowledge of the complex and difficult problem of neurotic anxiety and abnormal fears. In his clear presentation of the various aspects of these psychopathological manifestations, he has provided a well-organized synthesis of the major contributions made by the leading workers in the arduous field of psychology and psychiatry. It is especially important to us who advocate an eclectic point of view that this significant treatise coordinates those findings which have been tested not only by logic and theoretical investigation, but also by the more severe and exacting process of clinical investigation. We therefore find that the contributions that have been so skillfully synthesized by Father Devlin are in the main those of outstanding psychologists and psychiatrists such as Mowrer, May, Fromm, Freud, Adler, Rank, Horney, Sullivan and Goldstein. However, the application of these theoretical principles is entirely the product of Father Devlin's calm, clear, and penetrating appraisal and clinical judgment.

It is especially gratifying to hear the detailed description of normal anxiety given at the beginning of the paper. So much emphasis has been placed in many books and numberless articles on neurotic anxiety that one seems to discern a tendency in the direction of considering all anxiety as neurotic or abnormal. In this select audience no such conclusion can be accepted. For, normal anxiety, aside from its protective function in our interpersonal relationships, has the more fundamental spiritual function of rendering us aware of the call of conscience.

In the consideration of neurotic anxiety, Freud and his followers have consistently expressed the conviction that neurotic anxiety develops from fear of punishment (castration fear) which has its origin in libidinal desires. They hold that the neurotic individual develops anxiety as a result of the opposition of the superego to the gratification of the libidinal desires directed at the parent or parent-surrogate of the opposite sex, that is, in the Oedipus complex. In his presentation, Father Devlin clearly indicates that there is no such warranted limitation of the origin of neurotic anxiety to a libidinal, sexual element, but that it is the threat of the loss of security provided by the parents, usually the mother, that leads to the development of neurotic anxiety. The manner in which this occurs has been studied in detail by Karen Horney and Harry Stack Sullivan, but considerable research is being undertaken on this problem, which is all important for the understanding of the etiology of the neuroses.

The breadth of the concept of neurotic anxiety outlined in this paper is reflected in the consideration of anxiety both in infancy and childhood and onward through adult life. It might seem obvious that neurotic anxiety has its origin in the relationship of the child to his parents and that this anxiety is revived through the process of repetition-compulsion later in life. However, a problem arose in determining whether psychotherapy should be directed primarily and mostly at the early years of life, as seen in the analytic technique of many Freudian therapists, or mainly at the adult period of life, as in the therapeutic technique of many trained in the Horney school of analysis. I believe that the method to be followed is well expressed by Rollo May, who writes:

> The overall weight she places on present manifestations of conflict . . . does result in a tendency to by-pass the very dynamic sources of conflict (and hence neurotic anxiety) in the patient's early relationship with his parents. We would grant that Freud dealt too exclusively with childhood and infantile origins. We would grant also that the conflicts the child had (and has) with his parents carry over into all his present relationships as an adult. Nevertheless, the roots of the neurotic patient's problems lie in his relationships with his parents—a point which is one aspect of Freud's perdurable contribution. Therapy with respect to neurotic anxiety must certainly aim to clarify present relationships as the immediate manifestations of underlying conflict, as Horney insists. But at the same time the early conflicts with parents, carrying over into the present in the patient's emotional life, must be clarified as well (May, 1950, pp. 145-146).*

Father Devlin has dealt at length with the topic of conflict. He has outlined the elements of the interpersonal factors that give rise to conflicts within the individual. In the strictly instinctual theories of Freud, conflict is considered to be caused by the struggle between the demands of the instincts and the internal resistance which is set up against them; the conflict is between the repressing and the repressed forces. As a result, the energy or libido of the instinctual force is diverted to other aims and in neurosis is transformed into symptoms. But Father Devlin aptly points out that the threat of frustration of a biologic urge does not cause conflict and anxiety unless the urge is identified with some value essential to the existence of the personality. And he later states that probably the more positive expression of the conflict may lie in the deeper groundwork of man's twofold need for independence and dependence or in man's twofold relationship to himself as an individual and to others and God as a social being. He quotes Rollo May who maintains that there is a common denominator in these conflicts which underlie anxiety. This common denominator is found in the mutual relationship of the individual and his community.

Some very interesting investigations have been conducted on the role of the community and on the role of culture in producing neurotic

---

* May, R. *The meaning of anxiety*. New York: Ronald, 1950.

anxiety. Horney, Sullivan and Fromm, among others, see personality development as occurring at every moment within a social matrix, and have emphasized that the problem of anxiety must always be viewed in the context of the interrelation of the individual with his culture. For example, our culture stresses competitive success and it is held that failure in the struggle to achieve competitive success involves not only social contempt, but more important, self-contempt and feelings of worthlessness. The vicious circle of this process is seen thus: competitive striving causes intrasocial hostility which leads to interpersonal isolation and produces anxiety, which in turn stimulates increased competitive striving. But is it commonly accepted that our culture is more anxiety producing than those that have preceded it? Could we not view our cultural forces as generally producing normal and therefore potentially constructive anxiety, instead of destructive neurotic anxiety? It is especially in this area that Christian morality, through the teachings of moral theology, can and does set the various factors in proper perspective and clarifies this immensely intricate and complex issue.

Father Devlin describes the neurosis accurately: it is an intrapsychic compensatory pattern by which security can be preserved despite conflict; it involves some form of repression and the inhibition of those activities which the individual considers dangerous to himself. The symptoms are forms of compromise which facilitate the avoidance of the danger situation.

In general, although in more intense form, this is also what occurs in the psychosis. However, in the neurosis the personality of the patient is not as markedly changed from what it was before the onset of the illness; that is, there is not the fragmentation of the personality that occurs in the psychosis. To the neurotic, reality appears to be essentially as it is to the others in his environment, but to the psychotic, reality has changed in a gross and often bizarre manner. The neurotic is able to speak without distortion of language, but the psychotic often shows language deviations such as markedly irrelevant speech, disconnected phrases, the jumbling of words without connection between the words (known as word salad), to the extreme of the frequent use of neologisms which have meaning only for himself. And although we may find an occasionally paranoid attitude in the anxiety neurosis, it is vague, not fixed, and it is the anxiety that is uppermost, not the paranoid trend. Moreover, such projection is very slight and fixed in the neurotic. But in the psychotic, projection is the main mechanism and gives rise to the bizarre symptoms of delusions and hallucinations, which are not found in the neurotic patient. Finally, the neurotic individual has some appreciation of the fact that he is ill and his drives are in the direction of desperately seeking to return to his place in society, that is, to take his place again in his family and in his social group, whereas the psychotic has broken away from the reality of these relationships and indeed considers them a great threat.

Of course there are many more subtle symptoms which help differentiate the psychosis from the neurosis. We shall not enter into differential diagnosis, but let it be said that it is just as important for the pastoral counselor to recognize the probably psychotic person, as it is for him to determine whether an individual has normal anxiety or a neurosis.

I would say, therefore, that the first step in diagnosing a neurosis is that of ruling out a psychosis. After that we can go on to determine the type of neurosis with which we are dealing. Father Devlin has given a full description of the anxiety neurosis. He emphasizes the presence of free-floating anxiety in which the patient feels tense and intensely anxious for no apparent reason and frequently experiences a foreboding feeling of impending disaster, even though he can think of no realistic reason for this. It is in this type of neurosis that the patient has frequent physical disturbances. These sensations can be any of the following: frontal or band-type headaches, difficulty in swallowing, with the sensation that there is a lump or impediment in the throat, tightness in the chest, occasional chest pain, palpitation, difficulty in breathing, tightness and heaviness in the gastric region, vague abdominal pains, feelings of faintness, excessive perspiration. All these physical symptoms are caused by the overstimulation of the autonomic nervous system through the overstimulation of the hypothalamic area of the brain by the excessive anxiety. And it will be noted that the various organs affected are just those that cannot be regulated voluntarily, that is, by the patient's desire to do so. On the contrary, in conversion hysteria the voluntary muscular functions are impaired as in the hysterical paralyses and in addition, the anxiety is minimal, or entirely absent.

In the phobic type of psychoneurosis the question of diagnosis presents no great difficulty. The fears expressed are obviously not realistic as the patient himself recognizes, and the history of the patient's life situation quickly indicates that there is no objective basis for the fears. In this condition we can clearly see how the anxiety has been greatly displaced, perhaps to an object or situation symbolic of the threatening tendency, but certainly far from the original and true source of the anxiety. Psychotherapy of the phobic patient is interesting and rewarding in its results, but we frequently find phobias associated with obsessions and this presents not only a significantly different neurotic picture, especially in the personality development or type, but a very difficult illness to treat, often without success.

The treatment of the neurosis is dynamic psychotherapy—dynamic in the study and understanding of the interpersonal influences of early life and the present and in the discovery and investigation of the underlying, repressed conflicts that have led to the development of illness. As Father Devlin has well emphasized, analysis or discovery of the causes is only the first step in the treatment. Synthesis, or re-education, is the second indispensable step. Now in re-education, standards and values must be considered, discussed, studied and applied. Here the therapist cannot be passive or mechanical in the sense of dealing only with the technical interpretation of psychological mechanisms. Of necessity, the moral and philosophical background, knowledge and convictions of the therapist are bound to play a leading role in the therapeutic scene, and we hope, constructively so.

The pastoral counselor has a delicate and difficult task in helping his parishioner who complains of, or displays, great anxiety. He is in an excellent position to determine whether the anxiety is normal in character because his reassuring status as spiritual advisor enables him to obtain more easily than anyone else a detailed history of the person's situational stresses and problems.

In the case of episodic anxiety the personality structure is usually fairly strong and still able to prevail over the neurotic elements, for there are periods free from anxiety. I believe that here an objective evaluation of the individual's present life situation, of his behavior and attitudes, both psychological and moral, will lead to a deeper appreciation and acceptance of spiritual help, and will greatly strengthen his efforts to work out his psychological problems and decrease or eliminate his anxiety.

But in dealing with those suffering from a neurosis the clergyman not trained in psychology is limited to the recognition of the condition and referral to a psychologist or psychiatrist. Those who have some knowledge of abnormal psychology can be most helpful to the patient in cooperation with the therapist. Here we have the concept of the team approach which has been so productive in the treatment of mental and emotional disorders. The pastoral counselor is in a unique position to deal with the religious and moral questions, and often misconceptions, of the neurotic person. Through the explanation of the more easily understandable psychological mechanisms, illustrating with examples from the patient's behavior, he can reassure him on the need for therapy and enable him to accept the fact that the treatment will take some time. Then important imparted information (of course I do not mean the secrets of the confessional) can be given to the therapist who will advise on the further means of reassurance and suggestion that can benefit the patient.

There is no set formula; there is no way of relieving anxiety in all those who suffer from it. Only the trained psychologist or psychiatrist can, and even then often with difficulty, benefit the patient through the process of therapy described by Father Devlin. The pastoral counselor who has not had this training can help the neurotic person by emphasizing to him that the condition stems from sources out of the patient's awareness; that the only way to clear up the condition is by means of psychological methods and treatment; that the patient should prepare himself to accept a long period of treatment, and finally that however indirect the method of treatment seems to the patient, he will eventually be benefited by it.

William J. Devlin, S.J.

I am grateful to Dr. D'Isernia for his illuminating comments which I am sure you all feel to be a valuable complement to my original paper. As a further supplement, I should like to add some comments on the various approaches that might be used in pastoral counseling of those who suffer from anxiety and fear.

The psychologist speaks of personality types, frames of reference, and fixated personalities. There are various stages of personality development. The first is the oral stage which is characterized by certain psychological, biological, and physiological phenomena. It lasts for about fifteen months, during which the child is truly dependent on the mother or mother surrogate.

Things change when the child begins locomotion, at which time bowel training is important in our culture. This stage is referred to as the anal stage. Prior to this period, the child's impulses are all gratified. Activity is going on largely at a vegetative level, and the rational level is totally quiescent. At this stage the groundwork for the self is laid, and if satisfactions are not forthcoming the person may later feel quite inadequate.

At the end of the oral stage the child is a natural psychopath; he is impulse ridden; there is no inner control. During the second stage, while the child is operating on the autonomic and sensory-motor levels, the need for discipline arises. The child is now psychologically working out his own experiences of self and laying the groundwork for the self-concept. Here it is very important how the mother handles the child's impulses since there is no internal control. The lack of conscience makes it necessary to help him handle his impulses. Thus when the mother imposes external limits on the child's behavior she is furthering the development of the superego. If the child feels mother love he takes into himself these limitations and thus incorporates the attitude of the mother. Since his outward activity is directed, this is the beginning of internal control which precedes the growth of the superego. All of this is accomplished in the preconceptual stage of development. With the growth of the superego the child is beginning to function simultaneously on three levels: the rational, the sensory-motor, and the vegetative.

In the picture of the psychopath there is a rejecting mother. The psychopath hates and rejects the internal control and the attitudes of the mother, and this is the reason that he is referred to as an impulse-ridden personality. The scrupulous person, on the other hand, has parents who are rigid, and their attitudes are reacted to with fear and hostility. Fear is introcepted by this type of person, but he doesn't like it and there is constant internal conflict involving conscience. Another type of personality is the "Swiss-cheese" type with holes in his superego. These types emerge as consequences of parental example which is weak and lax. There is some guilt and therefore he is not a psychopath although he may be psychopathologically inferior in some areas.

It is clear that the first two stages of development are very important for psychological growth and personality maturation. The big problem is handling the child's impulses. There is within the child a drive to grow, the drive for pleasure. The drive for development and maturity, and thus growth and development, are purposeful; these are the dynamics of human personality. It is the psyche with its drives and needs that gives direction and finality to our lives. This is the core of personality, and it must be developed along proper lines if eventually it is to reach maturity.

In the first two stages, the directional urge has two sides—the self and others. The real goal in personality development is the "I and thou" relationship. Man is an individual and a social being. First he has a self and in the first two stages the self develops. It is only in what Freud called the Oedipal stage that the child begins to move about with others and develops the concept of sharing. The child now reacts to and interacts with environmental stimuli; he must learn how to share; sibling rivalry is prominent during this period. After he learns to share with his peers, he must learn to share with someone of the opposite sex. It is during this period of sharing, or when sharing is being learned, that most personality problems arise.

We are all aware of how personality types merge. The oral personality breeds schizophrenia, manic-depressive psychosis, and psychopathy. From the anal stage, the obsessive-compulsive personality appears. In the Oedipal stage the hysterical personality is foreshadowed. In these types life proceeds with basic behavioral patterns set down in infancy and early childhood. Impulses that stem from the depths of personality are drives which have an affective component (emotion) and a physiological component (the autonomic nervous system). These developments antedate reason, and thus the intellectual approach does not readily provide cure of neurotic and psychotic patterns. In the neurotic and psychotic person, emotions are so strong that they dictate to the intellect which becomes a conative element entirely under the sway of emotional experience.

In abnormal cases fixation occurs at one of the three levels and behavior reflects the level where personality development has been arrested. Each has its own frame of reference, which constitutes basic personality patterns. Behavior manifestations are the resultant of the basic personality core—the end condition of a conative response. The interaction of this frame of reference and the environment, particularly people, determines the behavior patterns.

When working with such persons, let us say a schizophrenic, the patient must be taken as he is here and now. Whatever present problems they show, their frames of reference will reflect the stage at which fixation occurred. These people are neurotic or psychotic because they are using a frame of reference dating from childhood. In therapy the past must be unravelled. Analytically, controlled regression to the point of fixation must take place, and this must bring about awareness of the events at this time of development. The emotional life must be untangled, but this is difficult since the problem began in the pre-conceptual stages and is in the unconscious. The intellectual approach is not helpful. The best approach, and one that can be used by spiritual directors, is to get the patient to express his feelings and attitudes so that he becomes aware of them. This is the basis of client-centered therapy. The therapist merely clarifies the feeling that the patient is expressing, no more. A sympathetic ear for one thus unburdening himself frequently gives relief. The same thing can be done in the confessional.

Psychoanalysis adds to this the interpretation of the patient's mental events. Both systems synthesize by reaching the point where development went wrong, and from that point bringing the patient through the successive stages that were missed and leading them on to maturity. Most unsuccessful therapists are those who direct analysis along intellectual lines rather than on the basis of particular emotional experience. The priest's training in philosophy and theology is so highly intellectual and abstract that he tends to approach people's problems in an intellectual manner.

Conflicts leading to abnormal conditions are initiated by the parents. There is an axiom in child psychiatry which reads: "Problem children, problem parents." In children who eventually develop conflicts the parents seem to be incapable of emotional giving. In the case of the schizophrenic, the mother is an "as if" mother. In the neurotic, the mother so confuses the child that he is forced to split mother and father emotionally, and conflict ensues. Deep security needs of such children are adversely affected. Neurotics are unhappy people and must be helped. The best way for the priest to help most of these cases is just to sit, listen with understanding, and keep your mouth shut.

SUMMARY OF ANXIETY

Father Devlin's treatment of anxiety had stressed its derivation in infancy and its essential characteristics. Together with hostility and guilt, anxiety accounts for a large portion of human suffering. It may be considered as non-specific pain or helpless uncertainty that accompanies objectless fear. The anxious person is helpless when he is unable to cope with threats and when he has no stable security pattern. Mobilization of energies against this threat is impossible because of the deterioration of self and interpersonal relationships.

Several types of anxiety can be identified. Normal anxiety has teleological value insofar as it appears as part of a normal progression through the stages of development to maturity. It involves an adjustment to the world of other people and thus a progressive release of emotional dependencies for social growth. It is the family which is the primary milieu that evokes anxiety and that emphasizes worthwhile goals as *bona ardua*. In some instances growth does not occur. There is a limitation of the capacity to master anxiety or anxiety-producing experiences.

Neurotic anxiety is anxiety which is not confronted constructively on the level of conscious awareness. Reaction in this case is disproportionate to any objective threat, yet is not disproportionate to the subjective threat occasioned by intrapsychic conflict. Subjective inability to cope with environmental stresses stems from conflictual patterns set up in early childhood, during which the child could not meet the difficulties of threatening interpersonal situations, and was unable to admit consciously the source of the threat. Repression of anxiety is central to neurotic anxiety.

Psychotherapy is difficult because of the early age at which the nuclear conflicts took shape. Therapy based on appeals to the intellect on a rational level is ineffective. The non-directive approach is found to be the best method of treatment. Helping him to gain insight is one of the most effective methods of treating the anxious neurotic.

The Sense of Guilt

GREGORY ZILBOORG

A native of Russia, Gregory Zilboorg came to this country in 1919. He received an M.D. degree from Columbia University in 1926, and in the years which followed he devoted himself principally to the private practice of psychiatry in New York City. He became one of America's truly distinguished psychoanalysts and he was one of the founding editors of the Psychoanalytic Quarterly. *He was the author of six books, among them* A History of Medical Psychology (*with George W. Henry, 1941*), Mind, Medicine and Man (*1943*) *and* Sigmund Freud: His Exploration of the Mind of Man (*1951*), *and somewhat in the neighborhood of 200 articles on various aspects of psychiatry. In his later years, Dr. Zilboorg was an outstanding proponent of the reconciliation between psychiatry and religion. Dr. Zilboorg died on September 17, 1959 after a brief illness.*

We are all familiar with the amusing display of impatience on the part of the queen in Alice in Wonderland: "Let the jury consider their verdict," the king said, for about the twentieth time that day. "No, no!" said the queen. "Sentence first—verdict afterwards."

There is something more than mere impatience in the queen's exclamation, and there is a great deal of her attitude in all of us—regardless of age, civil status or vocation. We all want to "know the end" in advance of reading the details in the many pages preceding the dénouement of the story.

If this particular leftover of our childhood impatience were the only form that impatience took, there would be considerable cause for amusement and almost none for concern. The trouble, however, with this little childishness of ours is that often it appears in many more earnest guises and is uttered in less obviously childish speech by people of considerable stature and prestige. Then, issues become confused, conversations, contentions, and exchange of opinions turn into argumentative sparring.

The sense of guilt is one of those topics that arouses impatience in us more often than not; it is a kind of prejudice against which one ought always to be forewarned. Whenever a topic like the sense of guilt is discussed, we recall at once the modern psychological descriptions and concepts which were offered us by Freud; we then almost automatically recall the apparent clash between "Freudian" guilt and the guilt as morality and religion traditionally know it; then we pronounce the sentence that Freud, or psychoanalysis, or Jung, or Adler is doomed to the sea of errors. We then proceed to examine the evidence which psychoanalysis has to offer, and the confutations which religious morality has to offer. This mode of "examining the evidence" cannot be very fruitful because, the verdict having been pronounced in advance, the *ex post facto* "examination" of evidence in the light of the previous verdict does not possess even academic value.

The process I have just described almost never manifests itself in the simple and crude form in which I have presented it. Our manners, intellectual gyrations and emotional preoccupations express themselves in forms both more complex and more delicate, so that our prejudice remains frequently unnoticed either by the participants themselves or by the observers of the argument.

The trouble is that we have not yet learned to study such official antagonists of religious faith as Freud. We listen to their empirical findings with that skepticism which is almost a form of anxiety, lest their findings might seduce us into following their positivistic or antireligious argument. I have always felt that this anxiety, so very well concealed under the cover of a sincere desire to keep one's faith, masked a not less sincere desire to defend one's self against one's own, perhaps unconscious, religious uncertainties and even doubts. It seems to me that it is this unconscious uneasiness that prevents us from reaching to the very core of the matter. The problem is a grim, obscure and confusing one, and I doubt whether I can succeed here in doing more than reformulating and restating the issue with a little less uneasiness and/or less insecurity than is often the case.

CONSCIOUS AND UNCONSCIOUS GUILT

We must start with the usual seemingly simple and clear statement that there is a conscious and an unconscious sense of guilt. We can then proceed, as certain psychoanalysts do (and quite wrongly, I dare say), to state that conscious guilt is normal and unconscious guilt is abnormal—neurotic or psychotic, as the case may be. A closer glance into the meaning of this formulation will at once make us aware of some difficulty. A depressed, or let us say a sad, person may say that he is not a very successful person, that in his most recent conference with his business partner he was rude to him and offended him without any reason; that he does not know "what got into him," but he is not so kind as he ought to be to his employees.

If we proceed to examine the facts on which this person seems to base his self-reproaches, we may find some justification for his sense of guilt, but not enough to explain the keenness and the pain of it. The quality and the quantity of his sense of guilt seem too great as compared with the facts consciously seen and consciously presented. Thus, we have here a conscious sense of guilt, or a full awareness of the apparent causes of it, which is real enough, but not entirely sufficient for the emotional reaction described. But in the light of modern psychology we are forced to assume if not to admit that there are other unconscious sources of guilt that have attached themselves to the consciously perceived and consciously stated factors as added psychological determinants, and have produced the intense sense of guilt which presents itself to our observation. In other words, in addition to the conscious determinants, we may safely state that unconscious determinants have played a definitive role in the sense of guilt in question.

On the basis of what I have just said, we may say without hesitation that it is almost a postulate that our psychological reactions are always a result of a multiplicity of determinants—they are *over-determined*. The psychic economy (i.e., the economy of the psychic apparatus) depends upon the nature of the determinants that produce a given reaction. Our reason and our will are always in danger of being partially or considerably or almost totally impeded—depending upon the number and the intensity of the unconscious determinants.

Thus, a person may constantly seek to destroy himself because, he says, he is no good at all, and because he is a murderer and a cannibal to boot, and because he has always been a bad son, a bad friend, a bad husband and a bad father. We may proceed to study the life history of this unfortunate man and to our surprise discover that he never killed anyone, that he never was a cannibal, that he never liked meat, that, as a matter of fact, if on occasion he did take a piece of meat, he insisted that it be so well done that it looked and felt like leather. We shall, in other words, find that his ideas are delusions. Yet we shall also find that it was true that he was a bad son, a bad husband and a bad father. Suppose that we succeeded in consoling this man so that he felt at least easier in his conscience for having been a bad son, husband and father; his delusions would not seem diminished, and his intense horror of the monstrosities he had allegedly committed would continue to torment him unabated.

Evidently there is something more to his avowed sense of guilt, no matter how conscious he is of it; the ideational content, in which the sense of guilt is rooted, seems buried in the unconscious and thus continues through its unconscious emotional connections to cloud his reasoning and impede the function of his will, and it does all this as efficiently as a drug or a brain lesion.

FORMULATIONS OF THE UNCONSCIOUS

When the importance of the ideational content of the unconscious was first discovered, it was rather difficult for the psychologist or the layman to accept the idea that thought and ideas can be unconscious. Gradually it became easier to speak of unconscious thoughts, as if we really knew what we were talking about. I say "as if," because I am not so sure that even now the most confirmed psychoanalysts and the most glib protagonists of what is routinely known as "dynamic psychology" really know what they are talking about in this connection. "Unconscious thought," "unconscious ideological content" as I put it when I spoke of the sense of guilt—are empirical working concepts, but they are not really understandable, not as yet at any rate.

The unconscious by definition and description is subject to the primary process; that is to say, its elements and components are all mixed together so that it knows no time, space, causality, or contradiction. How does it happen that we yet recognize unconscious thought and ideas, an unconscious logic of emotions—how does it happen that the disorder contains within itself definite groups of order, that the absence of "because" and "despite" yet permits rather definite even though special unconscious syllogisms? We might try to invent an explanation, but at the present state of our knowledge your explanation would be as good (or as bad) as mine. For we have no adequate explanation of this puzzle. What is more important, however, than taking notice of this ignorance, is to note that this is not entirely a psychological question. There was a time when psychology was defined as the science of human behavior; today, this purely phenomenological, "external," definition will no longer hold. Moreover, no sooner do we try to probe a little deeper than the empirical crust of the newer psychology, than we find ourselves confronted with philosophical (particularly epistemological) questions, metaphysical (particularly metapsychological) and ontological problems which the most skillful and most scientific psychologist is unable to penetrate.

The above digression seems to me quite proper and even necessary because during the past half century we have sort of grown accustomed to take for granted the various extra-psychological, and I must say pseudo-philosophical, excursions of modern psychologists, and assume that these excursions were inseparable parts of the empirical systems which they represented or discovered. So much that is truly superficial, and untenable even on a superficial level, was silently considered as part and parcel of the sociological matrix of Alfred Adler's psychology that his true empirical contribution was lost in the mist of his "theory," which at best was an ad hoc semi-materialistic construction and at worst a superficial adaptation of an amateurish sociology. So much that is of an oriental-cosmological mysticism was added by Jung to his original empirical findings that the human being, the person in the individual sense, was almost lost in the Jungian system. When we speak of Jungian analytical psychology, we are either confronted with the embarrassment of the riches of the Universal and the Infinite, or with some inwardly self-contradictory, empirical metaphysics—*a contradictio in adjecto.*

When we now turn to the theory of Freud, we find that it is much less difficult to separate the empirical data of psychoanalysis from their purely theoretical superstructure. Freud's great advantage lies in the very disadvantage which he has as compared with Adler and Jung. He was a poor sociologist and a poorer philosopher, but somehow neither his sociological nor his metaphysical excursions seem to be really a part of his scientific empirical system. What happened to Freud was something rather unique and, I may say, fortunate: Freud was a clinician despite himself. A scientific empiricist by training and bent, he indulged his coldly contemplative, slightly speculative mind by pondering every now and then in a rather impersonal way on life, death, and God. But instead of allowing himself to follow his own spiritual trends, he preferred to depersonalize them, and thus deny as illusions many of those things which in the light of recent publications were part and parcel of his spiritual search and struggle (Bernfeld & Bernfeld, 1944; Jones, 1953). What happened as a result was this: the clinical, empirical system of Freud seems to stand very well the test of time and experience; his metaphysical excursions stand apart from his clinical findings as something personal which is of Freud, to be sure, but no more of psychoanalysis than Freud's purely personal and cherished possessions. To me Freud's *Moses and Monotheism* (1939), or his *Future of an Illusion* (1928), are as much of Freud as the Etruscan vase which he owned, or the Egyptian statuettes which he cherished. But that which is of Freud is not necessarily of Freudian psychoanalysis.

And yet all the above qualifications, even if fully accepted, leave our problem far from clarified. For it is not only that certain unconscious ideation seems to lead to a conscious sense of guilt and harsh self-accusations; the sense of guilt itself may get buried in the unconscious and from there affect our behavior in such a way that the whole gamut from neurosis to psychosis, or from total inability to act to recidivistic criminal activity, may be produced by various types of the unconscious sense of guilt. The problem is truly baffling.

REALITY OF UNCONSCIOUS SENSE OF GUILT

Very early Freud observed a type of person whom he called "a criminal from a sense of guilt" (Freud, 1915, p. 343). At that time it seemed to Freud that mostly, if not only, young people are afflicted with this trouble. Later, case studies by Franz Alexander (1931) and Marie Bonaparte showed that a severe, complex, unconscious sense of guilt may lead to gruesome crimes, including murder. This is what Freud had to say in fact about the problem:

> In our analyses we discover that there are people in whom the faculties of self-criticism and conscience—mental activities, that rank as exceptionally high ones—are unconscious and unconsciously produce effects of the greatest importance; the example of resistances remaining unconscious during analysis is therefore by no means unique. But this new discovery, which compels us, in spite of our critical faculties, to speak of an 'unconscious sense of guilt' bewilders us far more than the other and sets for us fresh problems, especially when we gradually come to see that in a great number of neuroses this unconscious sense of guilt plays a decisive economic part and puts the most powerful obstacles in the way of recovery. If we come back once more to our scale of values, we shall have to say that not only what is lowest but also what is highest in the ego can be unconscious (Freud, 1923, pp. 32-33).

To return for a moment to Freud's remark about "a criminal from a sense of guilt," the following lines of Freud are very instructive:

> It was a surprise to find that exacerbation of this Ucs sense of guilt could turn people into criminals. But it is undoubtedly a fact. In many criminals, especially youthful ones, it is possible to detect a very powerful sense of guilt which existed before the crime, and is not therefore the result of it but its motive. It is as if it had been a relief to be able to fasten this unconscious sense of guilt on to something real and immediate (Freud, 1923, p. 76).

Please note that in the above quotation Freud uses once the term "sense of guilt" without qualifying it, and once he adds the adjective *unconscious*. This is a very important aspect of Freud's writing, as well as of the writings of the greatest majority of Freudian psychoanalysts: the concept of the unconscious is so familiar to them, they work with the unconscious so much more than with the conscious, and more often than not they concern themselves with the conscious only in so far as it reveals the unconscious—that as a result they frequently omit the qualifying term "unconscious" and speak merely of "the sense of guilt," of the wish to do this or that, of the thought concerning this or that. The uninitiated would not suspect at first that it is about the unconscious thought, the unconscious desire, the unconscious sense of guilt that they are speaking. The moralist and the theologian, like anyone else, are frequently and legitimately confused by the looseness of the language, and out of this confusion more than one problem arises which the moralist and theologian are hard put to resolve.

ALLEVIATION OF UNCONSCIOUS SENSE OF GUILT

It is difficult, at first glance, to accept almost as a postulate that one should strive to reduce, limit or abolish entirely the sense of guilt in a given individual. The painful question always arises: how could anyone continue to live as a human being if he were relieved of his sense of guilt? However, we must recall that the sense of guilt in question is not the realistic, conscious feeling of guilt in relation to a consciously perceived and willfully carried out act which is immoral or legally forbidden, but the unconscious sense of guilt which literally may play havoc with our behavior before our reason and good will take cognizance of what has happened and try to correct, to make amends, or otherwise to compensate for the moral or legal transgression.

Yet, even with all these qualifications, our difficulties are far from alleviated. Unconscious sense of guilt may "drive" a person to suicide and to murder without the individual in question appearing at first too compromised intellectually, or emotionally. These are the most difficult cases to assess clinically, and it is easy to imagine how more difficult it would be to assess these cases in the confessional, or during talks with the spiritual director. The penitent's unconscious sense of guilt might be such that a given penance would only spur him on to want more and more penance. In other words, instead of being relieved by penance and absolution, the penitent might find himself feeling "just as badly," or "worse." In psychoanalytic practice such cases are known as showing the so-called "negative therapeutic reaction."

A certain interpretation seems indicated at a certain point of psychoanalytic treatment; the patient seems psychologically ready to accept it; the interpretation is given; the patient accepts it; and next day some of his symptoms, instead of having disappeared, become accentuated, and a new symptom or two may even appear.

How can we recognize such cases? What can we do with them? In some such cases the task of the confessor might prove a little easier than that of the clinician.

It is necessary to recall in this connection St. Thomas Aquinas' simple but keen insight into the psychology of the sacrament of penance. The act of contrition, he points out, is accompanied by sadness (we could call it a mild depressive state, today) because the penitent is sad for having sinned, for having offended God. But penance is not accompanied by sadness, because penance is performed with hope of forgiveness. Here you have your differential diagnosis, so to speak. Whenever a sense of sadness is carried over into the period of penance, and whenever the penance prescribed appears insufficient to the penitent, we probably deal with an unconscious sense of guilt whose characteristic is a well-nigh insatiable desire for more and more punishment. In other words we probably deal with a psychopathological problem which in its severer form has become known as masochism.

A FORM OF MASOCHISM

This is what led Freud to return to the problem when he discussed masochism and said:

> Patients do not easily believe what we tell them about an unconscious sense of guilt. They know well enough by what torments (pangs of conscience) a conscious feeling of guilt, the consciousness of guilt, can express itself, and so they cannot admit that they could harbour entirely analogous feelings in themselves without observing a trace of them. I think we may meet their objection by abandoning the term "unconscious feeling of guilt," which is in any case an incorrect one psychologically and substitute for it a "need for punishment" which describes the state of things observed just as aptly (Freud, 1924, p. 263).

Freud's suggestion is quite satisfactory from the standpoint of the formal clinical approach, but fundamentally it robs the problem of some of its psychological essentials. Freud, being a strict positivist, or rather trying all the time to be one, would be satisfied with the psychological economics of masochism, the crude formula of which might run approximately as follows: the stronger the need for punishment the greater the demand for ever greater punishment. This "quantitative" point of view eliminates the whole question of values. And Freud refuted himself in this respect when, discussing the unconscious sense of guilt one year earlier in the *Ego and the Id,* he pointed out: "If any one were inclined to put forward the paradoxical proposition that the normal man is not only far more immoral than he believes [himself to be] but also far more moral than he has any idea of, psycho-analysis, which is responsible for the first half of the assertion, would have no objection to raise against the second half" (Freud, 1923, pp. 75-76).

It is obvious, is it not, that Freud seemed to be quite reluctant to enter the area of morality. Immorality—yes, this he could dissect and expose to light in detail. In this he was like the pathologist who dissects a corpse to seek the cause of death and exposes to light the fatal wound; thus he serves science, forensic medicine, the law itself—but he is relieved of the necessity of passing on the morality of the murder, on the problem of life and death and immortality. Freud, it seems, almost deliberately avoided coming closer to the problem of values and morality. He merely limited himself to the cool promise not to raise objections to the idea that man is more moral than he has any idea of.

This admission may appear at first a little amusing, but in actuality it is rather disturbing to the clinician and the pastor who seek a point of convergence and a line of contact and cooperation. It is disturbing, because Freud in making the admission stated an enormous truth and then stepped aside, as it were, refusing us the benefit of his extraordinary perspicacity. What Freud admitted here is what he stated more or less directly on other occasions, namely: "not only what is lowest but what is highest in the ego can be unconscious."

It is here that the pastoral problem comes up against a very difficult task: if our highest aspirations and hopes can be unconscious, how is it that they become unconscious? Are they repressed because we are ashamed of that which is highest in us? This is obviously not the case. The unconscious does not contain anything positive, or directly good: the unconscious is made up mostly of those matters which we prefer not to admit into our consciousness because they are not acceptable to our conscience, our morality. In other words, that which is highest within us, if it be unconscious, is not a higher aspiration but a sense of shame, a sense of guilt (unconscious) for not following that which we consciously avow or proclaim; it is the eternal *mea culpa* deeply buried so as to permit us not to think of ourselves as bad, as we would actually consciously be if we got freed of this (unconscious) sense of guilt.

REFORMULATION OF THE QUESTION

The above consideration may appear somewhat enlightening to the professional psychologist and clinician, but actually they must carry with the little enlightenment that they contain a considerable degree of disappointment, if not a moderate amount of confusion. This I believe is as it should be, because the problem appears to become more complex instead of more simple as we develop what is commonly known as greater insight into the mechanics, or workings, or dynamics of the human mind. Granted, one might say, that everything thus far described and discussed is correct, it would seem that the two fundamental questions which confronted us from the beginning will continue to confront us with the same tenacity and with rather little hope for an enlightening answer.

Question One: After all is said and done, how is it that a sense of guilt which seems to vary in intensity and scope even though it be unconscious may be responsible for the commission of both criminal and virtuous acts—that is to say (to use a purely positivistic terminology) for social or antisocial behavior, ethical or non-ethical? Does the sense of guilt as it is understood by the present-day psychology of the unconscious represent something so paradoxical and strange that it just exists as a sense of guilt without any real moral content, so that neurotically or otherwise it might turn into something bad, even criminal, or something good, even virtuous—like humbleness or readiness to serve one's neighbor? What manner of guilt is it then that it seems suspended between right and wrong, being neither and embracing both? This leads us directly to

Question Two: Granted that clinical psychology is purely empirical, is it possible to proceed with it in any direction—investigative, therapeutic, or educational—without any set of values which are independent of the scientific hypotheses under which this psychology operates? By independent we do not necessarily mean in the sense of some superhuman and supernatural values which are beyond the scope and the ken of psychology, but independent in the sense of values not based on the scientific positivism of the given system, but on a moral tradition the essence of which lies inevitably outside science as such.

THE NEED FOR PUNISHMENT

Let us try to find some plausible answer to Question One first. It is not an easy task. Freud sensed the difficulty more than he seems to have been fully aware of when he suggested that the unconscious sense of guilt is psychologically untenable, and when he suggested that the term "the need for punishment" be substituted for it. He pondered at that time the psychic economics of masochism. At one time he suggested that a sense of guilt is apt to develop in a person if a strong aggressive impulse remains thwarted even without entering consciousness, that is to say, if it undergoes repression without ever having become conscious, if it is thwarted, held back, dammed up, so to speak, without ever being permitted to enter consciousness except in the form of that vague sense of malaise which goes with any sense of guilt.

Let us note now what the criminal, or generally aggressive act, antisocial or not, represents from the standpoint of the economics of the psychic apparatus. It seems that such an act represents a breaking through of some dammed-up aggression; and at the same time this antisocial act provokes social sanctions which produce a sense of suffering caused by the punishment. To put it very schematically, we deal here with a sort of devilish (unconscious) method for the establishment of an affective equilibrium, an equilibrium which hurts others, makes the individual himself suffer, and causes him to seek again and again the gratification of that singular thing which Freud called the "need for punishment."

Let us recall again for a moment *Alice in Wonderland*. We might be tempted now simply to pronounce some condemnatory verdict before the evidence is in, and be done with the problem. But we cannot afford this rejection, for it really is a matter of considerable importance, that "need for punishment." One cannot help but feel that there is something missing somewhere in this chain of psychological phenomena which, although hypothetical, does seem to be corroborated time and again by a wealth of clinical observations.

Let us accept Freud's term "need for punishment" in its literal sense. This term might coincide with the colloquial expression: "A glutton for punishment." What does it mean? To stick the label of masochism on it would explain very little indeed—if anything at all. In a general way these appellations imply that the individual who is burdened with the unconscious need for punishment might seek by way of murder or suicide (I deliberately choose extreme examples) to hurt his own self. This is obviously not an act of love, nor is it an act of justice, since: (1) it is unconscious; and (2) it is frequently performed by way of hurting someone else. It is not an accident that since time immemorial suicide has been looked upon as an act of aggression, of hostility, of hate; not until the latter part of the eighteenth century did the English- or French-speaking world know any other term for suicide than "self-homicide."

From the purely mechanistic point of view, what seems to be happening here is simply this: the hostile aggression, the drive to destroy, to annihilate, may come out and express itself momentarily in full force on something or someone outside the person who is the bearer of this destructive hatred, and murder or some similar act will ensue. However, we all know that for one reason or another this drive to destroy often becomes inhibited in us even before it shows overt signs of existence. What happens then is something akin to that which occurs to the man who for one reason or another is prevented from giving vent to his rage: he remains silent instead of breaking out in vituperations; he may even show tears in his eyes, his hateful glance fixed on the object of his hatred and he bites his own lips. Whether you call this biting of one's own lips a result of an unconscious sense of guilt or of a need for punishment, the fact remains that it is an automatic, almost reflex-like act which the psycho-physiologically or mechanistically-minded would and do speak of as "turning the aggression on one's own self."

So much for the purely mechanistic view, which would (at the suggestion of Freud himself) drop the term "unconscious sense of guilt." However, it is interesting that that term was retained in Freudian psychoanalytic literature. More than that: the term "need for punishment" gradually acquired the meaning of "need for punishment because of an unconscious sense of guilt." This view is not expressed exactly in these words as far as I know, but the whole trend of the psychoanalytic literature seems to be just this, particularly so since the development of ego psychology. It would seem that the simplest mechanism of defense against the pressure of accumulated aggression is the direct release of this aggression; for obvious reasons this creates untold dangers to the person involved and as a result a self-punitive mechanism is brought into play which is called "the turning of aggression on one's own self."

Would it were all so simple, but innumerable problems arise here. How does the feeling, the knowledge—even though unconscious— of the wrongness of the aggressive impulse come about? And how is it that, even before the aggressive act is committed, it is treated unconsciously as an act already committed, and the punishment is at once (unconsciously) meted out? This is really sentence first and verdict afterwards; it is even more: execution first, with sentence and verdict trailing incomprehensibly in the shadows of the unconscious.

I have said before and, in order to understand both the inner psychological phenomena involved and the moral issues concerned, it is worth repeating, that the act of aggression which we are discussing, and the act of seeking punishment or the act of self-punishment, are suffused with hostility. Now hostility is the quasi-respectable, quasi-scientific term meaning "hatred." And the mechanism of turning the aggression on one's own self is suffused with the same hatred, except that this hatred is directed onto one's own self instead of onto others.

Again, as I have said, this "turning of the aggression on one's own self" is not a direct psychological mechanism; it is either a derivative of a number of others or it is combined with them. For the sake of brevity, I shall here assume that the reader is either fully acquainted with the fundamentals of Freudian theory, or that he can easily turn to the published sources of information. The point is this: the whole thing hinges on the mechanism of unconscious, involuntary identification, and this identification with a person is seldom if ever based on love alone. It is always combined with either strong ambivalence, which means a heavy admixture of hatred with whatever love exists, or it is based predominantly on hatred, in which case we deal with so-called hostile identification. This identification is in turn expressed in the unconscious by a rather constant, even though singular, fantasy that the object, i.e. the person with whom an identification is made, is swallowed and thus incorporated into the individual in question. Such an individual, if he kills himself, actually (in the psychological sense) kills also the person against whom the unconscious aggression (hostility) is directed. In other words, tradition and the religious moralists as well as the psychoanalytic theoreticians like Stekel are actually right when they say that every suicide is also an act of murder.

It is easily seen that the incorporated object, in so far as it was originally feared and hated, is also an agent of hatred within the human personality. Its psychological role seems to cause one a sense of guilt, or a sense of insecurity, and/or a need for punishment, direct or indirect—by way of various displacements, substitutions or distortions, or by way of mild neuroses or severe psychoses. It may also therefore easily be seen that the incorporated thing is not a "kind" thing: it knows no charity; it acts in accordance with the primitive *lex talionis*; it always demands its pound of flesh. It is what is known as the superego.

SUPEREGO AND CONSCIENCE

This is the reason why those among psychoanalysts who recognize the existence of moral values as being independent of the psychological mechanisms described above are unable to accept the equation of the superego with conscience. Speaking on purely theoretical grounds, one is forced to say that the sense of guilt based only on superego pressure is not really a sense of guilt but a sense of fear of one's own superego. The so-called sadistic superego (there is never a permissive superego) frightens the individual into a sense of guilt in the same way as a strict and overdemanding father frightens a child; this fear appears as a sense of guilt and produces at times that intense insecurity the origin of which is betrayed by the popular expression, "being afraid of one's own shadow"—an expression that shows how we intuitively understand that which remains to us scientifically still obscure. My shadow is not myself, it is something that is thrown off me by the light of the day. If I have reasons to be afraid of something which I have within me, I begin to be afraid (by way of projection) of that which is outside myself, into which I read the danger that comes from within me.

It is at this point of our considerations that one feels the need of much more study than has been done. And one (almost hopelessly) wishes that psychoanalytic studies had learned to avoid passing on things so much beyond their scope as morality, charity and conscience, and that pastoral psychologists and moral theologians would refrain for a while from spending so much time and energy on pointing out the logical and theological errors of the psychoanalysts in matters of morality. The errors are obvious, and the more we try to understand the real psychogenetic nature of the psychoanalytic concepts in question, the more obvious those errors will become—by themselves, as it were.

What seems to be much more important in this state of confused issues is to appreciate the full value of the two orders of things: the psychological and the spiritual. Granted that the greatest number of present-day psychologists do not know what spiritual is, and deny its existence, and believe that the nonexistence of spiritual experiences can be proved by the translation of these terms into modern psychological terms. Let us grant all this. The error is too obvious; it is as if one would insist that if you can translate St. Paul's epistles into Eskimo, it is *eo ipso* proven that St. Paul was an Eskimo. However, he who appreciates the order of things called spiritual will at once be struck with the fact that the empirical generalizations of the psychoanalyst are actually correct, and that, far from refuting the higher order of moral issues, these empirical generalizations actually confirm it. This is particularly true of such concepts as the superego and the (unconscious) sense of guilt—both psychological factors of unconscious nature. I have said enough about both and alluded to some of their major characteristics to be justified now in offering the following general proposition.

The superego is not conscience for many reasons, but the major reasons are those we want now to put forward. Those reasons are obvious. The origin of the superego lies in the ambivalence and the fear of the child. And conscience is not made up of fear, but of regret for having done something wrong. The superego is by its nature unforgiving; it is the epitome of aggression and hatred. The superego cannot be quieted; it can only be pacified with direct or indirect "payment in kind," only to come up again and demand again and always the maximum penalty for acts conceived and perhaps never committed. Conscience is never nonrealistic, and it does not treat a fantasy, conscious or unconscious, as if it were a fact. Conscience does not condone indulgence in conscious fantasies at the expense of facts, but it will not accept fantasies for facts. Conscience *regrets,* where the superego is *angry*. Conscience glows with hope when its owner repents and makes amends. The superego never says: Go, and sin no more; it merely says: Wait until I get you next time, or: It is all right to be sorry, but you must pay for it time and again until the end of your earthly days. Conscience knows forgiveness, and cedes its position to charity; the superego concedes nothing and cedes less.

As you see, we are dealing with an unusually difficult and complex problem. For the superego is an unconscious agent, and its language is action or depression; in order to express itself in human language, it resorts to the language of conscience. It is obvious that the psychoanalyst who equates superego with conscience cannot differentiate which voice it is that is talking the language of conscience at any given time. Only the one who knows and truly understands both the actions of the superego and the actions of conscience will be able to assess how much superego and how much conscience there is in each of the steps and manifestations of the sense of guilt. In this connection, we must recall that it would be wrong to say that there are two types of sense of guilt; conscious and unconscious, or irrational and realistic. The point is that there are endless gradations between the unconscious, irrational sense of guilt and the fully conscious rational one.

These gradations depend upon a very striking psychological characteristic of the psychic apparatus: it does not react to a given situation realistically; it never really spontaneously evaluates any given situation as it is. Being a biopsychological apparatus, it is more or less automatic in its reactions: one might say that the psychic apparatus cerebrates, but never really reasons. The ego, even the healthiest one, is to some extent a captive of the superego and the id, and unless the given reaction is fertilized as it were by free reason, all the experiences of the past, all the automatic neurotic reactions, including all gradations of the unconscious sense of guilt, are mobilized. Thus, a true reaction of conscience might be and usually is colored by a host of reactions from the past, ranging the whole gamut from mild insecurities (anxieties) to severe self-accusatory and self-destructive reactions. In other words, both the ideational content and the quantitative, affective intensity may present a great number of gradations and variations.

It is the differentiation of these neurotic sources and reactions in quality and quantity which is the chief problem of pastoral psychology. Therefore pastoral psychology must always be the fruit of the joint efforts of the psychiatrist and the priest.

In this opening presentation I have deliberately avoided giving specific clinical examples and offering practical (technical) suggestions as to how to make the above-mentioned differentiation, for I considered my task here was to point out the outstanding aspects of the problem. I hope that, in the light of the above considerations, the discussion which is to follow will enable us to bring out some of the practical issues and difficulties.

REFERENCES

Alexander, F. & Staub, H. *The criminal, the judge, and the public: a psychological analysis.* New York: Macmillan, 1931.

Bernfeld, S. & Bernfeld, Suzanne C. Freud's early childhood. *Bull. Menninger Clin.,* 1944, *8,* 107-115.

Freud, S. Some character-types met with in psycho-analytic work (1915). In *Collected papers.* Vol. IV. London: Hogarth, 1925. Pp. 318-344.

Freud, S. *The Ego and the Id* (1923). London: Hogarth, 1947.

Freud, S. The economic problem in masochism (1924). In *Collected papers.* Vol. II. London: Hogarth, 1924. Pp. 255-268.

Freud, S. *The future of an illusion* (1928). New York: Liveright, 1949.

Freud, S. *Moses and monotheism* (1939). New York: Knopf, 1947.

Jones, E. *The life and work of Sigmund Freud.* Vol. I. New York: Basic Books, 1953.

DISCUSSION

Rev. William C. Bier, S.J.
Associate Professor of Psychology, Fordham University

The sense of guilt that is encountered in pastoral work is on the conscious level, but it is important for the priest to be cognizant of the unconscious factors that are often involved in the experience of the feeling of guilt. It is in this area that psychology can be of assistance to the priest. Because the notion of the unconscious appears as a recurring theme in almost all considerations of abnormal psychological states, I believe that it would be profitable for us briefly to develop the concept of the unconscious and then apply it to the sense of guilt, the topic which has been so ably presented by Dr. Zilboorg.

The unconscious is, by definition, that about which we are unaware, but since we are speaking of the psychological unconscious, more specifically the reference is to unawareness in the area of psychological functioning. In other words, the unconscious of modern psychology has reference to psychological activity occurring within the individual of which the individual is unaware. A point of major importance in the understanding of the unconscious is the appreciation of the fact that it is not merely a static storehouse, but is dynamic and active. It exerts an influence on the behavior of the individual, an influence of which, by the very fact that it is unconscious, the individual is unaware.

Applying these notions to the sense of guilt, we can view guilt on three levels. There is first the normal sense of guilt which corresponds theologically to sin and is adjusted to the reality situation and the feelings which stem from the deliberate violation of a moral precept. Both in conscience and objectively the subject "feels" guilty. When, however, knowledge or feeling does not correspond with the reality situation, and when the feeling is out of proportion to the offense, or when the person is not objectively guilty, this is unjustified or excessive guilt. This feeling may be characterized as general neurotic guilt. Even here, however, the sense of guilt is conscious. In contrast, unconscious guilt is below the level of awareness; the subject is not aware of the sense of guilt. Very often it leads to the need for punishment, and as Dr. Zilboorg pointed out, it is often the motive of deviant criminal behavior. In this we see the operation of unconscious factors, and it is impossible to explain the phenomenon without reference to such factors.

I should like to make three observations on Dr. Zilboorg's paper. I agree that the speaker has proposed a criterion by which a normal and an abnormal sense of guilt can be distinguished, as when he said: ". . . when a sense of sadness is carried over into the period of penance, and when the penance prescribed is insufficient for the penitent, we probably deal with an unconscious sense of guilt."

Secondly, Dr. Zilboorg has suggested that an amoral sense of guilt, that is, a sense of guilt neither right nor wrong from the moral point of view, may lead to behavior that is socially and morally good as well as that which is bad or unacceptable. An example would be good works which seem to stem from a sense of humility but actually are derived from an unconscious sense of guilt. We may call this "pseudo virtue." It is not genuine humility because it is not motivated by proper theological motives, but is determined by unconscious forces.

Finally, I would offer the following comment on Dr. Zilboorg's suggestion that we cannot categorically discriminate between normal and abnormal, conscious and unconscious guilt. I suggest a gradation of unconscious factors: a normal sense of guilt is predominantly a conscious process, excessive or neurotic guilt shows a predominance of unconscious factors, and unconscious guilt is determined almost exclusively by unconscious factors. These distinctions are fundamental to understanding the psychology of guilt. These several distinctions can be schematically presented in the following way:

Kind of Guilt	*Suggested Name*	*Source*
I. Normal feeling of guilt	Moral guilt (Result of sin)	Conscience
II. Objectively unjustified or excessive feeling of guilt	Neurotic guilt	Superego
III. Unconscious guilt (Not consequent to but source of crime)	Need for punishment	Superego

This schematic presentation brings together the various concepts of guilt and their relation to both conscience and the superego. It is clear that the normal feeling of guilt corresponds to moral guilt and is dominated or regulated by conscience, whereas both excessive feelings of guilt and unconscious guilt are more on the neurotic side and are dominated by the superego. Excessive feelings of guilt can be characterized then as neurotic guilt, whereas unconscious guilt is characteristically expressed in consciousness as the need for punishment.

Rev. Gustave A. Weigel, S.J.
Professor of Fundamental Theology, Woodstock College

With Father Bier's synthetic scheme before us I would like to make an observation which was explicit in the discourse of Dr. Zilboorg and implicit in the remarks of Father Bier. Father Bier, for schematic reasons of simplification and clarification, offers us three dictamina for action; three judgments of practical reason. As he made clear, these three can be reduced to two. Conscience gives a dictamen and the superego gives another and the two must not be identified. Conscience is objective, conscious and rational. The superego is subjective, unconscious and arational. This is excellent schematization but we must not be misled to the point of supposing that actually there are two distinct dictamina. There is only one.

It can truly be said that conscience is an abstraction. This does not mean that it is unreal, far from it. However, there is no faculty which we can call moral conscience except schematically. The intellect makes moral judgments for the agent. Insofar as these judgments derive from an objective moral code rationally achieved we call the intellect moral conscience. Such a judgment in its schematic isolation is emotion-free. It is right or wrong, but it is calm and uncommitted.

However, since a man as a totality is dynamized by drives and impulses other than reason, and by drives which are independent of and prior to reason, the same intellect which makes moral judgments in the light of objective and rational motives, simultaneously acts under the pressures of unconscious impulses emotionally charged and uncontrolled by reason. When these impulses operate in accord with a projected father-image which is inhibitory and punitive, we have the superego at work. In some sense the superego is more present concretely than is abstractive conscience, but the superego is no more a faculty than conscience is. Its concrete reality is the action-dictamen insofar as it is derived from unconscious, arational, rebellious and punitive drives. Superego and conscience are closely and tightly interwoven when the intellect makes its practical judgment.

These basic reflections must be kept in mind lest we speak and think as if conscience and superego were distinct, readily distinguishable dictamina, so that all that need be done by the spiritual director is to make his penitent concentrate on conscience and ignore the superego. If this were our technique, we would be missing the point which modern psychology has so successfully made. In the concrete moment and in the concrete person the voice of superego and the voice of conscience fuse; nor is there any awareness of which is which. Only an analyst could extricate the different threads. Moral theology gives us the content of conscience but it does not give us the content of the superego. In the direction of human beings moral theology alone cannot be an adequate guide, just as dynamic psychology cannot be an adequate guide. The two together must be used in the guidance of the concrete human person.

Gregory Zilboorg, M.D.

In reply I would like to emphasize that it would be dangerous to accept the existence of the unconscious only by inference, for then we may ascribe to the unconscious all wrongdoing and evil, and as a result fall into difficult theological waters. There is a certain part of the unconscious for which we must be held accountable, not in a sense that we should be punished, but in a sense of requiring a careful examination of conscience. I would stress that rather than regard it as an evil source we should also look upon it as the source of many good things, such as intuition. The unconscious binds psychological energies and releases them, and at times ties them up in a chaotic manner without conscious reasoning and will. Since it is dynamic and a source of energy, it is an actual force that constantly controls certain areas of behavior, and we must therefore think of it in positive terms. The unconscious is negative only insofar as we cannot observe it.

It may be helpful to draw attention to the fact that the term "sense of guilt" is also used to mean a feeling of guilt. The latter term means being aware of being guilty, being convinced of guilt, as some neurotics are convinced that they are guilty even though they have done nothing wrong. Some non-neurotics are convinced they are guilty but on a realistic basis. It is impossible to relegate the conviction of guilt and the sense of guilt to two different orders. Some very depressed people have self-accusative trends of paramount conviction but not based on actual fact.

Let us conclude with the case of a woman who had committed an abortion on herself, who confessed and was absolved, and yet who remained in a profound depressed state. During this woman's childhood, adolescence, and adulthood, she had cared for her sister who was a cripple and a mental defective. Upon hearing that the child had died, she impulsively performed the abortion the next time she was pregnant. The death of her unborn child was the fulfillment of an intense unconscious wish—that the child who took her youth away should die. The confession of the sin she had committed, that is the abortion, was unacceptable to her. From the standpoint of her super-ego she killed her own child because she had been a bad sister and naturally wanted the death of her younger sister. Thus it was an act of devilish justice that she performed. The real sin was a life-long wish that the sister should die. Sometimes the superego and the unconscious become so inextricably combined that it is impossible to distinguish between the sense of guilt that is not real and the real guilt (conviction or feeling of guilt) which is concealed.

GUILT FROM OTHER POINTS OF VIEW

Joseph S. Duhamel, S.J.
Professor of Moral Theology, Woodstock College

We have all been enlightened by Dr. Zilboorg's analysis of guilt from the point of view of the psychiatrist and in the subsequent dis-cussion, from that of psychology. In turn, I should now like to speak as a moral theologian. The theologian, of course, is glad to accept the clinical findings of psychiatry, but I believe it valuable for us to look to some of the problems that seem to arise as a result of the data of psychology in the realm of morality and responsibility.

I see the problem as existing on three levels: the preventive, the diagnostic, and the therapeutic. Regarding the first issue, can we ask persons to teach religious doctrine in a way that may prevent the forming of a sense of guilt, or at least not add to existing guilt? We are faced here with a fact of religious experience and teaching. This is the fact of sin, both personal sin and original sin. Do we believe in these facts? To what extent do they help us or harm us in understanding and helping people with a guilt problem? We must face the fact that sin is a violation of one's conscience, and an offense against God. It is natural, therefore, that a person who knows that his act has offended God should find in himself a sense of guilt, and that in the sight of God he is an object of punishment.

The problem then is that we must teach the fact of sin and accept-ing the consequence of sin, but we must do it in a way that will not give rise to a neurotic sense of guilt. The solution is not only to teach that God is a God of justice and of wrath as a result of sin, but also to teach that God is a God of love and of mercy. The sinner should learn to look upon himself not only as an object of wrath but as an object of love and mercy, and therefore the sense of guilt that he has should be normal, and have no overtones of neurotic guilt. Once the penitent feels that he can be forgiven, God will no longer appear as a menace. In spiritual teaching it should be made clear that there is a difference between the indeliberate results of original sin—the involuntary impulses to evil that go contrary to the will—for which we are not responsible, and deliberate acts of the will that occur in line with these instincts. The clergy must present both sides of the truth without over-emphasis or exaggeration.

Regarding the problem of diagnosis, I would ask what we as clergy are expected to know when directing souls so that we can determine precisely when a case is no longer within our competence and should be referred to a professional psychologist. With his present knowledge the priest can only do so much in determining impediments to willful acts. If priests are to be able to decide when they have a case that should be referred to a psychologist, we must train them to some extent along these lines.

In the matter of treatment, we ought to know what priests can do without the help of a psychologist when the penitent is troubled with a sense of guilt. Because guilt is closely related to sin, one of the first persons to whom the guilty naturally turn is the priest. Moreover, many people will not go to a psychologist or psychiatrist because they feel this is a religious problem and only a priest can understand it.

Priests should certainly use whatever spiritual means they can as an initial step in the therapeutic process, but if these do not work then referral is in order. Such referral should not be hasty, for the priest may well act as a therapeutic agent in curing the sense of guilt; nor should we fail to consider the action of divine grace as an element in the therapeutic process. We must also, of course, consider the value of the channels of grace, namely, confession and Communion. Admittedly, in certain cases confession may only add to a person's difficulty, but in other types the sacraments and God's grace can accomplish what no man can do. There is a stage in the therapeutic process in which it is the cooperation of the patient that brings about actual cure, and here God's graces can enlighten his mind and his will so that he does cooperate with the therapeutic method in a way which would not be possible without the help of divine grace.

V. Rev. Msgr. James F. Cox
Catholic Chaplain, Rockland State Hospital

In my experience as a chaplain in a mental hospital, I have found that guilt enters into a great many of the abnormal psychological states seen in institutions for the mentally ill. In such a setting the severity of the problem of guilt is strongly highlighted. While a chaplain's work involves administering to the mentally ill, the clergy should be acutely aware of important theories and facts which psychology and psychiatry offer at the present time. These disciplines have made important contributions that can help clergymen in their work. However, the clergy should hold fast to the unchanging teachings of the Church on such doctrines as sin and punishment, heaven and hell, etc., and teach these doctrines to the normal and abnormal alike. Psychiatry may stress the psychological impact of such subjects, but they should not define or deny the basic teachings. The clergy faced with the problem of guilt often feel helpless, and the findings of psychology and psychiatry have served to reduce this feeling. However, it must be recognized that often we simply do not know what causes guilt feelings.

For patients suffering from pathological guilt, I propose that the priest recognize that this is a deviation from normality and that many such persons are not actually guilty of wrongdoing. The clergyman should not feel that he cannot do anything for such persons, but also he should beware of trying to treat the emotional abnormality. The priest can always administer the sacraments to confer grace on the abnormal patient. It is a fallacy to think that such patients cannot make intellectual judgments sufficient for a good confession. They may be just as guilt-ridden afterwards, but they will have received grace and the priest will have fulfilled his main functions. It is for the psychiatrist to relieve the emotional state associated with guilt.

In talking to patients of such things as heaven and hell, sin and punishment, we must remember that they frequently understand even though they do not react appropriately. These truths should be presented in a matter-of-fact way to the mentally ill. Sometimes it is beneficial to explain to a patient that there is a difference between objective guilt and their feelings of guilt. Confession will act on the objective guilt but will not help to relieve abnormal feelings. Ordinarily the parish priest is incapable of dealing with guilt feelings of this type, and should refer the penitent for proper treatment. The priest should be careful in dealing with such cases because of potential suicide.

I have one brief comment on the use of tranquilizing drugs and their effect on guilt feelings. There is no evidence to support the notion that the use of reserpine and thorazine removes conscience and thereby renders the person amoral. Guilt feelings abate under such treatment but the conscious sense of guilt seems not to have been impaired. Patients under such treatment show a better objective approach to their actions and to the integrity of their confessions, but this seems to be related to the reduction of their intense guilt feelings. Electric shock treatment seems to relieve intense attacks of guilt feelings and is regarded as instrumental in preventing suicidal attempts. Frequently shock eliminates guilt feelings and the patient may become anxious as to whether his confessions are adequate. These cases should be treated in the same manner as we would treat anyone who is anxious about his confession. The patient should be reassured that if he is telling the truth the confession is valid. After all, persons suffer from guilt feelings because they are sick, and the suffering induced by the sickness unites them with Christ in somewhat the same way that physical suffering unites one with Christ on the Cross.

Dr. Walter J. Coville
Chief Clinical Pychologist, St. Vincent's Hospital, New York City

At this stage it may be helpful if I, as a clinical psychologist, conclude our discussion of guilt in terms of a case referred to our department of diagnosis and treatment at St. Vincent's Hospital.

This is the case of Mary, a 26-year-old school teacher who was referred for treatment soon after her engagement to a young man whom she initially did not love, but whom she accepted and learned to love, since he had the complete approval of Mary's parents. On initial contact Mary was sad, tearful, and blocked severely in the description of her problem. She explained that she was compelled inwardly to analyze all her thoughts before voicing them to determine whether they were sinful or not. She felt bad and sinful. She feared that she was losing her mind because of obsessive preoccupations with impurity and a constant evaluation of everything in the light of moral standards.

Mary described persistent feelings of guilt. She felt guilty for talking assertively to her parents, for raising her voice in conversation, for collecting pay for teaching, for using a spoon on Friday that she feared had touched meat, for many confessions and communions which she interpreted as sacrilegious, and even for the fact that she was forced to seek help. She described herself as discouraged, hopeless, different, unworthy of attention, and acknowledged that she was thinking of dropping her faith and committing suicide. The thought of revolt against God, however, was abhorrent and created more anxiety and guilt.

Mary's guilt problem is not uncommon. Every clergyman and confessor has met this problem in his work. The tenacity of guilt in the absence of a reasonable basis can be baffling, and evaluation and treatment can both be most discouraging unless one understands the dynamics underlying such feelings. The confessor also faces the problem of accurately evaluating the guilt and the moral responsibilities involved, a situation that presents a challenge to theology.

As already indicated, Mary interprets everything as sinful even where there is no sin. Guilt feelings pervade every aspect of life and cripple normal productivity. The guilt here is a feeling or sense of guilt since she is not consciously nor deliberately committing sin. If she did, her guilt would be normal and constructive and it would motivate her to make amends and thus alleviate her guilt and anxiety. Mary's guilt, as distinct from this objective or conscious guilt, is a sense of guilt which is subjective, neurotic, and unconscious. Thus her problem is essentially an emotional rather than a moral one, based on erroneous concepts.

This type of guilt is beyond insight and self-direction. In fact, Mary described how for years she had tried to work the problem out by herself. She failed to free herself from these crippling anxieties and guilt feelings because defensive pride would not allow objective and unbiased evaluation. Repeated confessions and spiritual advice offered her no help. In fact, these enhanced both the guilt and the anxiety. There was a strong tendency for atonement through some type of punishment and released aggression to gain relief. These aggressions, however, caused more guilt and a further need for punishment—a vicious circle in which Mary felt hopelessly trapped.

An evaluation of Mary's background and life experiences makes her problem understandable and a solution more probable. People struggling with problems of neurotic guilt feel that no one can understand them and that a solution is hopeless. Reassurance is in order in situations like this, letting the patient know that his problems can be understood and that there are solutions. To understand Mary's problem, we must turn to her early childhood experiences.

Mary was an only girl, the second of three children in the family. She recalls that she felt that her mother was disappointed in her because she never did what her mother wanted her to do, or that it was never done correctly. Her mother was extremely critical of Mary and the young girl began to feel inadequate and inferior to her mother who was perfect in everything. As a child, she was forced to practice the piano which she hated and feared, because she could not please her mother who was an excellent pianist. Mary was scolded for her slowness and inefficiency in household duties by her mother, who anticipated her in everything, making the girl feel that she had to conform and obey even though she felt resentment and rebellion which was quickly repressed. Thus Mary developed into the model girl, known for her conscientiousness, obedience, and respect for elders.

This story of Mary's background demonstrates how a child subjected to severe criticism and control will develop feelings of inadequacy and dependency on her all-perfect parent. The standards so persistently imposed upon the child, who is anxious to please the parent, are absorbed and internalized by the child. These internalized standards become the superego or the idealized image, which is purely a result of learning and reflects the mores of the environment rather than true morality. The superego supersedes the parental standards, and failure to satisfy its demands leads to feelings of guilt just as failure to satisfy parental standards earlier led to feelings of shame and guilt. This superego is not the conscience, since it is unconscious in its function and associated with considerable anxiety. It is closely related to the idealized image that an individual constructs for himself, and the greater the discrepancy between the real self and the ideal, the greater are the anxiety and the guilt. Conscience, on the other hand, is a conscious function of the intellect and, as such, is subject to error just as any judgment of the intellect.

In the present case, emotional factors contributed to the development of an erroneous conscience, which compelled Mary to interpret almost everything as sinful. These interpretations were unconsciously motivated by her strong need to maintain security in the face of the rigid demands of the superego and her idealized self. Several other phases of her development, however, must be considered. Mary's father was a professional man with a high standing in the community, and her mother never allowed the children to forget the family's social position. Thus from early childhood Mary was indoctrinated by her mother in correct behavior. "Don't disgrace the family" and "what will people think" were important determinants of Mary's behavior.

Despite this intensive indoctrination, Mary saw the family somewhat differently, observing that her mother was an aggressive woman given to spells of weakness associated with lapses of memory. She experienced many embarrassing moments with her mother and was often ashamed of her. The family atmosphere was tense and quarrels between the parents were frequent. These quarrels revolved around the father's drinking and his boisterous and destructive behavior. Witnessing these parental conflicts and recalling her mother's conception of family status caused Mary to become confused, ashamed, and guilty. She felt herself playing a deceitful role and attempted to compensate by gaining favor with girl friends and teachers.

Mary's personality development also involved compliance and dependence, since most opportunities for independence and responsible behavior were denied her at home. Her parents did everything for her, so much so that even at 26 Mary could make no decisions without consulting her parents and receiving their approval. If they disapproved, Mary complied with their wishes regardless of her own feelings. Thus she was completely dependent upon her parents and insecure in the face of responsibility. This uncertainty and dependence became an additional source of confusion, anxiety, and guilt, especially when confronted with marriage and its subsequent responsibilities. Thus the occasion of her engagement enhanced her guilt feelings to such an extent that she agreed to seek psychological aid.

It is well known that emotional conflicts contribute to the development of an erroneous conscience involving matters of morality. In the case of Mary, her first conscious experience of guilt occurred at the time of her first Holy Communion. During the preparation for the sacrament, she became aware of the sinfulness of impure thoughts and actions and recalled an occasion when, as a young child, she slept with her father and on another occasion indulged in sex curiosity with a girl friend. This recall was traumatic and she dreaded her first confession. Having made her confession, she returned to the confessional to repeat it. The confessor told her that all was right now and to forget it. However, neither this admonition nor the Communion that followed satisfied her sense of guilt and need for atonement. From then on she was haunted by vague doubts, fears, and guilt feelings, always wondering whether her many confessions and communions were sacrilegious. She became scrupulous about modesty, and had many misconceptions about sex and heterosexual relations. Defenses were set up to alleviate anxiety and to control guilt. Thus, she projected blame on her parents and teachers, rationalized her failures, and developed compulsions to siphon off her anxieties. She felt inferior to others but managed to cover up by attitudes of solicitude in a somewhat superior manner.

The onset of heterosexual interests precipitated a flood of doubts and guilt about such relationships. Superficially, she impressed one as conscientious, well-adjusted, and desirable. Only she herself was aware of the inner turmoil. The engagement and prospect of marriage, together with its responsibilities, was too much for her to handle. She felt too inferior, inadequate, and guilty. Her dependent relationship upon the father was a source of much guilt, for she felt that she came between the mother and the father and ruined the relationship between them. Aggressive and resentful feelings toward the parents and her religion tormented her and enhanced her feelings of guilt.

In the treatment of guilt feelings, reassurance should be used to impress the client that the problem is not unique and that it is understandable. Obviously, a simple knowledge of the facts does not effect a cure. Emotional re-education is necessary, and the emotional relation between therapist and the subject is probably the most important factor in the eventual resolution of the conflict and the consequent development of emotional security and independence. For this reason it is imperative to avoid moralizing and preaching. The therapist should adopt an accepting and non-critical attitude toward the patient. He should provide release for the accumulated anxiety. As the patient becomes more secure through this relationship, the therapist retraces the causes of the problem and shows how the early life experiences and early reaction patterns determined the development of guilt, inadequacy, and anxiety. Particularly important is a clarification and resolution of the relationships with the parents.

It is obviously important for the therapist or counselor to be free of anxiety himself in dealing with such problems. Emotions are contagious, and emotionally unstable people are quick to react to the feelings of the therapist. The therapist should know himself, since self-knowledge will help him in recognizing and controlling his own involvements with the patient. The therapist must be confident and optimistic in his outlook. He must believe that repressions can be removed and that patients can be freed from their guilt and anxiety for more secure and productive living. He should have a clear concept of the aims of the therapeutic process, and should be realistic in recognizing that the scrupulous person with obsessive-compulsive traits is very difficult to treat, and that it may involve long-term therapy with sometimes unpromising results.

SUMMARY OF GUILT

The problem of guilt in pastoral work was considered from four points of view: the psychiatric, the psychological, the theological, and that of the Catholic chaplain in a mental hospital. The psychiatrist considers the effect of underlying stress on unconscious factors as they lead to the feeling of guilt. This emphasis is in keeping with the view that the unconscious is the fundamental source of abnormal behavior. The unconscious has three characteristics: first, it is below the level of awareness; second, it is predominantly psychological in nature; and third, it is active or dynamic. Our evidence for the unconscious is indirect.

Guilt can be classified on three levels depending upon the degree of unconscious activity. Normal guilt is guilt in the moral and theological sense of the term. It implies consciousness and conscience. It arises out of a deliberate violation of conscience or moral principle. It is normal because the feelings conform to the reality situation. Unjustified, excessive, abnormal, or neurotic guilt does not conform to reality, either because there is no objective wrong-doing, or because the feeling of guilt is disproportionate to the offense. Since this type of guilt cannot be explained in terms of the objective situation, we must appeal to causes in the unconscious forces within the individual. The feelings of guilt so experienced are conscious but the person is unaware of the reasons for this guilt. These reasons are unconscious. Unconscious guilt is on a deeper level of abnormal guilt because the person is unaware of both the cause of guilt and of guilt itself. The feelings of guilt are buried in the unconscious. Because the guilt is not the result of wrong-doing but is rather the cause of it, the individual manifests a definite need for punishment. Unconscious guilt is considered amoral, that is, the tendency itself is neither good or bad. Just as a force of this kind can be directed toward unacceptable and immoral actions, it can also be induced to serve behavior which is socially acceptable and commendable.

The distinction should be drawn between conscience and superego in this connection. In normal psychological development, the superego is formed earlier than conscience. In the abnormal person, they do not coincide; to explain abnormal behavior we must appeal to the superego as its basis.

In working with persons who have guilt feelings, the priest can function in three capacities. In terms of prevention, he must treat sin as a religious fact. But to the guilty God must be portrayed not only as a God of punishment but also as a God of love and mercy. Diagnosis in these cases will not be technical but can be practical. The priest must ask himself if the penitent's feeling state is justified by the objective situation. If not, he should inquire about the chronicity of the acts. If behavior is not episodic, additional help should be sought. In treatment, the priest must remember that he is not a psychiatrist. If he should feel the need of additional help, several rules should be followed: 1) don't get panicky; 2) do not take the attitude that immediate referral to a psychiatrist is always necessary; and 3) it is often wise to take a middle course by discussing the case first of all with a psychiatrist.

Scrupulosity in Pastoral Work

NOËL MAILLOUX, O.P.

*Father Noël Mailloux, O.P. has a B.A. (1930)
and a Ph.D. (1934) from the University of
Montreal and a Licentiate in Sacred Theology
(1938) from the Angelicum in Rome. He was
the founder of the Department of Psychology at
the University of Montreal and served as its
Chairman until 1957. Currently, he is Vice-
Dean of the Faculty of Philosophy at the University. On the Canadian national scene, Father
Mailloux served as President of the Canadian
Psychological Association from 1954 to 1955
and in 1959 was the recipient of the first
Career Research Award presented by the Canadian Mental Health Fund and the Canadian
Mental Health Association. He has been Secre-
tary since 1960 of the International Catholic
Association for Medical-Psychological Studies,
and since 1954 he has served as a member of
the Executive Board and Treasurer of the International Union of Scientific Psychology.*

The most striking characteristic of pastoral work is undoubtedly
the universality of its scope. The young priest who is assigned to a
parish discovers very soon that he is confronted with an appalling task,
the proportions of which extend far beyond merely human possibilities.

The young curate is expected to propose all the Truth capable of
inspiring a dynamic faith, exempt from any superstitious tinge; he is

called upon to enlighten any receptive conscience with the basic principles of virtuous life, and to supply it with proper guidance through the vicissitudes of its moral ascent; finally, he is empowered with means of salvation equal to the needs of everyone who only cares to make use of them. Although this involves tremendous responsibilities, the inexperienced priest has no reason to be disturbed or fearful in regard to such duties. In return for his total dedication to their fulfillment, he can rely on the reassuring promise of the Lord to assist and sustain him whenever the enhancement of providential designs is at stake. For him, indeed, the most crucial problem encountered in his pastoral work consists of understanding the actual needs of all those put under his care and of finding the way to meet them adequately. Unlike specialists in other fields of human endeavor, he cannot restrict his attention to a particular group for whom he feels natural sympathy on account of his own interests and preoccupations. The saint and the miscreant, the temperate and the drunkard, the faithful and the infidel, the educated and the illiterate, the wise and the foolish, the rich and the poor, the old and the young, the sane and the insane, all are equally entitled to receive his help and mercy. From his supernatural viewpoint, there are no desperate cases, and no one exists for whom nothing can be done.

THE SCRUPULOUS PENITENT

As it is well known, there is a whole group of penitents who deserve particular solicitude on the part of the priest, precisely because they suffer in their conscience. Commonly designated as scrupulous penitents, they present more or less severe symptomatic disturbances in the functioning of their moral conscience. To safeguard their internal peace, moral theology attempted to formulate some generally applicable rules derived from the basic principles which regulate the morality of human acts and individual responsibility, looking forward to the development of effective guidance methods based on precise empirical data. After resorting to these rules, the ordinary confessor could only rely on intuition, patience, and kindness to give reassurance and undertake a difficult process of moral re-education.

It has become customary to look at scrupulosity as the equivalent of an obsessive-compulsive symptom which happens to develop in the field of conscience and to affect moral behavior. However, a careful and prolonged observation of more than a dozen very severe cases has convinced me that scrupulosity may present extremely variegated patterns, emerging from totally different dynamic backgrounds. It seems that every neurotic or psychotic personality constellation is liable to produce some more or less typical forms of scrupulosity, and, sometimes, it is even difficult to assert that this symptomatic reaction belongs to any of the known specific syndromes.

At this stage of complete confusion, an attempt at formulating a more comprehensive interpretation would hardly avoid the risk of being premature. We must rather concentrate on the various aspects of conscience functioning, and try to define what kind of disturbances or distortions can be observed in this particular sphere. From such systematic and factual descriptions of observed phenomena will likely come the possibility of a more concrete and better oriented approach to individual cases. Also, we might arrive at some clear-cut working hypotheses which could be profitably submitted to empirical verification.

As generally recognized, the normal operating of moral conscience involves the adequate exercise and close integration of three major functions or abilities. First, conscience has to bear witness to the objective morality of a contemplated action as well as to the subjective intentions instigating its performance within the framework of well-appraised circumstances. This evidently presupposes the capacity for implementing acquired values in actual life situations on the basis of adequate reality testing and of undistorted insight into one's conflicting motives. Second, conscience is expected to supplement its initial estimation with the eliciting of internal commands and prohibitions which derive their compelling or restraining power from uninhibited natural inclinations to achieve the total human good, from a free-choice capacity highly perfected by virtuous habits, from well-developed inner control over instinctual impulses, and from an autonomous acceptance of moral regulations which gives rise to the power of self-obligation. Finally, conscience involves a deep but realistic sense of responsibility. When the action is completed, its judgment of approval or disapproval brings an increase of self-esteem or self-depreciation or guilt, and as long as such reaction remains healthily effective, it guides and stimulates unlimited further moral progress, inciting one to straighten out whatever appears to be wrong or to take the initiative toward new accomplishments.

In the light of this summary description of conscience functioning, anyone will perceive clearly enough that scrupulosity can hardly perturb some specific part of this extremely delicate mechanism without affecting its whole organization. However, clinical observation has revealed that such more or less generalized disturbance is liable to present significantly differentiated patterns, according to the nature of the particular conflict in which it is rooted, as well as to the individual motive which was at the origin of the latter and continues to influence its whole development. Of course, time limitations and lack of clear-cut empirical data forbid me to think of offering a complete picture of these variations. On this occasion, I will merely attempt to draw on whatever material I have been accumulating for outlining a systematic and meaningful re-interpretation of the most familiar categories of scrupulous penitents. They may result, on our part, in better awareness of the help we can provide to these penitents, as confessors and as spiritual directors.

ANXIOUS SCRUPULOSITY

If we examine our records carefully, it is easy to isolate first a whole group of cases in which the total picture of scrupulosity is dominated by the characteristic feature of anxiety, regardless of the object or situation that becomes the source of overwhelming uneasiness. These persons are submerged by some intense and incontrollable fear as soon as they are confronted with circumstances involving the mere possibility of temptation or sinful conduct. Exposing themselves even to the remotest possibility of wrongdoing appears just as formidable as putting themselves in some proximate occasion or as actually committing a sin. Thus, for example, an adolescent enters the school only at the ringing of the bell for fear of hearing "dirty jokes" in the school yard; he is afraid of going to communion because a tiny piece of food from the evening snack might have remained between his teeth which he had forgotten to brush before bedtime.* A young lady hesitates to wear some nice, although perfectly modest dress, because she might appear too attractive and arouse sensual desires in men; she is also upset by the idea of leaving town on the week-end with her husband, because her neighbor might be unable to get a baby-sitter and would

* These lines were written when Eucharistic fast from the previous midnight was still required.

find it impossible to attend Mass on Sunday morning. An older man is scared to accept his promotion to a well-paid supervisor's position, because he would be then responsible for checking all the sales bills and might do some injustice to clients through occasional errors.

These same persons are again overwhelmed by tremendous anxiety whenever they are confronted with some moral obligation and actually compelled to make a responsible decision. Even if they know exactly what to do, they feel an uncomfortable uneasiness of being locked up in some threatening situation which may amount to real claustrophobia.

Incapable of autonomous regulation, they refuse to face any obligation having realistic moral implications, while they often impose on themselves a very heavy burden of factitious obligations which involves nothing more than far remote possibilities of actual sinning. Moreover, the time soon comes when even such imaginary obligations become also a dangerous source of anxiety. And, to make things worse, if they are being forced by necessity or persuaded by their spiritual director to surmount their anxious hesitations in order to engage in some course of direction where they have to assume some real responsibilities or to deliberately overlook some self-made obligations, they feel immediately submerged by the fear of having yielded to some indefinite temptation, of having consented to some imperceptible intention, or having transgressed some privately recognized rule of their conscience. While constantly coming to grips with mounting anxiety, these scrupulous persons develop increasingly severe symptoms. After a period of annoying hesitations, they begin to feel hampered by troublesome specific or generalized inhibitions which betray the presence of a neurotic conflict in the process of crystallization, and finally, such conflict being fully internalized and remaining active independently of the particular situation where it was generated, they are deeply disturbed by fearful avoidance reactions which may well be qualified as moral phobias.

OBSESSIVE-COMPULSIVE SCRUPULOSITY

If we now turn to a second category of scrupulous penitents, usually characterized as obsessive-compulsive, every experienced confessor will feel himself on familiar, although distressfully confusing, ground. Clinical observation has led to the discovery that, probably under the threatening influence of shame, these persons develop some private morality and religion, imbued with amazingly superstitious requirements and beliefs, which they constantly try to impose on their environment including their spiritual director.

Of course, these hermetical systems remain impervious to any clear-cut rational attempt to evaluate such conduct according to basic moral principles, and especially, according to any sense of responsibility even in regard to most obvious violations of moral regulations. Every confessor is familiar with these penitents who admit being constantly pre-occupied by reprehensible thoughts and desires, or yielding to rather questionable impulses, but display a most obstinate reluctance at recognizing some concealed connivance, and insist on obtaining absolution without being compelled to accuse themselves of anything more than some vaguely possible sins. If they indulge in masturbation, this always occurs in circumstances which escape their control; if they miss Mass on Sundays or break the rules of fast or abstinence on prescribed days, it is simply because terrific headaches, digestive pains, or anemic attacks seem to choose precisely these moments of the week to afflict them.

These people cannot tolerate any impairment of their self-esteem and feel deeply hurt or humiliated by the slightest allusion to some suspicious passivity on their part. They usually go to great length to force moral regulations into their distorted schemata and finally to do away with any subjective responsibility. In the meantime, they often feel morally obliged to comply with fantastic internal threats and commands, e.g., washing their hands so many times, putting things in certain order, etc., which are so obviously foolish that their violation cannot constitute a "serious" misdemeanor.

Their contact with social reality is well preserved, but seems to be totally absorbed by a strong narcissistic need to rely on others to maintain their self-esteem. To anyone around them, appearing as a potential accuser who might use their confession as an opportunity to shame them, they present their case in such an abstruse way that this painful experience is adroitly prevented, and at least tacit approval has to be given to their paradoxical viewpoint. However, as this attitude is progressively reinforced, we readily observe some very well known symptomatic reactions. At first, these persons seem to succeed in establishing quite effective devices for "saving face" through a noticeably high degree of intellectualizing. Personal conflicts are considered exclusively in terms of ideas and words, which permit them to escape from concrete troublesome situations into a world of abstractions lending itself to easy wishful manipulations. Unfortunately, it is not long before the second stage sets in when obsessive doubts and uncontrollable compulsions make their unwelcomed appearance to increase the bewilderment of the harassed spiritual director.

GUILT-RIDDEN SCRUPULOSITY

The third category of scrupulous penitents we now intend to examine seems to present characteristics which are just the reverse of those attributed to the other two. Instead of being appalled by the mere shadow of wrongdoing or of minimizing any intentional participation therein, they insist on the fact that they have committed so many sins that they can never be sure of their being able to identify them all correctly and adequately. Far from dreading or repudiating responsibility, they seem to endorse it so indiscriminately that they give the impression of having developed an *overwhelming sensitivity to guilt.*

They repeat their accusations again and again, and remain unsatisfied even after describing the most minute details. Having just left the confessional, they cannot resist the urge to come in a second time and start all over again because they are quite certain of having omitted something important. Oftentimes, they feel deeply upset by the persuasion arising from some casual attenuating remarks, that the priest is not taking their accusations as seriously as they pretend them to be. Also, they would like to delay the rite of absolution indefinitely, being quite sure that some forgotten sin will be remembered as soon as confession is completed; and when the priest insists on putting an end to their beating around the bush by suggesting that he might absolve them for whatever could be remembered at this particular time, and by assuring them that anything they will recall afterwards could very well be taken care of at some other time, they declare flatly that this provisional absolution will be quite useless and should be regarded as just another sacrilege added to their already long series of crimes.

Deeply convinced that the spiritual director cannot feel any genuine interest for them as persons, and should be terribly annoyed for being entangled in such a hopeless attempt to relieve them of their irretrievable sufferings, they display an attitude of utter annihilation and despair. They also torment the priest by insisting that whatever attention and sympathy he is lavishing on them can only be the result of his sense of duty and does not derive from truly felt love. Thus, they submit his charity to the most severe test that can be imagined as long as they are waging this desperate attempt to compel him to grant love, protection, security, and forgiveness. By demonstrating their misery and even by blackmailing in this disguised way, they obstinately try to influence him to return their lost self-esteem. In such instances, as can be readily observed, the whole symptomatology is chiefly emanating from a core of devastating moral masochism leading to overt self-accusation, to insuperable despair, and often enough to suicidal attempts.

SUSPICIOUS SCRUPULOSITY

The aforementioned three categories of scrupulous penitents can be rather easily identified by any confessor even of limited experience. However, to complete this gross classification, it seems useful to point out a fourth one, which is often rather difficult to diagnose correctly, and which is a frequent source of unpleasant complications. All who belong to it generally approach the priest with a basic feeling of mistrust, although this is at first carefully concealed. They admit having made several attempts in the past to discover an adequate solution to their moral perplexity, but add promptly that all these attempts ended up in deceptive failures and painful experiences. After declaring that they are deeply disturbed, completely mixed up, and totally incapable of seeing what is wrong with their conscience, they sink into obstinate mutism and wait for the confessor to take the initiative by asking questions. Of course, to his questions they seem to pay no attention at all, or they give only the vaguest answers, such as "perhaps," "I cannot remember," "it might be so," "I don't know," etc. While displaying such distressing pseudo-imbecility, they make keen deductions about the sort of reactions the priest would have toward them had they ventured to verbalize what bothered their consciences. Thus, they secretly supply themselves with a sure weapon to be used when the time comes for the vote of confidence. Then, it is not rare to see them explode in a sudden outburst of rage and express their hidden mistrust with utmost aggression, insisting that they have been quite right in keeping their mouths shut, since otherwise they would just have exposed themselves once more to the already too familiar disappointment of being misunderstood and misinterpreted.

If we examine carefully the life history of such persons, we immediately notice a deplorable lack of consistency on the part of their early environment in the presentation of values. As children, they listened to adults' recommendations trustfully and developed high aspirations, which remained dear to them even in later life. However, they were bitterly disappointed when they progressively discovered that the persons they expected to be their models and whose examples they were prepared to follow, were trying to get away with transgressions which they could no longer tolerate in themselves. For a prolonged period of time, they often persevere in making strenuous attempts to live up to ideals which exert on their conscience an extremely powerful attraction, and which can never be definitely abandoned. This goes on until they discover that their efforts remain hopeless, because they are never provided with the adequate means for achieving this long-contemplated perfection on account of a total lack of trustworthy models and proper guidance. Suddenly, they find themselves torn apart by one of the most dreadful conflicts in human life. While they keep a strong attachment to moral and religious ideals, they are overwhelmed by an intense feeling of hatred for and rebellion against anyone or anything symbolizing them, namely the priest, the Church, the sacraments, and even God himself. As can be easily deduced from the above proposed observations, the chief factors of this complicated symptomatology, which is liable to develop along paranoid lines, consist in a particularly strong ambivalence and in an insurmountable suspiciousness.

GENERALIZED PATHOLOGICAL SENSITIVITY OF CONSCIENCE

In compliance with the principle of economy, it has been customary simply to assimilate scrupulosity to the paralysing endless doubting, which is a typical reaction of obsessive-compulsive neurosis. To many authors it seems sufficient to say that in certain cases these doubts happen to develop in the field of morality and to center around matters of conscience to give an acceptable description of scrupulosity. As to those who see in values something more than arbitrary social demands and prohibitions, and whose thinking is in close agreement with the spiritualistic tradition, they undoubtedly made a crucial contribution by establishing a clear-cut distinction between superego and moral conscience, and by showing, through repeated clinical observations, how the rational functioning of the latter may be disturbed by the former's *modus operandi* which tends to remain schematic, automatic, and crudely retaliatory.

However, in the eyes of the experienced spiritual director, the phenomenon of scrupulosity has a much wider scope and requires a much more elaborate interpretation than is generally supposed in contemporary studies. As it were, no one will deny that obsessive mechanisms are at work in most manifestations of scrupulosity; but clinical observation has led us to believe that several others at least are also intervening, the dynamic interplay of which is introducing significant modifications in the general picture of conscience functioning. Oftentimes all of them appear to be active and may assume a predominant role in some unpredictable sequence. For this reason the spiritual director will feel more inclined to consider scrupulosity as a rather generalized pathological sensitivity of moral conscience, which through the distortion of any one of its functions is bound to upset the pattern of its dynamics as a whole. This more comprehensive notion is far better in accounting for the various aspects of the phenomenon as observed from the viewpoint of the confessor, and I would dare to say, of the moral theologian, who is trying to analyse the vicissitudes of prudential judgment. Underlying these vicissitudes, we can expect to find the well differentiated constellations that were tentatively described above together with several others which are still in the process of being empirically circumscribed.

However, more can be said in favor of this typically moral construct. Indeed, normal conscience functioning is rooted in sound religiosity, i.e., in man's sound attitude toward God, just as its right functioning is dependent on the virtuous assertion of this attitude. This means that scrupulosity cannot be interpreted only in terms of conflicts arising between id impulses and internalized reality or social representatives. Since, in the religious man, conscience is inevitably applying moral regulations to actual conduct with constant reference to God's will, it is evident that the appearance of scrupulosity indicates that deep transformations are taking place in one's religious life. As the superego is the inner proponent and supporter of society's ideals, the *lumen conscientiae* is in the individual's nature the inner expression of the "voice of God," promulgating His commandments and formulating the universal values which supply the necessary basis for a fully evolved moral life. It goes then without saying that this natural instance, emanating directly from the Creator, has inevitable primacy over the superego, the acquisition and development of which makes it possible merely to reap the fruits it has been able to produce. Therefore, it is only when we have more precise information about this essential factor, which has not yet been systematically submitted to empirical investigation, that a decisive step will be made toward a full understanding of scrupulosity as a symptom *sui generis,* not merely affecting but actually involving the moral and religious life of the individual. Of this we must be keenly aware as theologians and as spiritual directors. If we intend to adequately fulfill our responsibility toward those who, quite involuntarily, are meeting almost insuperable obstacles on the way to salvation, we will not hesitate to start gathering observational data until the most intolerable secret sufferings of human conscience are thoroughly understood and effective means have been found to relieve them.

These remarks will serve as a clear warning that the few schematic clinical descriptions presented in the beginning of this paper should be regarded merely as an indication of the initial approach we might use to improve the art of spiritual direction by giving it the necessary empirical basis it is still awaiting. Quite often, the psychopathologist is given a well-deserved reproach for forgetting, under the spell of his professional bias, that some human acts at least are emanating from clearly conscious judgment and free determination. On the other hand, we must humbly recognize that, as human beings, theologians are no more than others exempt from the temptation of neglecting the facts which do not immediately fit into the sphere of their current personal thinking. Totally absorbed in building up the well-integrated structure of moral virtues, destined to become the flexible and efficient instrument of divine grace, we often show some reluctance at giving due consideration to serious obstacles encountered in the acquisition of fully rational functioning which supplies the normal basis for the higher achievements of supernatural life. No wonder, then, that we can do so little for those who require our help in all confidence and with the best of intentions, while they feel desperately hampered in their spiritual development by uncontrollable vicious habits, degrading addictions, and neurotic impulses or inhibitions.

SOME PRACTICAL SUGGESTIONS

Now that it has become clear that satisfactory interpretation of scrupulosity is beyond the expectation of immediate possibilities, we shall feel free to propose at least some few practical applications which can be derived from our present knowledge. Certainly, they cannot be considered even as the elemental principles of a still to be elaborated psychotherapy of moral and religious disturbances, since we cannot think of providing the art of spiritual direction with adequate techniques before we have achieved at least a rudimentary dynamic study of conscience functioning and of moral symptomatic formations. However, the experience gained from general clinical practice with deeply disturbed individuals has suggested some fundamental rules which may be recalled with great advantage in our guidance work and, perhaps, may serve as a practical frame of reference in our attempt at collecting further observations.

To start at a most superficial level, let us first point out that the confessor should be careful not to let all his attention be captured by apparent symptomatic reactions, and thus be deterred from centering his chief corrective effort on more essential causal factors. Referring to the aforementioned instances, one would suspect that the inexperienced spiritual director will hardly resist the temptation to discuss with these penitents their constant hesitations or doubts, their grossly exaggerated accusations or their obstinate mutism. He forgets quite naïvely that they are already only too familiar with this awkward attack on their personal difficulties, having discussed precisely the same points with many other priests or would-be listeners. This can only shake their wavy confidence right from the start, increase their basic insecurity, and confirm their expectation of having to face a new failure. Moreover, through such repeated experiences, they slowly gain the impression that their main trouble lies in the symptom itself, and, what is worse still, they develop a formidable intellectualizing or rationalizing ability which is bound to strengthen their defenses tremendously. These endless efforts aimed at reassuring, clarifying, rectifying or encouraging, in regard to what can be only a superficial manifestation of a deeper problem, usually end in utter confusion and bitter deception.

This will explain why, while presenting some constellations possibly resulting from the crystallization of moral scrupulosity, we never omitted to stress the dominant motive which seemed to supply the key to the mobilized defensive system and to give us excellent clues to grasp the nature of the reactivated conflict. Evidently, it is particularly important here to draw the penitent's attention, as soon as it happens to be verbalized, to his fearful free-floating insecurity, to his dread of shame which forces him to be constantly on the lookout for new devices for "saving face," to his extreme sensitivity to guilt which tends to turn all his aggression against himself, or to his basic mistrust which has made it impossible to eliminate unnecessary confusion from his value system. Then, indeed, there are good chances that the symptomatic formations will cease to be the focus of immediate preoccupations and that the desire to gain increased insight into the original conflictual situations will be greatly reinforced. When such orientation has been definitely taken, the spiritual director may hope for a more satisfactory and fruitful contact with his penitent, although much remains to be done that will require great skill on his part.

Another aspect of the problem of scrupulosity, on which one can never lay too much stress, consists of the fact that the apparent moral conflicts submitted for solution are merely a screen which serves to disguise much earlier conflicts of rather infantile nature, which are constantly revived for the simple reason that they were never given proper solution. Here we are confronted with the fundamental factor of *regression,* the intervention of which always introduces unexpected complications in any neurotic process. To propose an adequate explanation of the various ways along which this particularly important mechanism is operating is out of the question in such a brief lecture. However, one must remember that here lies the main source of misunderstanding between a harassed confessor who is attempting to cope with a moral difficulty by offering a mature solution, and a baffled penitent who is systematically discarding such a solution simply because it does not answer the difficulty as it continues to be perceived from his immature viewpoint. To put it in other words, the dialogue is pursued at different levels of communication, and, sadly enough, oftentimes without the slightest realization of the fact that neither one is actually comprehending what the other is talking about.

Finally, as we have already hinted above, the confessor must be constantly aware of the possible implications of neurotic transference, through which the penitent is strenuously although unconsciously attempting to push him into the role he wishes the confessor to assume to assure the satisfaction of his pathological needs. As can be easily deduced from our earlier description, the anxious-scrupulous penitent will require fròm the priest that he allow him to remain an irresponsible child by accepting the role of the reassuring and protecting parent, while the obsessive-scrupulous penitent will try to secure in him a favorable witness who will bear testimony to his innocence. Much could also be said concerning other categories of scrupulous individuals. However, what calls for special notice here is the tremendous and most embarrassing confusion which inevitably results from a naïve indulgence in so dangerous a game. One finds himself, then, before he has time to realize it, inextricably involved in a neurotic relationship that renders any efficacious attempt at straightening out the spoiled situation utterly impossible, and often generates almost insurmountable complications.

Arriving at the end of these all-too succinct considerations, I feel rather upset by the inescapable necessity which has forced me to formulate them in a somewhat dogmatic way. I hope that this will not prevent you from raising a number of interesting questions which this very incompleteness is bound to stimulate. As a concluding remark, I would only like to add that it would be extremely gratifying to have made a modest contribution to the Fordham Pastoral Psychology Institute, if we could foresee in it the starting point of a lasting concerted drive toward the building up of an elaborate art of spiritual direction. Such an art, as I have tried to indicate, will not develop from the mere adjoining of a psychological supplement to moral theology or from the acquisition of some existing psychotherapeutic techniques. It will emerge from a theologically inspired synthesis of empirically controlled data collected in the immense realm of man's moral and religious life.

DISCUSSION

Dr. Alexander A. Schneiders
*Professor of Psychology, Fordham University**

In his presentation of scrupulosity Father Mailloux has supplemented the traditional approach to the problem with an analysis of

* Now at Boston College.

what he has termed "conscience functioning." It will, I think, help to lend perspective to the interpretation of scrupulosity provided by Father Mailloux to look briefly at some of the other interpretations of scrupulosity offered in the literature.

We are all aware that various authorities have related scrupulosity to anxiety, to obsession and compulsion, to neurotic pride, and to pervasive guilt. Moore (1944, pp. 35-44) interprets it as a special type of anxiety, Allers (1931, pp. 356-357) as a true neurosis and a personality type, and Nuttin (1953, pp. 140-145) as an expression of guilt. The French psychologist, Janet (1908), had linked it to psychasthenia. Moore (1944), Allers (1943), Nuttin (1953), and Stafford (1950) all see pride as a basic quality and dominant feature in scrupulosity. The incidence of this condition is relatively high, Mullen (1927) estimating that more than 26 percent of 400 girls in his study manifested scrupulosity.

Regarding treatment, I would suggest that we develop our knowledge of etiology as outlined by Father Mailloux, and that we explore carefully the nature of this disorder and hold to the distinction between scrupulosity as a moral defect and scrupulosity as a psychological difficulty. I would agree fully with Father Mailloux's suggestion that scrupulosity be subjected to empirical study, and that the theological approach be integrated with therapeutic treatment.

REFERENCES

Allers, R. *The psychology of character*. New York: Sheed & Ward, 1931.
Janet, P. *Les obsessions et la psychathanie* (2nd ed.). Paris: Alcan, 1908.
Moore, T. V. (O.S.B.) *Personal mental hygiene*. New York: Grune & Stratton, 1944.
Mullen, J. J. Psychological factors in the pastoral treatment of scruples. *Stud. Psychol. Psychiat. Cath. Univer. Amer.*, 1927, 1., No. 3.
Nuttin, J. Psychoanalysis and personality. Trans. by George Lamb. New York: Sheed & Ward, 1953.
Stafford, J. W. Psychology and moral problems. *Homiletic Pastoral Rev.*, 1950, *51*, 118-124.

Rev. Noël Mailloux, O.P.

In reply, Fr. Mailloux observed that when we study the pathological mechanisms in scrupulosity, we must remember that these mechanisms are normal and hence that they can be found in normal people.

A normal person, however, has the capacity to change or to manipulate the situation so that it can be controlled. Father Weigel remarked on the reluctance of penitents to name a sin according to the violation itself, that is, they often use a euphemism as a substitute. These "scrupulous actions" are common to all people. Scrupulosity, then, is a matter of degree, and only when there is a neurotic process at work should we call it true scrupulosity.

Any interpretation of scrupulosity in terms of neurosis is insufficient. A neurotic condition will have some repercussions in the moral and religious attitude of a person, but even when a normal person is unable to solve a conflict at the higher non-neurotic level, these symptoms also appear. The basic factor in scrupulosity, according to Fr. Mailloux, is something *sui generis;* if something happens at the higher level first and the person cannot cope with the problem, neurotic reactions appear. We must conceive of scrupulosity as a typical symptom of moral or religious conduct which has not been sufficiently studied or clearly understood. Sometimes, when a neurosis is cured, the person will appear more normal on the religious or moral level, but the real scrupulosity has scarcely been touched. This indicates that they are not the same thing.

An additional point concerns the problem of angelism, a reaction recognized as a defense mechanism typical of the adolescent period, and more or less universal. This reaction is natural, and consists of an awkward attempt to get rid of impulses by denying them. Thus, when they reject impulses, scrupulosity may appear; they see the sin not so much in the consent given, but in the fact that they have such impulses. It is important to inform these young people that such impulses are not bad or abnormal in themselves, and in fact they would be abnormal if the impulses didn't exist. In this way guilt may be detached from the impulses.

With respect to the problem of absolution for the scrupulous, it is important to note two things. First, refrain from telling the penitent that he is scrupulous, for this only increases his guilt; second, it must be made clear to him that sins are one thing and obsessions another, and that absolution is given only for sins. Too many scrupulous persons expect that the sacraments will cure their neurosis, and if they do not despair sets in. Thus they rebel against the sacraments and refuse to go to confession. They must be reminded that the sacraments give grace, but do not cure neuroses. If the confessor can get across the idea that this is a neurosis he can be of great help to the psychiatrist.

The problem of scrupulosity cannot be dealt with successfully by known objective means. The essential core of the problem is that, as far as reason is concerned, a scrupulous person knows that his behavior is foolish and unreasonable but the battle rages at an unconscious level and he cannot come to grips with it. The unconscious looks at objects and behavior in a primitive way, and thus the problem of scrupulosity becomes displaced and not amenable to a direct approach. An additional complication is the difficulty of communication with the neurotic. In many areas of living the neurotic is totally unaffected, but in the problem area a semantic barrier is encountered. In any case of scrupulosity emphasis must be put on the difference between the symptoms and the sin. The entire problem of the scrupulous person and the obsessive-neurotic is an extremely important one which has not yet received the attention and the research it justly warrants.

SCRUPULOSITY FROM OTHER POINTS OF VIEW

Rev. Gustave A. Weigel, S.J.
Professor of Fundamental Theology, Woodstock College

In spiritual writings the term and the question of scruples has long been known. The masters of ascetical theology have dealt with the problem from the Middle Ages onward. Needless to say, they dealt with the whole issue more practically than theoretically but there was an implicit theory in all of them, nor was it always the same theory. For some, scruples were a trial sent by the devil to vex souls striving for moral perfection. For others it was an almost inevitable phase in the development of those who gave themselves seriously to the religious life.

OLDER VIEWS ON SCRUPULOSITY

In general, spiritual writers and directors did not consider the phenomenon of scruples a psychological disorder until the nineteenth century. I believe that it was Janet who first classified the scrupulous disorder with a psychological label, and he considered scrupulosity to be a simple obsession. Even writers in our day still follow Janet and his theory of neurasthenia, whereby the psychic energy is considered quantitatively with the result that scrupulous persons are people deficient in psychic energy, which must be built up. The way it is built up is by exercise, for the psychic energy was considered to be like a muscle, which can become flabby if not used. This kind of thinking, though it still can be found in relatively modern books, will hardly conform to the best findings of psychology.

For all these older writers scruples meant an overly rigorous demand of conscience beyond what was dictated by the objective precept. Doubtless, there are people so afflicted, but scrupulosity as a term includes phenomena which are only superficially described by the definition just given.

But perhaps the most dangerous element in the older books on scruples was the treatment prescribed. All insisted that the scrupulous person was to follow blindly the counsels of the director. This tactic was justified practically as well as theoretically. The practical justification was that only in this way could the scrupulous person live. If left to his own devices, he would abstain from action because he was always concentrating on the over-rigorous precept relevant to the action. The result would be collapse. The theoretical justification was that the will had to be strengthened like a flabby muscle. This would only happen if the person decided for action. Repeated decision would render the will strong and so it would overcome its neurasthenia.

This over-simplified technique has caused much suffering and very little good. The reason for its inadequacy was the lack of reflection on the total phenomenology of scrupulosity.

The generally accepted supposition that scrupulosity is nothing but the tendency to see sin where there is none needs questioning. It has been often noted that people can be scrupulous in one field of moral endeavor and totally callous in other fields. The political grafter can be puritanically strict in the matter of family morality but totally amoral in his public life. This should give us a key to the nature of scruples. It is not sin itself which frightens the scrupulous person. It is a certain kind of sin, really or supposedly such.

ADOLESCENT SCRUPULOSITY

This preoccupation with a certain kind of sin is especially clear in the maturation of young people. Unfortunately, among Catholics in general though not universally, sex morality is so stressed in their formation that for many of them there is only one sin—sex offense and sex misdemeanor. The small child's norm of right and wrong is more external than internal. Of course children have consciences but they are so inadequately formed that they rely on the precepts given and imposed externally by their elders. In adolescence morality comes from within, and this new experience causes the youth difficulties. There will be an awkwardness in applying rules and this awkwardness is easily labelled as scrupulosity, though the youngster is really very far from pathological scrupulosity. The maturing of the sexual powers with the concomitant psychological interest in the matter will make the youth prone to exaggerate the demands of the law, because when he first heard it, it meant so little to him that he gave it vaster meaning than it actually had. The generality of youths usually survives adolescent "scrupulosity" without traumas.

A phenomenon which is referred to as "angelism" is involved here. The ideal held up to young people in order that it be taken seriously by the young is communicated by the teachers with the usual pedagogic devices of exaggeration and simplification. Teachers know that simplification is the best way of proposing a principle. Hence, the immature student is prone to accept as absolute what was really only intended to be relative; to take as universal what was only meant to be general. In consequence in the minds of many youngsters the precept of chastity means asexuality. The moral doctrine of chastity is quite opposed to the notion of angelism. An angel just because he cannot be unchaste cannot be chaste either; an angel cannot be sober in food and drink any more than he can be immoderate in their use. Sex and food simply are beyond the life of an angel. Chastity as a virtue leads us to the use of the sexual apparatus in accord with its inner rational structure, and therefore the structure is supposed as present, not absent. What is more, in the light of the doctrine of original sin, there is the supposition that the sex drive like all other innate drives in man, will operate spontaneously without the control of reason and even contrary to the dictates of reason. Consequently, the Catholic doctrine of chastity so far from being a doctrine of angelism is really the denial of such a view. However, I think that we must admit that it is a fact that for so many Catholics chastity is conceived as angelism, a condition in which there is no sexual activity, and that man must achieve this situation and the absence of it means moral fault in the subject. Such a frame of mind is not necessarily a state of scrupulosity but rather an effect of bad instruction. When the bad instruction has been corrected, and the striving for angelism still goes on, then we have scrupulosity.

As has already been observed, this scrupulosity derives not from conscience but rather from the superego, the punitive device and inhibitory influence of a cruel father-image. This kind of scrupulosity neither supposes a strong attachment to morality nor does it deny it. It is a mistake to consider scrupulosity as a sign of virtuous striving. It is just psychic disease affecting the intellect's capacity for moral judgment, ranging from the mild but inevitable neurotic disorder in all men to extreme psychosis.

SCRUPULOSITY A DISEASE

As long as the individual is led to believe that his scrupulosity is really a credit to him, he will cherish and nurture it. If he is made aware that he is suffering from a mental disease he will be better able to rid himself of it. Spiritual directors should therefore treat scrupulosity as a disease and make it clear to the subject that it is not the sign of holiness but rather of amoral sickness.

Scrupulosity is not merely an obsession, a concentration on one minor aspect of the real to the exclusion of attention to all its other phases. It is also an anxiety, a fear-state which may be all pervasive or aroused by the problem of chastity or any other moral issue. Its consequences can be compulsive too. The scrupulous person may develop neurotic automatisms because of his anxiety. The advice to have recourse to prayer, though certainly sound in itself, can mean to the scrupulous person the need for some prayer action which he is compelled to perform, such as making the sign of the cross or speaking to himself with words like "I won't," "I refuse," etc. Consequently scrupulosity involves obsession, anxiety, compulsion, and other motives. It may also be masochistic self-torture in a perverted attempt to satisfy the sex drive.

Dr. Coville in his case history of Mary showed a typical characteristic of the scrupulous person. There was much introspection and much self-examination. Scrupulosity frequently involves narcissism, and when it does there is a deep-seated self-centrality in the subject.

There is a lack of awareness of the objective world and the ego seems the only reality worth considering. Such persons are characterized by selfishness and indifference to others. They do not take part in social activities, not even in religious social activities.

Nor must we think that if the scrupulosity concerns sex there will be no consciously induced sex activity. The compulsive nature of scrupulosity will produce all kinds of sex acts ranging from the more obvious to the most bizarre. The scrupulous person will complain that he does not want these outlets or actings-out, and in a way he speaks the truth. There is a compulsion involved in the whole matter. The scrupulous person lives through the picture so vividly painted by St. Paul in the Epistle to the Romans (Rom. 7:15-16) and comes to the conclusion that within himself there is another agent who does things which the higher or conscious agent does not want at all.

Scrupulosity need not be bedded in narcissism. It can also be a schizophrenic or paranoid manifestation. After all, the schizophrenic has a double life; one peculiarly his own built up in fantasy and the other in terms of the objective environment in which he lives. In the fantasy world scrupulosity can develop nicely in as far as it is a central and controlling obsession.

Once more angelism can enter in its most vicious form. The subject may unconsciously set up the angelic ideal in order to punish himself in an aggression directed to the subject. Precisely because there is sexual activity in fantasy or in deed, the angel-ideal can punish the agent and punish him severely and constantly. Oedipus complex and angelism can easily go together, and usually do.

In brief, scrupulosity is not a sign of virtue; it is not a sign of good will; it is not a token of submission to God and His law. This is the first thing which must be recognized. Secondly, it is not merely an obsession. It involves anxiety and compulsion as well. It may be radically narcissistic or radically paraphrenic or depressive. It may be masochistic. In some cases one feels that it is all these things. Thirdly, the initial awkwardness of the adolescent in applying the moral law to himself should not be declared scrupulosity though it contains some of its signs. In the average adolescent it is a passing phase doing neither harm nor good. Only when it survives adolescence or is clearly neurotic in the adolescent can we call it true scrupulosity. We can define scrupulosity as the pathological disturbance of the intellect's capacity for moral judgment.

HANDLING OF SCRUPULOSITY

What to do with the scrupulous person? We are again faced with the limitations of the priestly power. The priest as priest is not a psychiatrist, and when a definite scrupulous syndrome is a true neurosis it cannot be handled adequately by the non-trained priest guide. If it is not a true neurosis or psychosis but only a neurotic tendency, the priest can do much. First of all he can bring peace to the penitent. Secondly, he can ward off the development of a neurotic tendency into a true neurosis. When the true neurosis is present, then the penitent can only be referred to a psychiatrist, or at least guided by the priest instructed by a psychiatrist for this particular case.

There are certain commonly used means which seem totally counter-indicated. The suggestion that the penitent have recourse to little prayer formulas when temptation comes seems harmful; a compulsion is being induced and the compulsion will only strengthen the temptation which is now officially declared as beyond the powers of the subject's resistance. Even a general prayer habit directed to this problem exclusively only strengthens the obsession of the penitent. The priest should try to direct the penitent's attention away from the object of his anxiety, not lead him to it.

Secondly, the oft-used advice to be obedient to the confessor and do what he says, even though the reasons are not apparent to the penitent, is not helpful. The subject is not being cured. He is being turned into an automaton. Needless to say, the advice is rarely followed because it cannot be. Moral action always supposes personal choice, and the choice of the confessor is not that of the person. Personal choice always supposes an intellectual vision of the choices possible, and if the intellectual vision is not sound, the choice will not be sound.

Here is where the work must be done. The penitent must be shown that his problem is not moral at all, but rather psychic. His anxiety must be traced to its roots. He must be led to see that his angelism is either neurotic pride or father-rebellion or a strong unconscious desire to indulge in a certain line of conduct which his conscious moral code does not allow. Let us not forget that the person scrupulous in the matter of chastity is sexually very active in fantasy or deed. He is merely trying so hard to deny that he is doing so, and his denial takes the form of evasion of the law by legal techniques. When he accuses himself in such a way that it is clear that the law has not been violated, he is unconsciously trying to justify himself, though he cannot feel the justification because he has not faced the true law in the whole matter. This incapacity to face the true law is repression; it is not lack of intelligence nor absence of good will.

Ultimately it seems to boil down to this: the priestly attitude to the scrupulous person must be psychiatric, even though no true psychiatry is done. The priest's work must be analytic, bringing out by a long treatment of questions the inner drives and unresolved past conflicts which produce the malaise. If the case is difficult, then the penitent must be referred to a competent therapist.

And what do we do when we cannot send the penitent to a psychiatrist? I think the answer is obvious enough. We do what we can. If we are not doctors, we can at least be nurses. The nurse takes care of the sick person even after the doctor has given him up. With patience and sympathy the patient's needs are satisfied in the proper fashion. If the doctor cannot come or does not come, the nurse does what she can, but she always remembers that she is a nurse and not a doctor. This I think is the answer to a question which has been vexing us during all our discussions. Often enough good nursing produces a cure, and even when it does not, it is still in demand.

Thomas L. Doyle, M.D.
*Consulting Psychiatrist, Fordham University**

For generations and centuries before we as physicians dared to specialize in the field of human behavior, churchmen, clergy and religious were attacking the problem of excessive guilt and concern over sin. Because of this tradition, experience, and know-how, I as a psychiatrist, feel a deep humble emotion in assuming the privilege of talking to you about this problem. My heart tells me that I should

* Shortly after the 1955 Institute, Dr. Doyle resigned this post to enter the armed services. He is now engaged in private psychiatric practice in New York City.

take the lowermost seat and listen. It is only because of my training and my experience with the medical approach to these cases that I feel that I can add anything at all. It is the seriousness and urgency of the reaction—the heartache and suffering of the scrupulous person that truly urges us to be here today and attempt a solution. The problem is serious because it affects not only the less significant layman, but also the cloistered religious and important clergy. Let it be said first of all that the scrupulous person is a good person. He is conscious of his moral duty and wishes to serve God. It is just this trait that runs rampant because of a personality disorder or even a serious psychiatric illness that makes up the matter of scrupulous pathology. Although help and efficacious good help is extended to the person by clergyman or physician, some cases are resistant to help and go on to total mental breakdown. It is here especially that the psychiatrist grounded in good moral and medical principles can play his greatest role.

The scrupulous person is not a rare entity and you in pastoral work could inform me far more on the high incidence of the problem. We here at Fordham in the Department of Psychological Services see at least 30 percent of our emotionally disturbed students having some form of scrupulosity. We enter treatment on a total approach basis promptly and vigorously. It is my impression that every pastor has a certain definite proportion of his flock afflicted with the malady.

SCRUPLES A PSYCHIATRIC ILLNESS

There is a large cultural factor which conditions the individual to the scrupulous state and is important in its etiology. Persons of Roman Catholic faith are more prone to the reaction than those of other denominational groups. The person raised in rigid compliance to a strict religious code and way of life when he becomes emotionally disturbed is more liable to show scrupulous symptoms. It is not because of the religious training that this occurs, but in spite of it. The individual with a healthy psychological adjustment has no need to probe the most simple incidental action into a sinful serious meaning. In doing so, he loses sight of the aim of his religious fervor and turns the energy upon himself in a destructive way. To do this one must be ill. Thus the conclusion which we must stress today is that the person who shows the signs and symptoms of scrupulosity at the height of the reaction is demonstrating a facet of a serious psychiatric illness.

Like all psychiatric illness, it is the quantitative aberration which determines the pathology. Thus the degree of the scrupulosity is all important. Fleeting reactions of concern for sinfulness bordering on near excess are normal and occur in all persons attempting to lead a sound or heroic moral life. We all suffer on occasion from anxiety, depression, frustration, day dreams, and scrupulous thoughts. There is nothing new under the sun and scruples are not unique. It is when the concern over committing sin becomes the major concern of the day, and disrupts the healthy free flow of emotions, that scrupulosity becomes a major problem.

Scruples may be seen at times in the sensitive child. This may represent undue emotional stress, particularly tension at home and parental rejection. Seven to ten years of age is the most usual time. The reactions are usually short-lived, they clear up without specific therapy, and they leave no lasting damage.

The next period for appearance of the scrupulous state is seen in adolescence—just at puberty or shortly thereafter. Such a reaction carries a dangerous prognostic sign and is accompanied by great emotional turmoil, "hysterics," weeping, etc. In nearly all cases the onset of serious scruples at this time may portend an acute dissociating disease—schizophrenia. The young person feels that he has personally wronged God far more than has any other of His creatures. Such persons become tense, sleepless, withdrawn, and suffer from bizarre thought patterns. A recent case that I saw in consultation had all of her guilt stem from the fact that she had broken a drinking glass in her parochial school—all by accident—but this signified harm to the Church and God. Rejection and lack of love at home were demonstrated as some of the major factors in her incipient schizophrenia. Treatment included therapy for the parents even more than for the scrupulous child.

ADULT SCRUPULOSITY

Scruples as we commonly think of them are seen in adult life. The highest frequency is in the twenty-year olds, but the reaction is by no means limited to this decade. One sex is no more prone to the reaction than the other, so that it occurs equally in males and females. In the adult scrupulous person the symptom complex represents deep-seated conflict or frustration. The reaction frequently represents a frustrated sexual drive. Healthy sexual energy is bottled up and transferred into masochistic scrupulous symptoms. In the clergyman or religious, in whom sexual outlet is limited by the vow of chastity, the scrupulous state may represent a failure of healthy sublimation and proper channelling of normal instinctual drives.

The largest number of scrupulous persons belong in the category of the psychoneurotic reactions. They fall into the illness termed the obsessive-compulsive neurosis. These persons appear as rational as you and I; they do not appear sick on the surface; they can deal with reality in nearly every sphere of their lives; they hold down good jobs. However, they are tense people, troubled and restless. They feel that they have not found their purpose in life. Deep in their unconscious they are in conflict, and they cannot satisfy their pathologically high ideals. Anxiety breaks through to disturb their equilibrium. The cause of the disturbance cannot be understood by them, and if the therapist approaches the solution the answer is so harsh and hard to take that they cannot accept it. Thus anxiety is channelled into obsessive preoccupation with the possibility of sinning. This preoccupation with sin, past, present, or future, can take over all of their thinking. This type of obsession is like other neurotic obsessions concerned with health, salvation, and the like. In Freudian terms the scrupulous person has an excessive need to be clean—to be free of dirt and sin.

In such people normal, healthy drives and inhibitions become exaggerated and out of proportion. The normal desire for holiness and sinlessness swings to pathological self-destructive avoidance of sin or even the most minute innocuous act. In his hatred of self for falling short of ridiculously high ideals, the person assigns evil to events and actions that are completely innocent. These scruples are a symptom of the anxiety stemming from the deeper conflict.

The next largest group of scrupulous persons is seen in those who are in the process of developing schizophrenia where the total personality is breaking down and dissociating. Scruples are on occasion seen in the patient who is in the early stages of paranoid dementia praecox whose efforts at holding the personality together are breaking down. Here we observe the ideas of grandeur which are twisted to make the person feel that any act might be sinful and unworthy. Symbolically and paradoxically they may wish to take over God's place—the Jehovah complex—and as this idea approaches consciousness they are overwhelmed and flee into scrupulosity.

Other cases—somewhat more infrequent—are seen in the simple withdrawn schizoid person. These people are so fearful and tense that they withdraw almost completely into a shell. They are unable to face reality or to be objective. This scrupulous overconcern may persist for years resisting all therapeutic efforts. Here the scruples are a defense for the patient to hide behind, making him the center of attention and at the same time representing his own frustrations, weakness and inadequacy.

The scrupulous pattern is rarely seen in the deeply or even moderately depressed person. It can occur and therefore should be mentioned. In the patient who is essentially depressed the scruples are a self-deprecating phenomenon and fit in with a whole trend of self-imposed distrust, lack of self-confidence, and dissatisfaction. As the depression is lifted, the entire chain of scrupulous symptoms will disappear and will not return unless the depression recurs.

SOME INSTANCES OF SCRUPULOSITY

The obsessive-compulsive neurotic reactor is seen most commonly and I am sure you have encountered several cases in your pastoral work. I was called to see a patient in a convent of Sisters —a semi-contemplative order that also performed vigorous active work. The patient was in her late thirties and had been in the convent for over fifteen years. She was a tense, thin, wiry, obedient, but troubled person. For the past ten years of her religious life she had suffered from scruples. There was an excessive need to be clean, and she feared that she might spread germs and contamination to others. Any small act, or fleeting aggressive thought, meant serious sin to her and she could no longer measure the reality of her actions. She went to confession in every church near her convent up to six and eight times a day. She was restless, sleepless, paced the floor at night, and disturbed the Community. A change of assignment, spiritual direction linked closely with psychiatric care, ultimately broke down the persistent obsessions. Insight increased, and she began to understand many of her deeper conflicts, aggressions, and frustrations and could handle them better. She is much improved, but under duress the same symptom pattern is prone to recur.

A young Catholic male in his late twenties was referred to me by a close friend who is a curate in one of our large parishes. A graduate of a non-Catholic high school, he was then working for a chemical supply house. The family background and culture was Spanish and different from the usual family in the neighborhood. However, the patient was thoroughly Americanized. For the two years prior to examination by me, the patient had developed a gradually increasing scrupulosity. He could not date a girl or even permit himself to look casually at a woman on the street. He truly believed that even the thought of sex fleeting through his mind could be a mortal sin, inviting possible loss of heaven and demanding immediate confession to a priest. The patient was under much pressure and was becoming more and more compulsive in all his actions.

Careful psychiatric evaluation revealed that on two occasions in the past months he had been hallucinated and had heard voices telling him he was sinful and calling him dirty names. Here clearly was a case of early paranoid schizophrenia developing out of the obsessive state. Intensive therapy was instituted immediately. He was placed on the new psychiatric drug, chlorpromazine, and gradually in psychotherapy he became more extroverted and self-assured. The schizoid qualities became dim and lessened as insight developed. Ultimately scrupulous thoughts no longer occurred to him. He dated girls and made new friends. Because of conflict with his parents the patient finally left home to travel West and enter the hotel business. I have heard from him subsequently and he seemingly has developed a sound moral life and a healthy personal adjustment.

The simple withdrawn schizoid reaction described previously was exemplified in a female patient I treated in a large psychiatric hospital. The patient was approximately fifty years of age and for the last twenty years had been an Anglican nun. For the past eight to ten years, she had become particularly tense in the cloistered life, and fearful of her duties and of the other persons in the Community. She would remain by herself for hours and was convinced that even her slightest action or glance was gravely sinful. She would weep, was withdrawn, refused to eat and was sleepless. Ultimately her condition warranted psychiatric hospitalization. Under intensive care and by changing her whole environment she was brought out of her withdrawn state while at the hospital. She has returned to the Episcopalian convent in a new assignment. She is a sensitive person and not particularly active or aggressive. Still she has something of a sense of humor now and she is no longer subject to scruples.

The last case is one of scruples in a depressed person. This patient, also treated in a psychiatric hospital, was a large, roly-poly construction engineer, married and of Jewish extraction. He had been extroverted, jolly, and self-assured until nine months previously. Suddenly, previously insignificant actions appeared wrong and sinful to him and he berated himself. He became more and more scrupulous and self-deprecatory until he felt totally useless and immoral. Soon a deep depression took over and he was hospitalized. Under electro-shock and psychotherapy, the scruples were eradicated, and now three years later he is happy, stable, and at ease. Here the scruples reflected essentially his depressive illness.

TREATMENT OF SCRUPULOSITY

My description of these cases has revealed something of the therapeutic approach to these problems. The treatment must be well grounded. The first consideration is the religious approach, and here prayer and the petition for grace to overcome the problem under the guidance of the spiritual director is most important. The clergyman must give reassurance and attempt to develop insights in the person which will lead to desensitization of feelings resulting from the deep conflicts. By transference to himself and confidence in the person, the priest, minister, or rabbi can lead the individual to a more extroverted reaction and the gradual maturing of the personality.

If the case does not respond to treatment or is showing resistance, increasing tension, disorganization of the personality, or paranoid symptoms, the patient must then be referred for immediate psychiatric help. The priest and the psychiatrist then work as a team, each caring for his own area of readjustment. With the obsessive-compulsive patient the psychiatrist analyzes and loosens the deeper frustrations which leads to insight and healthier methods of sublimation. The person becomes more mature, and learns to "roll with the punch." He is no longer as sensitive, is more confident and more effective. Ultimately he is led toward a better heterosexual adjustment which permits the proper flow of instinctive needs.

With the schizophrenic patient, especially the paranoid, support, reassurances, and total direction play a more important therapeutic role. Ultimately the paranoid illness will precipitate out and then the medical approach will be exactly the same as in any such problem. These scruples are actually only a facet of the major disturbance and may disappear as the true projective symptoms are brought under therapeutic control. Depending upon the depth of the disease and the time when the patient receives treatment the outlook for recovery will vary.

With the person in a depressed state the affect and mood is treated and the scrupulous pattern will immediately lessen with recovery. Treatment of persons in religious life or clergymen is of course more difficult and requires special consideration. If the trends are deep, fixed, and chronic, only support and some insight may be developed. The new drugs, chlorpromazine and reserpine, should be used freely by the psychiatrist in attendance and to a full extent. A change of assignment should be considered which will permit wider efforts at sublimation and more healthy mental mechanisms to act. Therapy should be long-term and as thorough and complete as possible.

The prognosis and outlook for recovery depends essentially on the depth of the conflict and frustration and the degree of fixation present. In the young person entering vigorous therapy the prognosis is usually good. The outlook for the scrupulous schizophrenic is that of dementia praecox itself—25 percent should recover, and 50 percent should be greatly improved under proper treatment. Today with new techniques of medical treatment the prognosis for the depressed person is amazingly good.

I would make one closing plea. This is for close cooperation and understanding between religious and psychiatrist. There is no true dichotomy. We are on the same team working simply for the good and salvation of the troubled mind and soul. The resulting confidence in the patient will be amazing.

SUMMARY OF SCRUPULOSITY

In his presentation of scrupulosity, Father Mailloux had stressed the inadequacy of our concepts regarding the nature and treatment of scrupulosity. It occurs, he said, in the area of conscience which has three functions: (1) attendance to the objective morality of the act and the intention that governs it; (2) eliciting of internal commands and restrictions; and (3) a deep and realistic sense of responsibility.

Four types of scrupulous persons can be distinguished. The first type is characterized by anxiety and an uncontrollable fear of sin that often extends to imaginary obligations, what might be called a "moral claustrophobia." In such cases deep, severe conflicts are characteristic. The second type is found in the obsessive-compulsive neurotic, where the affective element is shame. The individual develops a private morality and religion and is impervious to reason. There is a pervasive and pathological self-esteem, and compulsions develop as protective devices for the scrupulosity. This condition tends to do away with responsibility; the individual escapes the consequences of his actions by the use of words and abstractions. The predominant psychological element in this category is narcissism. The third type is in a measure the reverse of the first two, in which scrupulosity is characterized by guilt. The penitent tells of having committed a great number of sins. He delays securing absolution; he develops feelings of despair and annihilation; and he demands from the confessor love, protection, and security. This is a type of moral masochism. The fourth type of scrupulosity is characterized by mutism, in which the paramount feature is mistrust in the counseling situation. He may burst forth with rage and aggression when once his antipathy is triggered. He characteristically mistrusts the ability and the good faith of the counselor.

One of the main background factors in the development of scrupulosity is inconsistency of behavior in the persons important in the patient's life. This situation acts as a source of pathological idealism; it leads to hopelessness in striving, stimulates conflicts, and shows up commonly as hatred for God, religion, and morality. The result is usually the development of a paranoid trend.

The scope of scrupulosity is far wider than that suggested by the older formulation that it is an element only in the obsessive-compulsive neurotic. Actually, it involves a pathological sensitivity in moral conscience which is seen in a large variety of clinical entities. The behavior of the scrupulous person is rooted in a deep religiosity. Remedy is directed not so much to a change in the superego as it is to a change in conscience, the inner voice of God.

Four rules are suggested for the priest-counselor in assisting the scrupulous person: 1) he must be aware not to be captured by symptomatic actions and thus be distracted from essential causal factors; 2) the counselor should draw the penitent's attention to his insecurity, shame, sensitivity to guilt, and to his aggression against himself and mistrust of the counselor; 3) the counselor must remember that apparent moral conflicts submitted for solution usually serve as a screen to disguise earlier conflicts of an infantile nature; and 4) the priest-counselor should be keenly aware of the possible implications of neurotic transference in dealing with scrupulous persons because they are excessively dependent.

The typical characteristics of the scrupulous person are immaturity, fixation and/or regression to an earlier level of functioning, anxiety, pervasive guilt, a pathological ideal, and the development of protective devices to escape the implications of scrupulosity.

Treatment of scrupulosity is dependent upon a number of factors. First, it is important to determine the nature of the difficulty itself. Second, therapists must arrive at a knowledge of basic causes. Third, it must be remembered that the condition is more psychological than moral in nature. Fourth, treatment should be complemented by research that will give us more insight into the nature of this condition. Fifth, therapists, particularly priests, should work toward an integration of theological and psychological therapeutic approaches.

In a brief discussion that followed, Father Weigel pointed out that the older treatment of scrupulosity was dangerous in that it was oversimplified and failed to take into account the seriousness of the condition and its possible implications for other areas of behavior. Scrupulosity is very often incidental to psychosexual development and is thus a tangential characteristic. In many girls there is a danger that scrupulosity will lead to angelism, and there is always the possibility of confusing angelism with true chastity.

Chastity is rightly conceived in the light of man's nature which is partly sexual, and thus angelism is inadequate to sanctity because it denies part of the basic nature of man.

Father Weigel also pointed out that scrupulosity is not virtuous striving; rather it is a disease and should be treated as such. It is largely obsessive in nature, but also presents other neurotic symptoms, and it is both egocentric and selfish in character. The scrupulous person is basically unsocial. He is prone to self-punishment and this is not true submission to the will of God.

In treatment, the priest must recognize his own limitations. Forcing the penitent to pray may lead to an increase in his already unhealthy feelings. The scrupulous person is worried about the practice of obedience because it deepens his sense of dependence and inadequacy. He should be made to understand that his problem is psychological rather than moral, and that he suffers from a neurotic pride which he tries to rationalize. The spiritual counselor must develop the right attitude toward the penitent and can be of great help in giving necessary support.

Emotional Disorders of Children

JOSEPH J. REIDY

Joseph J. Reidy, M.D., received his medical degree from Loyola University in Chicago in 1948. He spent the year 1953-54 as a resident in child psychiatry at the Neuropsychiatric Institute of the University of Michigan. From 1954 to 1957 he was Medical Director of the Astor Home for Children, Rhinebeck, N. Y., and from 1957 to 1962 he served as Director of Child Psychiatry, Department of Mental Hygiene of the State of Maryland. From 1960 to 1961, he was Assistant Commissioner, Department of Mental Hygiene, of the State of Maryland. Since 1962 Dr. Reidy has been engaged in the private practice of psychiatry in Baltimore. He is the author of approximately 25 articles in professional and scientific journals, mostly in the area of child psychiatry.

This paper presents a brief outline of the very important and complex field of childhood emotional development. Our understanding of this field is limited; there are many aspects which we cannot fully explain, and the number of research projects increases each year. But the classical psychoanalytic theory of child development, the substance of this paper, provides the most complete and coherent explanation of the facts.

The clergyman, like the teacher, should be acquainted with the principles of childhood emotional development and should be able to understand how persons achieve mental health and realize their potentials. He should be able to recognize children who are manifestly emotionally ill and refer them for appropriate diagnosis and treatment. The clergyman can give to children the counsel and support they need in times of trouble, sickness, and bereavement. We expect that he will help to provide the social and family setting which produces emotionally healthy children. In this paper I wish to introduce these principles of child development and to indicate how the clergyman can join forces with the other professionals in this field.

EARLY DEVELOPMENTAL PROCESSES

The infant begins life with instincts which have as their goal immediate and direct satisfaction. These instincts exist for the life of the person, seeking always to operate by this "pleasure principle," to obtain satisfaction independently of the outside world, or despite the demands of the outside world. But in order to adapt to reality, indeed, even to survive, the infant postpones some immediate pleasures, modifies some instinctual aims, and abandons other aims. This, the process of development, which is also the process of socialization, causes frustration, anxiety, and conflict.

From the psychoanalytic viewpoint instincts are not bad or harmful. They are the raw material out of which character and personality are formed, and it is the instinctual energy properly directed which leads to knowledge and civilization. Although instincts have the goal of immediate discharge and satisfaction, they are very flexible and can adapt to many life circumstances. This flexibility is one of the differences between the instincts of humans and those of animals. Not only is the instinctual life not bad, but an individual with strong instinctual drives will be able to gain satisfactions in many ways which make possible a full development of his potentials and a rich, satisfying life.

The instinct seeking direct satisfaction comes into conflict with the requirements of reality. To gratify the wish under these conditions becomes painful or dangerous; for example, it might entail the loss of love. The aim, or wish, is forbidden by reality and must be repressed. Repression does not mean a destruction of the instinct or even a lessening of its force, but a delay in satisfaction or a change of aim. The aim, the forbidden wish, not the instinct, is repressed.

Depending on the circumstances repression can be harmful or beneficial. This course of development is so inevitable that we must judge as unrealistic those training methods which promise freedom from frustration, anxiety, conflict, and repression. Child training which takes into account the child's instinctual life does not mean a lack of training of instinct, a "permissiveness," nor does it mean a rigid stifling of instinctual life. A person is so constituted that in an "average expectable environment" his potentials will unfold in an orderly and predictable manner.

Although the flexibility of instincts, the ability to choose when and in what manner to satisfy instinctual drives, is a feature of human life, this flexibility is limited. The person's inborn mechanisms of growth and adaptation are limited by his hereditary endowment which will include the degree of his physical health and bodily intactness, his intelligence, the strength of his drives and his ability to tolerate stress. These mechanisms will lead to normal development if the environment provides adequate stimulation and if the stresses and frustrations at each developmental stage are not excessive. There must be anxiety for the child to learn to tolerate anxiety and also to warn him of danger, there must be stress for the person to develop the ability to master life situations.

In the development of the embryo each organ has its period of "ascendancy," a critical period of growth; if injury occurs during this period the damage will be widespread and will affect succeeding growth; if injury occurs after this critical period the damage will be less.

> . . . there are critical moments in the development of every organ or part that are characterized by rapid cell multiplication. At such times this particular proliferating region is dominant and may even exert a depressing influence over the growth of other parts. If this favorable moment for differentiation is not taken advantage of, the transient supremacy of the organ is lost and it in turn submits to depression by other parts assuming their dominant periods. The result is a reduced or imperfectly formed region, which, having missed its opportunity, is never able to express itself completely or perfectly in competition with other parts now arrived at similar states of perferment (Arey, 1943, pp. 178-179).

There are also periods of ascendancy in emotional development during which injury or lack of stimulation causes damage. Since each growth stage is built upon the preceding one, a child whose needs have not been met adequately at one stage will attempt to overcome this handicap throughout succeeding stages and his behavior will bear the characteristics of pathology of that stage. For example, the child who has experienced severe deprivation in the period when his needs for feeding are predominant—the oral stage —may show disorders of eating, obesity, or alcoholism in later life. The adolescent who shows an extremely rebellious attitude toward authority may have struggled in childhood with parents who were extremely restricting and punitive. In general the earlier in life any fault or damage occurs the more widespread and serious will be the pathology and the more thoroughly it will effect subsequent development. The most severely damaged children, the organically mentally retarded, are usually damaged in the prenatal period or at birth. The childhood schizophrenics experience at least part of their hurt in the first year of life. Even the youngest infant is impressionable and damageable; from his earliest days the child has an emotional life which needs nurture and training of the proper kind to strengthen his ability to master instincts and adapt to reality.

IMPORTANCE OF PARENT-CHILD RELATIONSHIPS

"Nurture" means more than physical care and love, although it certainly includes these essentials. Unfortunately, there are many children in our time who do not receive these basics, who are unwanted, unloved, inhumanly treated, physically neglected. Nurture means protection, approval, stimulation, limit-setting, consistency and many other things to which every child is entitled. It means a parent-child relationship where the child is not seen as a cute plaything or an annoying burden or as someone to supply the satisfactions the parent should be getting from other relationships, but as a wonderfully important person in his own right. There is a connection between the emotional life of children and the quality of parent-child relationships.

> This assumption rests also on a genetic view of certain basic functions of the organism as inherited potentialities, fulfilled only with appropriate organic or social environments—it is assumed that an infant equipped with the potentialities for special response will suffer its loss or severe diminution if no social environment exists in which the response can

operate. The social object, mother, or mother substitute, who constitutes the infant's first social environment must presumably give emotional warmth during the process of infant care in the early months of life (Levy, 1951, p. 251).

One of the newborn's first tasks is to recognize his own distinctness, to differentiate between himself and the rest of the world. He must learn about himself through contact with persons, particularly his mother. He perceives that his mother's body or his mother's breast is part of himself when he is fed; but he comes to perceive that there are times when this person or this breast is absent. Although he can hallucinate the missing object, he finds that this does not satisfy his hunger and his need for comfort, so he must abandon this attempt to find the source of satisfaction within himself and he seeks it in the outer world. The giver of food and other comforts becomes an object distinct from himself and an object that the infant recognizes as having a special relationship to himself. The giver of food becomes the giver of love and the bridge to reality. Since nurture is more than giving pleasure and comfort and food, since it is also protecting the child and setting realistic limits to his instinctual aims, the nurturing person causes the infant pain and frustration. The infant has feelings of anger and opposition toward the person he loves, and his feelings of love and hate are incompatible. He can resolve these conflicts in a way that he will come to look upon the world as hostile and restricting, but if he feels assured of love and approval he can sacrifice his immediate desires in return for this love.

Often we have come to recognize the conditions for the attainment of object relations and object love by their absence. When there is a lack of this one-to-one parent-child relationship, as happens in large institutions for homeless infants and young children, there are very serious consequences. In very young infants there is retardation of physical and mental growth. These children do not reach out to take in their environment; they resemble organically retarded infants and this state often persists until the child leaves the institution. Adoptive parents are surprised at how rapidly some of these children learn to talk, for example, once they are in a family.

Some infants seem depressed, apathetic. Their physical needs are cared for in an excellent manner, but some lose interest in the world, indeed, some have died. There is another reaction which produces children who have been called "empty" or "affectionless." These children were first studied in institutions where they were reared during their formative years, that is, from birth to pre-school years, and where they had no consistent relationship to one person who could function as a parent to them, but were cared for in groups by an ever-changing line of adults. They developed little capacity for social relationships, did not trust people, did not experience the feelings of loving or being loved. They had to find a substitute for this absent relationship and often found it in material things; for example, some became chronic stealers. Often they failed to find a substitute for this loving relationship and they became restless, shallow people who had no strong feelings for other persons.

CHILDHOOD SCHIZOPHRENIA

The most severe pathology in object relations occurs in schizophrenia. In adults we see schizophrenia as a disease process characterized by a breakdown in thinking, a failure to perceive correctly and form rational judgments about the reality of the outside world, and a lack of an appropriate synthesis of thought and feeling. The breakdown manifests itself in the symptoms of being withdrawn from the world of reality and immersed in one's own thought processes, feeling that the people in the world are hostile and persecuting to the patient, hallucinations of sight and hearing, and moods which range from stuporous or flat states to those of extreme silliness, excitability, panic and suspicion. There are many variations in this clinical picture, and many persons who appear to function quite well in their life situations may show the tendencies which come to full flower in the clinically-ill patient. Whether there is one schizophrenia or whether there are several diseases falling under this broad classification, we do not know. At any rate, all of these states have certain common features, and there is one explanation common to the various states:

> The infant starts out in a state of "primary narcissism," in which the systems of the mental apparatus are not yet differentiated from each other, and in which no objects exist as yet. The differentiation of the ego coincides with the discovery of objects. An ego exists in so far as it is differentiated from objects that are not ego. Therefore, the following

formulae mean one and the same thing, only varying in point of view: the schizophrenic has regressed to narcissism; the schizophrenic has lost his objects; the schizophrenic has parted with reality; the schizophrenic's ego has broken down (Fenichel, 1945, p. 415).

At one time it was thought that schizophrenia did not occur until after puberty, but we know now that there are children whose adjustment to reality is so incomplete that we can say that they have failed to form object relations. These children are called schizophrenic and the terms "autism" and "symbiotic psychosis" describe special groups of these children. When this illness is present in its severe form the child does not communicate at all with others. He may not talk or may talk only in meaningless words or repeat stereotyped phrases or questions. He is constantly trying to master particular aspects of reality, fails to master, continues to try, but cannot integrate them as other children do. He may be almost constantly rocking himself, or running up and down, or spinning objects around and around. He cannot orient himself in relation to place, space, time, or other persons, and often does not know the limits of his own body. Many of these children, when they do speak with some meaning, will reveal abnormalities in object relationship. For example, some will never call themselves "I" or "Me," but "He," or refer to themselves by name. Many of these children do not view the world as a stable platform, but whirl and skip, attempt to jump off high places, even to fly, because of their disordered perception of the world. Piaget (1954) speaks of every infant as having an isolation within his own experience before he knows of himself or knows of a world with an existence apart from him. If the child cannot escape from this isolation, or if he needs to fall back to this state, he is a very seriously ill child, and one who may not respond to treatment.

While it seems probable that schizophrenia of childhood is an organic condition, and that it is inherited as a recessive physical trait, it is also probable that environment plays a part. Since the most important part of the child's early environment is his parents, many studies of childhood schizophrenia have considered the emotional health of the parents. Early reports in the literature pictured the parents as intelligent and educated, but cold and undemonstrative, who looked upon their infant as an interesting experiment, and who often intruded on his development with excessive demands for accomplishment and growth. Other parents were pictured as hostile, confused, guilt-ridden, or depressed. The child finds difficulty in forming his first object relations because it is difficult to relate to these parents, or because the parents are unable to provide sufficient incentive for the child to give up his own world. Perhaps some of these observed attitudes are the reactions of parents to this serious and puzzling illness of their child. Because of the difficulty in assessing the contribution of the quality of the mother-child relationship or of emotional illness of the parents to the occurrence of schizophrenia, we must be cautious lest we accentuate feelings of guilt and unworthiness in these parents.

The infant's task in knowing reality and in making object ties and the difficulty of the schizophrenic child in accomplishing this task illustrate how very important issues are decided quite early in life. There are other emotional illnesses which occur when the child fails to meet the demands at later epochs of development. Even when the recognizable clinical illnesses of childhood are absent, damage in any of these periods will lay the groundwork for the emotional illnesses and character disorders of later life.

CHILDHOOD SEXUAL AND AGGRESSIVE DRIVES

The sources of these disturbances in childhood and in later life are the sexual and the aggressive drives. Not only does every child have active sexual and aggressive drives, but normal emotional development cannot take place unless the energy of these drives is used. Many persons will deny the existence of infantile sexual life, and it is not surprising that the adult has little recollection of his infantile drives. The physical limitations of the child and the requirements of reality prevent his attaining his infantile sexual and aggressive goals; these goals are forbidden, they must be repressed and become unconscious. The repression often leads the adult to negate the existence of these strong drives in infancy and childhood. Because of this repression the adult constructs the fantasy of the happy child, and this fantasy leads him to overlook the real problems of childhood. When the adult acts in accordance with this fantasy he may contribute to the problems of the child.

The parent who denies the existence of an infantile sexual life may be the parent who encourages nudity in the house or takes little precaution in keeping his sexual activities from his child's awareness. He (or she) may be allowing intimacies with his children which he will characterize as "affectionate," but which in fact are sexually stimulating. The physician who denies the existence of infantile sexuality and scoffs at concepts such as "castration anxiety" will be oblivious of the serious effects of hospitalization and surgery for children. Adults who deny the existence of these drives will not see the necessity for carefully explaining realities of death and illness and birth and the many other events which the child cannot handle unaided.

We have considered that the aim of instincts is immediate satisfaction, but the infant learns that immediate satisfaction sometimes brings pain rather than pleasure. His curiosity attracts him to touch the hot stove, the pain induces him to give up this goal. We see the child express anger toward inanimate objects which limit him, and we see him express hostility toward his mother who frustrates his desires. The child learns only gradually to distinguish between his wish and the fulfillment of his wish, he equates thought and act, and when he wishes to revenge himself against his frustrator he considers his action accomplished by the magic of wish fulfillment. This accounts, for example, for the anxiety of young children when separated from their parents. In some children this anxiety, stemming from their hostile wishes, will be so great that they are unable to go to school. So long as they are not separated from their mother they can be reassured that their hostile wishes have not been carried out. Since the child can only imperfectly distinguish wish from act, he will fear punishment for his forbidden wishes. When the child has a need for the person toward whom he feels hostile, when he feels love for the frustrating parent, he must somehow handle these conflicting feelings. If he directly expresses his hostility he will risk the loss of love. If he is convinced that he is unloved, he will risk nothing; if he is convinced he is bad, he may act as a bad child, so that he will be punished and so regain the love. Or he may strive so hard to conform, to be good, that he becomes severely inhibited or overly-conscientious.

The outcome of the struggle of instinct with reality results in a "defense." The basic defense is repression, but the instinct uses its energy to escape this repression and the person calls upon other defenses to maintain the repression. The defenses vary from those which work with a minimum of expenditure of energy by the ego and so leave the ego with adequate energy to develop normally to those which absorb so much energy that the child is constantly occupied with shoring up this failing repression, and this keeps him fixated at one developmental level. A child must always make use of defenses and there are in every child times when his defenses fail and we have break-through of anxiety, minor and transient symptom formation.

DEVELOPMENT OF SUPEREGO

In concluding this part of my paper I wish to discuss briefly the superego. This concept is not the same as moral conscience or moral consciousness which are theological concepts, but it is a way to explain how the child who has needed his parents to set limits on his instinctual life himself takes over this limit setting. In the healthy personality we do not see the manifestations of superego functioning because then it works in harmony with reality and causes no difficulty. It is only when the ego fails to control the instinctual life that we see the superego manifested either as an excessively rigid apparatus which can control instinctual life at the expense of the impoverishment of the ego, or as an excessively permissive apparatus which allows gratification of the instincts at the expense of a continuation of infantile gratification and a failure of the ego to mature. Superego formation is built upon the defense of identification, by the child taking into himself, and making a part of his own ego, the limit setting of his parents. Into superego formation also enters the ego ideal, the goals and aspirations of the person, an internalization derived in large part from the model of his parents. If his parents provide "good" material formation for identification, the person will have a trustworthy superego. The end of the period of infantile sexuality is the time of maturation of the superego and if the child has not made a normal resolution of his infantile sexual problems faulty superego formation will result.

We expect that the parents' attitude toward instinct gratification will be decisive for superego formation. Children who develop antisocial personalities have been studied and it has been shown that the parents of these children have poorly controlled, although not always overt, delinquent tendencies.

> . . . anti-social acting out in a child is unconsciously initiated, fostered, and sanctioned by the parents, who vicariously achieve gratification of their own poorly integrated forbidden impulses through a child's acting out (Giffin, Johnson, and Litin, 1954, p. 669).

> Regularly the more important parent—usually the mother, although the father is always in some way involved—has been seen *unconsciously* to encourage amoral or anti-social behavior of the child (Szurek, 1942, p. 5).

Friedlander (1945) and Giffin, *et al.* (1954) speak of the anti-social nature of parental behavior as manifested by violent quarrels, by sexual scenes which the child witnesses and other displays of uncontrolled emotions. These are seductive to the child and stir up emotions and anti-social impulses which he is unable to handle. Friedlander (1945) also notes that an anti-social character can result from severe economic or other deprivations; this is somewhat like Levy's "deprived psychopath." Levy (1951) also mentions the "indulged psychopath," the result of inconsistent handling of the child with too lenient or permissive attitudes alternating with very severe frustrations.

ROLE OF THE CLERGY

The most important years for a child's development are those years when he has little contact with the clergy, but his parents will have contact with the clergy and it is here that the clergy can help to provide the "average expectable environment." If the beginning is made in the seminary, through courses and with some opportunity to observe normal and abnormal child development, then it will be the informed clergyman who will be advising parents who consult him, who will be able to see that the education of children in his parish school will promote normal emotional growth. His knowledge of children will be a factor in determining how he presents religion and morality to these children. Neurotic children can readily make a parody of religion, can use it as a defense. But if religion is not presented as harsh and punitive, if instincts are not viewed as intrinsically evil and life only a series of temptations, perhaps some children will not become scrupulous adults and others will not turn away from a religion which they have tried to use as a neurotic defense and which has failed them. The concepts of religion which have led to misunderstandings and divisions among scholars are certainly difficult for children to grasp. For they are still under the sway of infantile magical thinking, struggling to master their sexual and aggressive wishes, and their early life experiences will color their perception of religion.

The clergyman as a community leader can do much in the prevention of emotional illness. While it remains true that every child has the problems of mastery of his instinct life and adaptation to reality, and has to deal with anxiety and conflict and guilt, his struggle is aided by a favorable environment. Adequate housing and income and health services, diminution of racial and religious discrimination, reduction in crime—all of these social advances will reduce the number of emotionally handicapped children. Once these children have become seriously ill and their personalities are cast in a neurotic or anti-social mold treatment is long and expensive, and there are not enough social workers and psychiatrists to give this treatment. More and more treatment services are provided— family counselling, foster care, aid to dependent children, psychiatric clinics, services to delinquents. These are worthwhile, but so long as they remain treatment services rather than preventive services they will not be sufficient.

There is the problem of illegitimate children, as one example. It is a psychiatric problem as well as a social problem because great numbers of these children become dependent, neglected and emotionally ill. Proposals and actions to reduce this social evil have been many and some controversial—casework or psychiatric treatment for the unwed mother, supplying contraceptives, sterilization, stopping financial aid to mothers, jail sentences for fathers. We should do whatever we can to treat the women who need treatment, but what are we doing for the children. Some are adopted by very capable families and they gain a chance for a healthy life. But of the great numbers who are not adopted many go into foster homes. This is better than sending them to child-caring institutions, but typically the foster homes are overcrowded, are inadequately supervised, and many of the children will become as disturbed as their parents have been. We have the knowledge to help many of these children, but public money is reluctantly doled out for their care, and few families from the educated and professional classes, who should be well equipped to raise emotionally healthy children, come forth to help. This is one area where leadership is needed.

The clergyman, like every other professional whose work concerns children, should not only seek knowledge, but should look at his own attitude toward the child's emotional life. It will be colored by his own infantile experiences, his identifications with his parents, his defenses.

REFERENCES

Arey, L. *Developmental anatomy*. Philadelphia: Saunders, 1943.

Balint, A. *The early years of life*. New York: Basic Books, 1954.

Fenichel, O. *The psychoanalytic theory of neurosis*. New York: Norton, 1945.

Fraiberg, S. *The magic years*. New York: Scribners, 1959.

Friedlander, Kate. Formation of the antisocial character. In O. Fenichel, *et al.* (Eds.) *Psychoanalytical study of the child*, Vol. I. New York: International Universities, 1945. Pp. 189-203.

Giffin, Mary E., Johnson, Adelaide M., & Litin, E. M. Specific factors determining antisocial acting out. *Amer. J. Orthopyschiat.*, 1954, *24*, 668-684.

Levy, D. M. The deprived and indulged forms of psychopathic personality. *Amer. J. Orthopsychiat.*, 1951, *21*, 250-254.

Piaget, J. *The construction of reality in the child*. New York: Basic Books, 1954.

Spock, B. *Problems of parents*. Boston: Houghton Mifflin, 1962.

Szurek, S. A. Notes on the genesis of psychopathic personality trends. *Psychiat.*, 1942, *5*, 1-6.

Waelder, R. *Basic theory of psychoanalysis*. New York: International Universities, 1960.

Childhood Origin of
the Psychopathic Personality

JOHN I. NURNBERGER

John I. Nurnberger received his early education and professional training in his native Chicago, with his B.S. degree from Loyola University in 1938 and his M.D. degree from Northwestern University in 1943. He spent the year 1949-50 as a Research Fellow in cell chemistry and genetics at the Medical Nobel Institute in Stockholm, Sweden. Upon his return to this country, Dr. Nurnberger spent several years at the Institute of Living in Hartford, Connecticut. Currently, Dr. Nurnberger is Professor and Chairman of the Department of Psychiatry and Director of the Institute of Psychiatric Research at Indiana University Medical Center. He is co-editor with S. R. Korey of the four-volume work Progress in Neurobiology *(1956-1959). More recently he has collaborated with C. D. Ferster and J. T. Brady to produce an* Introduction to the Science of Human Behavior *(1963). In addition to these books, Dr. Nurnberger is the author of some thirty articles in various medical and scientific journals.*

It is tempting for those of us who are repeatedly unsuccessful in the treatment of certain emotional and mental disturbances to ascribe these failures to mysterious, constitutional, and inherited defects in personality structure or organization. It is even more tempting for us to turn to such comforting explanations of the behavior of those individuals who seem to have the capacity to appraise and evaluate their actions, who may insist on their deep distress at past transgressions, who may protest their strong resolve to mend their ways, and yet who, in spite of this, continue along the same familiar pattern of aggressive, destructive, impulsive behavior with little detectable remorse for distress inflicted and social damage done. Those disturbances characterized by remorselessly repetitive, impulsive action against self and environment are referred to as psychopathic or sociopathic personality disturbances.

INFLUENCE OF MATERNAL ANXIETY AND TENSION

The speculative formulation concerning the genesis of sociopathic trends which follows depends heavily on two factors. The first of these is maternal anxiety, tension, and attitudes of rejection as communicated to the infant; the second is the nature of acceptance or rejection of such communicated experiences in the infant. There can be no serious doubt that the level of anxiety as well as the methods for relieving it vary significantly in different people and therefore, of necessity, in different mothers. Also, experience confirms that mothers vary in their attitudes of personal acceptance or rejection of their own newborn. The communication of rejecting and anxious attitudes and states to the infant is the core of Harry Stack Sullivan's (1953) brilliantly elaborated thesis on human development. Though Sullivan details clearly the occurrence and manifestations of such communicated anxieties, he provides no specific mechanisms by which such attitudes and feelings can be communicated to the infant in the pre-verbal stage of development.

Certain recent clinical experimental studies suggest such plausible mechanisms. It is known, for example, that the anxious individuals show detectable alterations in the tone of their skeletal muscles. These alterations are readily detected by electrical recording techniques during periods of anxiety. They can frequently enough be observed clinically as well. Not only are these states manifest in arm and leg muscles but also in the laryngeal musculature so that the tone, rhythm, and control of speech may be significantly altered during such conditions. The heightened tone of the muscular system, therefore, serves as a highly sensitive mechanism even for distorting otherwise smooth voluntary movements. These become more brisk and are of somewhat greater than normal amplitude. The result is that the smooth, co-ordinated movements of the person at ease are transformed into the quick, jerky movements of the person under tension.

Among the basic physiologic needs of the newborn infant are not only warmth, satisfaction of hunger, and adequate rest, but also stable physical support and relative quiet. We know that among stimuli most provocative of seemingly distressful responses in the infant are loud noises and rapid changes of position. Such responses are readily veri-fied. I would propose on purely speculative grounds that significant communication of maternal anxiety and attendant rejection is effected through the altered muscular performance of the mother and through insensible changes in intonation and verbal expression. Thus, the new-born of the anxious mother may come to realize that the world indeed is a harshly noisy and frightening place and that its own state of sup-port in this environment is frequently enough unpredictable and un-reliable as communicated by the jerky movements of such a mother. Certain it is that the bombardment of the infant with such a variety of noxious auditory and vestibular stimuli may well serve to com-municate harsh frightening data to the newborn. Whether, in fact, in some such way as this the first crude picture of the external world as a dangerous and threatening and inconsistently sustaining environment is drawn is, of course, not definitely known. This formulation is proposed for what it is worth in the absence of any definite physiological or psychological data on this matter. Suffice to say that the formula-tion is reasonably consistent with what we know of the physiology of anxious individuals. It is also entirely in line with known behavioral responses in the very young.

It might be expected that the mode of reception of such noxious and distressful stimuli would vary from individual to individual infant. Perhaps so-called genetic factors are operative here. Surely if these factors be physical, they must manifest themselves almost exclusively in the emotional or affective aspects of behavior. A vast body of clinical and experimental data indicates that the only close corollaries between physical somatic functions and human behavior are on the strictly emotional level. Two possible responses to such stimuli have been noted. One of these is compliant and clinging, the other, rejecting and rebellious. Why one individual should react in one way, another in almost the opposite, is entirely unclear. We are forced to seek in the affective aspects of personality for answers to such provocative questions. It is to be hoped that such answers will be resolved in clinical and behavioral research in the future.

It is probable that communications transmitted non-verbally by the anxious, tense, rejecting mother spell out in unmistakable terms the fact not only that the world is a dangerous and frightening place, but also that the individual so exposed is of little intrinsic worth. Much thought has been given to circumstances which favor the growth of self-respect and a sense of worth in the individual, and those which hinder or prevent the development of such attitudes. These are questions of fundamental import in a discussion of the sociopath since clinical experience confirms that these individuals are disgusted with and revolted by the pictures they have of themselves.

PERSONAL ATTITUDE OF MOTHER TOWARD INFANT

My own experience with such patients would indicate that an early formative influence of profound importance is the personal attitude of the mothering one toward the infant. I would divide possible attitudes into two classifications. One is the attitude which may be paraphrased as follows: "You are my infant, totally dependent upon me by the circumstances of your birth, but you are also an individual, a person, who will develop into a free, independent, and mature agent. It is my central responsibility as a mothering one to do all things necessary to support and assist in that development." The second attitude might be paraphrased as follows: "You are my infant, my own, my very property, a thing rather than a person. You exist primarily for my own personal gratification and satisfaction and you will be trained in the business of doing and thinking for my satisfaction and not yours." The former statement is the almost miraculous viewpoint of the mature and broadly virtuous mother who loves in the most important sense of that misused term. The latter is the statement of the immature, frustrated mother who is incapable of participating in adult activities or of securing the necessary gratifications from adult sources and who, in desperate need, turns to her infant for the satisfactions which she is incapable of appreciating or obtaining on any other level.

It is evident from this formulation that I consider the direct influence of the mother to be of profoundest importance in these phases of personality development. This is unquestionably true. It is not my intention, however, to point a finger of blame at mothers merely because their role is so profoundly important as well as difficult. The role of the father and the husband as a participant particularly in the first year of the infant's life, is more related to his attitudes toward his wife than to his operations with the newborn. It is, of course, not at all unusual for a mother to turn to her infant for comforts when she has failed repeatedly to find in her husband a source of any of the adult securities and gratifications which any normal human being desires and needs. Only the heroic and unselfish mother will refuse to turn to her infant for substitute gratifications under such circumstances.

EARLY DEVELOPMENT OF ATTITUDES TOWARD AUTHORITY

The developing infant probably does develop (sometimes during the first year) a very strong and permeating impression that the world is a dangerous and threatening place, and that he himself is a thing rather than a person if he is exposed to the anxious, tense, and immature mothering figure whom I have already described. It is equally probable that the fundamental patterns which later manifest themselves either in schizophrenic withdrawal or in sociopathic attacks on society, its things and its people, are traceable to such first impressions. The basically compliant infant with a physical-emotional structure ill-suited to acting out may well revert to autistic reverie and retreat from the persons and things of the outside world when he comes to learn that they are hostile and threatening. This retreat may provide the fertile nidus for later schizophrenic reactions. By contrast, our other type of infant with an affective system impelling toward acting out may come to attack his threatening environment and those who deny his value and individuality. Thus it is that the primary attitudes toward authority figures elicited by maternal attitudes can set the stage for maturing general attitudes toward authority whether represented by parents, teachers, companions, church or state. I would like to continue this discussion very largely as it relates to the maturation of such attitudes toward constituted authority, since developmental distortions of this attitude provide the most vivid data to explain the repetitive and at times compulsive aggressions of the sociopath.

With the development of verbal understanding in the child a further distinct representation of the outside world is established. This is best exemplified by the varying attitude of parents toward the curious, seeking, experimental activities of developing children in and around the home, also in parental attitudes toward information sought and questions asked. In this area two gross deviants from the usual parental attitude may be mentioned. There are, thus, the so-called "no-no parents" who restrict and limit the activities of their children exclusively in the interests of their own peace, comfort, and contentment. While I am wholly in favor of an ordered and reasonably tranquil home, and agree most emphatically that the experience of such an environment is a highly important factor in the developing social sense and responsibility of the child, I do not agree that such a home can be maintained by preventing every noisy and potentially disturbing innocent activity of the growing child.

Thus, a parent who by verbal interdiction blocks every type of normal exploratory activity in and around the home, and who rewards the innocent aspects of such activity with dire threat or physical punishment, is indeed communicating to the growing child by word as well as attitude that the external world must certainly be a frightening and threatening one since his every tentative contact with it is forbidden. The compliant child, the child thirsting for approval, may accept such limitations and mold his life to the comfort and peace of his parents alone. There will always be some subtle rebellion even in the highly compliant, however. We see this rebellion in the violent, hostile, psychotic impulses of our schizophrenic patients who, too often, are described as having been phlegmatic infants, ideal children, models of propriety, who have always done precisely as they have been told and yet who, after a quiet and withdrawn adolescence, merge into adult life with all the pent-up fury of their beings in explosive disequilibrium. The alternative course is that manifested by the aggressive, acting out child who rejects every interdiction and becomes consistently recalcitrant to correction and intolerant of denial.

At the other end of the spectrum is the relatively uninvolved parent who is convinced that there is no substitute for trial and error in learning, who works on the assumption that denial or restrictive attitudes toward children are unhealthy manifestations of hostility, and who permits children an unending array of exploratory experience. Childhood curiosities being what they are, it is inevitable that such unprotected children must encounter many daily sources of pain and distress in their exploratory activities. By bitter, personal experience they come to discover, unprotected and alone, that the world is indeed a hostile and dangerous place which is best coped with through hostile defense or prompt attack. I am not convinced that the interdicting "no-no parent" is any more sincerely involved in the welfare of his children than is the completely permissive and equally uninvolved parent. The end effect in that certain group whom we refer to as sociopaths must be the growing conviction that the world is dangerous and threatening. This is further grafted on the impression, which can usually never be verbalized, that the parental authority figures are not to be respected, they themselves respected even less.

HEALTHY ATTITUDES TOWARD AUTHORITY

Among the influences which create healthy attitudes toward authority, none is more telling, more pervasive, or more sustained than those emanating from the home environment. Since the activities of the sociopath so often represent an indifference to social custom and need, to the rights of others, and to the valid limitations on behavior implicit in authoritative legislation, it is relevant to consider certain fundamental home factors which work to create healthy attitudes toward authority. I am going to list these in a relatively diagrammatic way. They are so commonly discussed and recognized that it does not seem pertinent to develop them in detail in this summary. Among essentials for the development of a healthy respect for authority are the following:

(1) Natural authority representatives should be at home during early formative years. This applies very particularly to instances in which both mother and father work and are thus away from the home a great part of the day even during their children's crucial formative years.

(2) The authority representatives should be consistent, just, and benign.

(3) Auxiliary or substitutive authority figures should, whenever possible, be kept at a minimum particularly during formative years, first of all because there are no sound substitutes, and secondly, be-

cause fundamental agreement is relatively uncommon between the established and substitute representative.

(4) The limits of acceptable behavior should be clearly defined.

(5) Effective and prompt sanctions should be in evidence where behavior in the developing child is unacceptable to the standards clearly set in the home.

(6) The exercise and significance of authority should be manifest as far as possible in terms of example and action, as little as possible in terms of word and injunction. One need scarcely emphasize the terrible ambiguities which arise over serious inconsistencies between behavior demanded of growing children and examples presented. We may expect and anticipate that our children will imitate not only the good, commendable, and lovable aspects of our behavior but, in some perverse and mysterious way, even more vividly the disgraceful and destructive aspects of our behavior.

I would like to stress the fact that for the priest, too, the most impressive effect he will exert will be in working along preventive lines particularly with parents and potential parents, in leading them to a more healthy attitude toward themselves and a more precise appreciation of their roles and responsibilities as parents or future parents. This work with parents and potential parents is most efficacious in preventing the development of sociopathic trends and this must be stressed because the successful treatment of matured sociopaths, in terms of our current limited knowledge, is always difficult, frequently impossible.

REFERENCE

Sullivan, H. S. *The interpersonal theory of psychiatry.* New York: Norton, 1953.

Early Sexual Development

JAMES E. HAYDEN, O.S.B.

Reverend Dom Jerome Hayden, President and Director of Marsalin Institute, received his B.S. and M.D. degrees at the University of Pittsburgh. Upon the completion of his studies there he joined the Faculty of Medicine. After several years of teaching and practicing medicine, he attended the University of Louvain where he received a doctorate in philosophy. Soon after his return from Europe he entered religious life and following completion of his theological studies at the Catholic University of America he was ordained a priest in 1947. Following his ordination and after further studies in psychiatry and neurology at home and abroad, he joined the Department of Psychology and Psychiatry at Catholic University where, until 1957, he taught and trained residents in the field of psychiatry and clinical psychology. Currently, as President and Director, he is engaged in treatment, training and research in the field of Psychiatry at Marsalin Institute, Boston, Massachusetts, which he founded in 1957.

The word "sexual" has undergone considerable expansion of meaning as a result of Freud's systematic and scientific investigation of the problem. Though the term is used by analysts in a very broad sense there is no vagueness about the factors which they regard as manifestations of sexuality. Outside of psychoanalysis sexuality applies only to the restricted sexual life that is subordinated to the reproductive function. Freud extended the meaning of the word sexuality to include the sexual life of perverted persons and also of children. "Sexuality" has come to include "genitality" (a term which refers to impulses to normal adult intercourse) and all other aspects of life to which the term "love" is commonly applied—parent-child relationships, self-love, friendship, ideals, etc. A word which is more fittingly applied to this wide group of phenomena is "psychosexuality," which emphasizes the mental aspects of sexuality in contradistinction to the physical or bodily manifestations.

The manifestations of sexuality in human actions, conduct, relationships, thoughts, and perceptions are regarded as an expression of a certain power or energy which psychoanalysis calls libido. The term remains properly reserved for the instinctual forces of the sexual life both in their bodily and mental manifestations. Libido, therefore, is the dynamic energy which is expressed in the manifestations of the sexual instinct. Though the English definition of the word "libido" offers such meanings as inclination, desire, longing, appetite and passion, psychoanalysis uses the term exclusively in connection with sexual pleasure and sexual desire, but as we have noted above the psychoanalytic concept of sexuality also includes that to which "love" is commonly applied.

Sex or sexuality in psychoanalysis therefore includes all those trends that were once sexual even though they are now diverted to non-sexual aims. Likewise included are those infantile tendencies which are associated with adult sexual life and even those that are only generally sensual but which may persist as perversions. All of these are grouped under the heading of sexuality with various manifestations of parental instinct and of much that is love and hate—all that leads to establishing a relationship between the sexes which will ensure the propagation of the race.

All these tendencies which psychoanalysis refers to as infantile and adult sexual instincts pertain to the sensual order. St. Thomas pursued this problem with astonishing precision. In dealing with the acts which are natural to man he clearly distinguishes two levels from which they proceed, the rational and the irrational. The *natural human act* derives from a typically human and rational mode of existence while the *natural act of man* derives from a typically irrational mode, an impulsive product of the animal instinct. That which rises from nature to the inferior plane can escape the control of reason. To this force or power or dynamism St. Thomas applies the term of "sensuality." This word for him designates the forces of our sensible nature, precisely in the sense that they are the sources of inclinations rebellious to reason. St. Thomas clearly grasped the complexity of this problem and there is no indication of his using the concept of sensuality in the narrow sense of the word to indicate sexual indulgence alone. And so he holds that all things which are in us and common to beasts pertain in some way to sensuality. Sensuality then has its roots in the appetite; that which stirs or stimulates the appetite is the apparatus of sensible knowledge. That which follows the excitation of the appetite is movement or motivity. All of this is included in sensuality for St. Thomas who regards this complex structure as an organized structure. Freud too supposes all of this. He recognizes the existence of appetite, of knowledge and motivity but he does not consider it in its philosophical, moral or educational aspects, but in its temporal topographical aspects alone. He does not study the complex structure of sensuality or sexuality independent of time. It really is a matter of taste as to whether one wishes to use the Thomistic term "sensuality" or the Freudian "sexuality."

INSTINCTS

That basic power or energetic drive which enables all living things to accomplish certain ends and bring about a state of tension within the individual until it is gratified, Freud called "instinct." The use of the term may appear unfortunate because of the variety of ways in which it has been applied, but this was also true at the time when Freud first employed the word. He observed that no knowledge could be of more importance in establishing a sound psychology than some approximate understanding of the common nature and possible differences of the instincts. On no matter of psychology was the shedding of light more needed. Psychoanalysis considered that all mental occurrences must be regarded as stemming from a basic interplay of elementary instinctual forces. This viewpoint led to confusion since psychology had included no theory of the instincts. Consequently no one could say what an instinct really was and the matter was left to individual caprice.

The term instinct is not used by St. Thomas, since the term is of more recent origin, but it was very clear to him that besides man's ability to synthesize sensory data he has a further power in his sensory equipment which makes possible the recognition of objects as immediately or remotely useful or harmful to the organism. The estimative power or faculty is defined as "the ability to recognize, in a sensory way, the things that are good or bad for the organism" (Brennan, 1938, p. 224). This power is to be assigned to the psychophysical composite, the mental aspects of which are cognitive since the products of the "vis aestimativa" belong to the knowledge order of events. Since these products represent only one of the several features which are included in the modern description of instinct, Brennan defines instinct as "an innate arrangement of psycho-organic powers, which enables its possessor to immediately recognize the utility or harm of certain objects, to experience emotional excitement as a result of such knowledge, and to act or feel the urge to act in a particular manner according to the biological value of the perceived objects" (Brennan, 1938, p. 225).

This theory cannot be attributed to Freud since it was generally agreed upon before him, but through his discoveries certain new elements were added to it. Previously it had been assumed that the sexual instinct in man was quiescent until adolescence when the physical manifestations of sexual activity appeared. Freud pointed out that there are psychological indications of sexual instinct many years before this period is reached. What he referred to was sexual interests, pleasure-seeking interests in one's own body first and then in that of another. Freud clearly indicated that the child's capacity for interest in the outside world was due not to selfish tendencies but unselfish tendencies and that its origin is physiological as well as psychological. This interest which one is able to show persons and things outside of self must be withdrawn from the tremendous amount of affection which the child invests entirely in himself. Emotional growth requires an increasing capacity to draw upon this self-directed love for a wisely directed external investment of it. This investment of love in external objects is considered in essence to be sexual since it pertains to the creation and maintenance of life, the attachment of persons one to the other, and pleasurable reciprocal consideration and concern.

The libidinal or sexual instinctual forces may be classified under three main headings.

1. *Adult sexual instinct* universally recognized after puberty and responsible for the manifold love and reproductive phenomena of adult life. The term is not limited to the manifest erotic components of sexuality. Adult sexuality includes the psychic accompaniments of feelings of love, tenderness, appreciation, security, and an augmentation or extension of self which are of the greatest importance.

2. *Infantile sexual instincts* existing from birth which are gradually organized in the first two years of life and reach a peak in the fourth and fifth years after which they gradually or suddenly disappear. The quiescent period between the infantile and pubertal varieties of sexuality is called the *latency period*.

3. *Body or organ libido* which refers to the sexualized or libidinally charged tissues and organs of the body. Organ libido is a factor which is found in the conversion hysterias and in the psychoses. The distribution of libido in the various parts of the body determines to a great extent the locality of the conversion symptoms.

DEVELOPMENT OF INFANTILE SEXUALITY

An understanding of adult sexuality and its aberrations requires a knowledge of the developmental history of infantile sexuality. It is unreasonable to believe that without any previous conditioning the sexual instinct is dormant for twelve to fourteen years only to appear suddenly at pubescence in an individual totally unprepared for adult sexuality. Freud held that the preparations for adult sexuality are intensive and cover a long period and that during latency the sexual instincts are already given definite assignments for preparing the individual for the severest test of all, the harmonious union of the sexes for the purpose of reproduction. His formulation of the general characteristics of the sexual instincts is that they are numerous, derive from manifold organic sources, originally act independently of one another, and only at a later stage achieve a more or less complete synthesis. Only when this synthesis is achieved do they serve the function of reproduction, thus becoming recognizable as sexual instincts.

It appears that the infant's sensuality or sexuality at the outset is rather vague and widespread. It affects the entire cutaneous surface of the body but within a very brief time it becomes concentrated in a few erogenous zones and undergoes organization and development. Freud has maintained that the sexual life of the child consists entirely in the activities of a series of *component-instincts*. These instincts seek their gratification independently of one another in the child's own body and in external objects. The component instincts are named after the body zone from which the excitations are derived and their manifestations appear in a temporal sequence. The three most important sources of infantile sexual interest are the oral, anal (and urethral), and genital zones. With keen penetration Freud observed that the sexual instinct should be seen as developing out of the various components rather than being divided into them. For, if the sexual instinct is to reach its final form some of the component instincts must be suppressed or turned to other uses.

The First Oral Phase. The first organ to make libidinal demands upon the mind is the mouth, which is the first region of the body to make its appearance as an erotogenic zone. Any organ or body zone which is capable of transmitting sexual stimuli to the psyche is called an erogenous zone. The mouth is endowed with definite organ-pleasure largely through its being an organ of sucking. While it is true that the purpose of sucking is chiefly that of gaining nutrition it soon becomes evident that it also serves another purpose. This is a fact which is easily observed in all infants, since sucking is resorted to independently of the need for food. The sexual instinct detaches itself from the nutritional instinct very early and seeks its satisfaction independently. The intensity of this drive is demonstrated in the strength of the desire, and the pleasure-value of sucking can be estimated by the frequency and persistence of its practice. The connection between the self-preservative instinct and sexual instinctual satisfaction is to be noted here, as in the case of all other infantile pleasure activities.

During the early oral period there is the tendency to retain or incorporate all objects brought in contact with the mouth; it is a *constructive stage*. So the infant's existence centers around the accumulation and retention of energy, the chief efforts are bent on growing. The chief characteristics of the infant's early life are rapid growth and dependence, which are expressed in its great demands for food and a desire to be taken care of. Freud and his associates speak of this oral phase as including the pleasure sensation caused by suckling and thumb-sucking, and the dependent, passive, receptive and demanding attitudes toward the mother. This may be regarded as an erotic practice of the incorporative function which reveals a source of excitation beyond that caused by hunger.

The Second Oral Phase. This phase commences with the appearance of teeth when another emotional attitude connected with oral assimilation appears. It is often described as cannibalistic in type because of the biting, tearing, and swallowing characteristics. This is a *destructive* phase as is evidenced by the urge to break up, destroy and cast away. The new form of sexual satisfaction which replaces the activity of sucking consists in masticating and devouring. When the source of nutritional supply does not satisfy, the child bites. What is formerly passively received it now tries to take by force. Thus an aggressive oral attitude may be distinguished from the earlier receptive one. The pleasurable instinctual activity produced by masticating is easily discerned in a child of this period by the pleasure he derives from destroying things with his teeth and his attempts to chew up every attainable object and swallow it.

Pleasure-sucking after the weaning period is largely an autoerotic activity since the child finds its instinctual satisfactions on its own body—its hand, fingers, thumb, or toes. But with pleasure in biting there appear new contacts or relationships with external objects including human beings. Psychically these persons are brought into relationship with the oral zone as are the objects on which the biting pleasure is experienced. Because of the possessive nature of this oral tendency another emotional link with oral activity is envy. This is readily observable in a child when another child takes his place at the mother's breast.

The First Anal Phase. The eroticism now becomes shifted to the perineal region (the area between the thighs which includes the anus and more or less the genitals), where it is for a period concentrated on the anus. There are also two phases to anal sensuality but they are in the reverse order from that obtaining in case of the mouth—the destructive (rejecting) phase is first, the retaining (mastery and control) or constructive one second. The former is dominated by eliminative pleasure, the latter by retentive pleasure. The feelings associated with expulsion are quite different from those of retention.

The first anal stage is characterized by the predominance of pleasure experienced by the passage and expulsion of the stool. The intimate relationship between mother and child during the toilet training period must be borne in mind, if the feelings and attitudes which develop in connection with anal function are to be properly understood. The mother at regular intervals persuades the child to part with his stool and even offers him inducements of praise or tokens of affection to do so or for having done so. An exchange is thus made for other values and an identification between external love objects and excrement ensues. Psychically this symbolic identification is seen as an expression of esteem and with the expulsion there is also associated the feeling of pride over what is indeed the child's first accomplishment. With this aspect of the first anal phase we note the development of such attributes as pride, esteem, compliance, and generosity. The predominant feature of expulsion, however, is the hostile tendency in the instinctual satisfaction. We add therefore that the attitude toward excrement as an expelled object is ambivalent—it is positive as regards esteem and wish to retain and negative as regards rejection and expulsion.

The Second Anal Phase. It is a clearly observed clinical fact that children who indulge the pleasurable sensibility of the erogenous anal zone will withhold their stools to increase the pleasure of their later expulsion. The early interest which children manifest in their stools can seldom be expressed freely because of educational restrictions. This indulgence, however, is frequently observed in adult psychotics who have regressed to the infantile anal phase. When such a state is reached the patient lives out his pleasurable interest in feces by smearing himself and everything within reach with his fecal matter.

When the child's pleasure from anal retention is interrupted by parental insistence on regulated and controlled bowel function the child rebels. It has been widely observed by psychoanalysts that children and adult neurotics who reveal anal retentiveness display qualities of obstinacy, possessiveness, and independence. Possessiveness is clearly linked with the value placed on excrement by virtue of the symbolic significance of value attaching to it. It is the child's own possession to which no other has access. When he complies with the parental demands for an evacuation he presents something and that which he presents takes on the significance of a gift, even money. After all there is a bit of bartering that goes on during bowel training. The sense of independence is clearly linked with the mastery of sphincter control and obstinacy or stubbornness with unwillingness to give us his object of pleasurable interest.

The child's anal-sexual interests and the influence of adult (chiefly parental) inhibitions and attitudes toward them are of far reaching consequences in the development of *moral sense*. Such words as filthy, dirty, naughty, and bad become associated with anal function when the child does not comply with the adult restrictions placed on anal activities. The association, however, takes on a new and far more important significance since these first social, ethical, moral demands are of an anal nature. Overstrict demands during the toilet training period may result in excessive moral feelings of duty and consequently of guilt in matters that pertain to social obligations, law, and authoritative figures. Also trivia may take on the importance of major issues. These reactions are clearly discernible in scrupulous persons, obsessive-compulsive personalities who are anal in character, and who manifest a tendency to revive the anal-sadistic sources of pleasure.

Sadism and Masochism. Frustration experienced in excretory functions evokes *sadistic* aggression, just as oral deprivations occasioned oral aggression. The sadistic impulses of the oral phase are greatly increased during the anal phase which is commonly referred to as the sadistic-anal phase. Freud says that the inclusion of aggressive impulses in the libido is justified by supposing that sadism is an instinctual fusion of purely libidinal and purely destructive impulses, a fusion of elements which thereafter remain inseparably bound together.

The infantile forms of sadism which have been noted bear the names of the erogenous zones with which they are associated, oral, anal (or excretory), and genital. There being little distinction between the self and outside objects during the oral phase the most violent forms of organized sadism against objects is observed during the second year. The fact that control over bowel function is promoted by parental figures accounts for the fact that the hostility and hatred directed toward adults is strongly charged with anal (excretory) sadism. The clinical picture varies with the type of sadism involved. The direction of pleasurable aggression toward external objects is called sadism.

The characteristic features of this first phase are those of smashing, crushing, throwing, kicking, and trampling. The retentive or second anal stage is characterized not by destruction but by mastery. This form of sadism is very apparent in the crippling, restrictive, confining, tormenting, selfish interference with another's liberty. Such activities are aimed at complete mastery over the object.

The tendency to experience pleasure in pain exists in both active and passive forms. The term masochism is used to denote the passive form. Whereas sadism is pleasureable aggressiveness directed toward an external object, masochism is the tendency to enjoy aggressiveness directed toward self. Masochism is sadism in reverse. Masochism is the tendency to enjoy sexual satisfaction when pain, ill-treatment, and humiliation are inflicted upon oneself. It may express itself in an individual whose psychic life is controlled by the idea of being completely subject to the will of another person of the opposite sex, of being mastered, humiliated and abused by this person.

Masochistic expressions of aggression may be classified in the same manner as the sadistic types; they may be oral, anal, or genital. Contrary to the active functions of sadism (biting, expulsive and penetrating) we find the masochistic varieties associated with the receptive, retentive and pressure functions of the zones involved.

The Genital or Phallic Phase. The genital concentration of all sexual excitement is achieved at the conclusion of infantile sexuality. Interest in the genitals and in the genital masturbation becomes a dominant feature. Interest in the male organ so strongly dominates infantile genitality that Freud designated this stage the phallic phase, since the genital phase of childhood could not be taken as a complete model of adult sexuality. The erotic gratification at this phase involves urination and masturbation. It is difficult to define precisely the beginning and end of this period but in most cases it begins about the fourth year and reaches its peak in the fifth or sixth year.

The male penis takes on extraordinary importance for both boys and girls during this period. The female child discovers her rudimentary form of a penis, namely, the clitoris and in many psychic ways attempts to overcome this "defect." The diverse mental attitudes and neurotic symptoms which result from this discovery are easily discernible in that type of woman, who unwilling to admit the lack of what she believes to be a most important organ, behaves, feels and thinks as though she were a man; thus she develops a masculine type of character. As a compensation for her feelings of loss we often find the female reacting with violent aggression and hostility toward men in general and because of this attitude homosexual tendencies are increased.

On the other hand the little boy's high esteem of his penis causes him to fear the possible loss of it and thus he develops castration anxiety. The fear of castration is often precipitated by real or imaginary threats directed against the penis as a punishment for masturbation. Also his discovery of persons without a penis often horrifies the little boy. Seeing little girls without a penis he is led to believe that they once having one have lost it as a punishment for masturbation.

Though love at this phase is as dependent, possessive, and demanding as it was in the oral and anal phases it manifests some of the features of later sexual feelings. Sexual development does not run a smooth course, its course does not exactly parallel physical and mental growth. This discrepancy results in the emotional constellation of this age which is called the Oedipus complex, a mixture of love, hatred, jealousy, inferiority, and guilt resulting from the child's possessive sexual attraction toward the parent of the opposite sex (positive oedipal wish) or toward the parent of the same sex (negative oedipal wish).

This period of infantile genital organization is extremely important for adult sexuality since an object choice of the opposite sex is now made. It is but natural that such a choice would be made from among those who have cared for the child. The mother obviously becomes the object of the instinctual aim in the case of the little boy; the father in the case of the little girl. All the sexual urges of the phallic phase which include those stemming from the other erogenous zones are directed toward the object of choice. Naturally the process of excitation is centered around the genitals while the other instincts play a subordinate role.

During this period the love object is valued not only because of the pleasure deriving from satisfaction of the sexual urges—real or fancied—but because of the more stable and lasting relationship which is being established. Tenderness and affection are developing at this time and as a consequence the parent of the same sex becomes a disturbing influence in this erotic relationship—the parent of the same sex becomes a rival or competitor and his or her absence or death is wished for.

Latency. At the conclusion of the infantile genital period, which reaches its peak in the fifth or sixth year, the first important period of sexual development is ended. The period which follows the final abandonment of infantile genitality (by the sixth year) and the onset of puberty is designated the latency period. This period varies in duration but usually runs from the sixth to approximately the fourteenth year, depending upon the differences of individual physical maturation as well as the difference between the two sexes.

The child at the completion of the oedipal phase of the phallic period enters a period of calm in his life of instinctual satisfactions. Masturbation usually ceases as well as all other forms of sexual stimulation. The struggle of object relationships within the Oedipus complex is suspended because of the identification with the parents. Sexuality, however, does not disappear during this period but merely lies dormant or latent. The instinctual energies of the sexual life are directed toward adaptation and adjustment which are expected at this age and for intellectual expansion and interest.

During this period the child is far less absorbed in himself and being less interested in former forms of amusement reaches out for playmates and friends outside of the family. The child's desire to imitate the parent of the same sex is far more conspicuous than the latent heterosexual interests.

OBJECT AND AIM

The implications for sexual pathology (deviations of the sexual instinct) are seen in the deflections of sexual interest to those sources of instinctual pleasure associated with the early organization of the sexual life, namely, the component instincts. The sexual instinct is of a highly composite nature and is liable to disintegrate into its component parts. Each component instinct is unalterably characterized by its *source* (the body zone from which the excitation derives). Furthermore each component has as distinguishable features an *object* and an *aim*. Sexual instincts, therefore, may be considered according to source, object, and aim, and as regards object and aim they are capable of change.

The *sexual aim* is the aim toward which the instinct strives, namely, ultimate gratification. The aim is always discharge accompanied by satisfaction and is capable of being changed from *activity* to *passivity*. Though satisfaction is invariably the goal, there may be different ways leading to the same goal; an instinct may have various intermediate aims which are capable of combination or interchange.

The *sexual object* is that toward which the aims of instincts are directed. It is, therefore, the person or material object from whom the sexual attraction emanates; or that in or through which the aim can be achieved. It is variable and not originally connected with aim, but attached to it by virtue of its being peculiarly suited to provide satisfaction. The object need not be an extraneous one either, it may be a part of the subject's own body.

Extensive research has revealed that many, many human individuals exist whose sexual life strikingly deviates from the normal. Such persons are called perverts among whom there is a group who are aroused only by members of the same sex; the opposite sex has no attraction for them at all and can even be a source of repugnance. Persons of this group are called homosexuals or inverts who, though they have foregone all participation in the process of reproduction, nevertheless seek to achieve very much the same ends with the objects of their desires as do normal people with theirs. But there is another large group of people whose sexual activity becomes increasingly further removed from what is reasonable. These deviations become more understandable by dividing the varieties according to object and aim.

In the first group characterized by deviation of the sexual object are found persons who have substituted another organ or part of the human body (mouth or anus) for the vagina, thus dispensing with the natural union of the genital organs. There are others who still retain the genitals as object because of their excretory rather than sexual functions. In such people the excretory function is capable of attracting the entire sexual interest. Again there are others who, entirely disregarding the genital organs, substitute for them some part of the human body such as a woman's breast, arm, foot, or a plait of hair as an object of desire. There are also others who experiencing no interest in any part of the human body find the object of their desires in a particle of clothing, a dress, a piece of underclothing or a shoe. Such persons are known as *fetishists*. There are still others who make the horrible and gruesome demand of having the body as a whole in the defenseless state of a corpse. Such persons may be so driven by their criminal obsessions as to render the living body lifeless in order to enjoy it.

In the second group we find members who show a deviation or deflection of aim by the performance of an act which may be regarded as introductory or preparatory. Persons in this category seek sexual pleasure in such activities as touching, looking and exposing parts of their own bodies which should be concealed. There are those too, whose affectionate feelings combine with the desire to inflict pain or torture on the object of interest. Feelings of this sort may range from a tendency to humiliate on up to the infliction of severe pain or injury. The reverse situation is also true when we find the person's tendency to be a desire to undergo humiliation and suffering at the hand of the loved object. Finally persons belonging to the above two groups may be divided into those who seek their particular objects of sexual desire in reality and those who are satisfied to enjoy them merely in phantasy.

Freud has emphatically stated that we can never understand normal sexuality until we understand these morbid forms of sexuality and can relate them to what is normal.

Normal development requires that every effort be made to help the child to direct outward and toward others that originally undivided primitive energy. The self-preservative needs must be met, but with the passage of time the child must be encouraged and provided opportunities to invest love in others rather than in self alone—until his outgoing interests and satisfactions will bring about a suppression of his narcissistic (selfish) trends.

Compromises of a sort which are valuable to society are called for —such compromises are called sublimations and it is upon these that cultural, ethical and moral living depends. The sexual instinct must in the nature of things be more or less thwarted. If this thwarting is deflected into productive, constructive channels sublimation is successful.

Growth, as we have said, depends upon a real capacity for sublimation—a capacity to draw upon this self-directed, self-preservative, narcissistic love for wise investments in external objects. The final goal of normal sexual development demands that the component instincts be suppressed or turned to other uses. Frustration, therefore, is called for but it must not be too consistent nor too inconsistent. Patience, unswerving love, and proper substitutes for withdrawals will go far in enabling the child to develop the strength necessary to bear with the frustration of having to forego his own pleasures for the welfare or wishes of others.

At the conclusion of the infantile genital period as we have said above the average child attains the psychological consolation of latency. This is a stage when further wholesome relationships and enlightened training and education should exert a profound influence on his future life. Through an appreciation and thorough understanding of moral concepts, social demands, the need for virtuous living and the means of achieving it he will be able to build a strong ego capable of resisting the recrudescence of those earlier infantile interests which make their reappearance at adolescence.

REFERENCES

Abraham, K. *Selected papers on psychoanalysis.* London: Hogarth, 1938 (First published, 1927).

Alexander, F. *Fundamentals of psychoanalysis.* New York: Norton, 1948.

Brennan, R. *General psychology.* New York: Macmillan, 1938.

Brill, A. A. *Basic principles of psychoanalysis.* Garden City, New York: Doubleday, 1949.

Fenichel, O. *Psychoanalytic theory of neurosis.* New York: Norton, 1945.

Freud, S. *The basic writings of Sigmund Freud.* A. A. Brill (Trans. & Ed.) New York: Random House, 1938.

Freud, S. *The three contributions to the theory of sex* (1905). A. A. Brill (Trans.). New York: Nervous and Mental Diseases Pub. Co., 1910.

Freud, S. *Beyond the pleasure principle* (1920). C. J. M. Hubback (Trans.) (3rd ed.). London: Hogarth, 1948.

Freud, S. Character and anal eroticism (1908). In *Collected papers.* Vol. II. London: Hogarth, 1924. Pp. 45-50.

Freud, S. The infantile genital organization of the libido (1923). In *Collected papers.* Vol. II. London: Hogarth, 1924. Pp. 244-249.

Freud, S. Instincts and their vicissitudes (1915). In *Collected papers.* Vol. IV. London: Hogarth, 1925. Pp. 60-83.

Freud, S. The libido theory (1922). In *Collected papers.* Vol. V. London: Hogarth, 1950. Pp. 131-135.

Glover, E. *Psychoanalysis.* (2nd ed.) London: Staples Press, 1949.

Hendrick, I. *Facts and theories of psychoanalysis.* (2nd ed.) New York: Knopf, 1948.

Menninger, K. A. *The human mind.* (3rd ed.) New York: Knopf, 1947.

Nicole, J. E. *Psychopathology.* (4th ed.) Baltimore: Williams & Wilkins, 1947.

Sterba, R. *Introduction to the psychoanalytic theory of the libido.* No. 68. (2nd ed.) New York: Nervous & Mental Diseases Pub. Co., 1947.

Zilboorg, G. *Mind, medicine, and man.* New York: Harcourt, Brace, 1943.

Adolescent Sexual Development

ROBERT J. CAMPBELL

Robert Jean Campbell, III, M.D., is Chief of the Out-Patient Psychiatric Service at St. Vincent's Hospital; Instructor in Psychiatry at Columbia University College of Physicians and Surgeons; and Adjunct Associate Professor, Fordham University Graduate School. Prior to assuming his post at St. Vincent's Hospital, Dr. Campbell was Senior Clinical Psychiatrist at the New York State Psychiatric Institute. After graduating from the University of Wisconsin, Dr. Campbell received his M.D. degree from Columbia University. He is a Diplomate, American Board of Psychiatry and Neurology, a contributor to various medical journals, and is currently editor of Hinsie & Campbell's Psychiatric Dictionary *(1960). The 1957 Pastoral Psychology Institute was the first to which Dr. Campbell contributed, but since then he has become the series most consistent contributor, having participated in each of the three subsequent Institutes.*

The second decade, the period of adolescence, for many years was almost synonymous with the term sex until Freud effectively and convincingly demonstrated the presence of sexuality in infancy and childhood as well. Since then, however, there has been, not precisely an overemphasis of infantile sexuality, for recognition of this was much too long in the coming and its importance is not to be gainsaid, but rather a neglect of adolescence and the important changes in the sexual life which occur in this era. "If the sexual instinct ever plays a significant part in the life of man it surely is during the age of adolescence, for biologically, the essenial characteristic of this age is that it represents the achieving of sexual maturity. Few, indeed, are the problems relating to adolescence that can be solved without taking into account some sexual factor or other" (Jones, 1922, p. 390).

MEANING OF ADOLESCENCE

Adolescence, then, can be looked upon as the period in which sexual maturity is achieved; it can also be considered as the age of final establishment of a dominant positive ego identity (Erikson, 1950), the age in which "tu-ism" replaces narcissism (Wittels, 1949), the age in which for the first time both the sexual and reproductive instincts attain full maturity and unite into a single striving (Nunberg, 1955), the age in which sexual development dovetails into the development of object relationships leading to the mature, adult stage of impersonal object love (allo-erotism) and unhampered orgastic heterosexuality.

In any account of adolescence, three areas must be considered— the physical or physiologic or biologic, the psychologic or emotional, and the behavioral sphere—all interdependent, each acting and reacting upon the other. In other words, adolescence is from one aspect a period of physical growth and changing organic physiology. It is also a period of changing emotions and psychological development. And at the same time, adolescence presents a certain picture of behavior and reaction to the onlooker which is separate and distinct from any other period of life.

Adolescence is a critical period of life during which the individual is subjected to the heaviest strain, both physically and emotionally. We might arbitrarily set the age limits of adolescence as from 12 to 21 years, for these are the years which on the average encompass all of the changes that we shall describe, at least in the normal individual.

On the physical side (Zachry, 1949), adolescence is ushered in by puberty, with a tremendous upsurge of growth: the body lengthens, broadens and becomes heavier, babyish flabbiness gives way to muscular development, secondary sex characteristics appear and, more particularly in the male, the voice begins to change.

BEHAVIORAL MANIFESTATIONS

On the behavioral side (Moodie, 1949; Zachry, 1949), we find that the adolescent becomes self-conscious and shrinks from being different. He resents the protectiveness of his mother and resists the authority of his parents, or he tries to hide behind this authority to avoid responsibility. He indicates a multitude of interests: science, government, politics, art, philosophy; he shows an insistent, compelling push toward action and self-assertion. He avoids many things at home and in school as being too trivial and unimportant. He drives himself to compete, all the while retaining his childhood longing for perfection in achievement. Since the body symbolizes the self, he must be physically competent and is concerned with his speed, his strength, his agility. He wants to think and act for himself, to throw off the yoke of adult domination. He wants a good job, a good income, rapid advancement, and an ideal wife whom others will admire. Yet, at the same time, he has many doubts about his abilities, his capacities, his competence, and his attractiveness. He doubts the world, and disillusionment is never far away. "But the urge toward adulthood continually comes into conflict with another, the urge to remain a child. And the result of this conflict between strong and opposing tendencies is strain and tension, anxiety and fear" (Zachry, 1949, p. 4). His behavior is conflicting, vacillating, contradictory and unstable. He varies between extremes: egoism and altruism, pettiness and generosity, sociability and loneliness, cheerfulness and sadness, silly jocularity and overseriousness, intense loves and sudden abandonments of these loves, submission and rebellion, materialism and idealism, rudeness and tender consideration—all are typical.

These behavioral characteristics give some hint of what the psychological and emotional changes are in this period. We find that in the main the adolescent is faced with three challenges psychologically: the achievement of independence and emancipation from authority; the expression of aggressivity and dominance; and sexual maturation (Schonfeld, 1951).

The individual ego at this time is invaded by a new id, which is stronger, more forceful, more insistent than ever before (Erikson, 1950). This invasion disrupts the psychic equilibrium and threatens to overwhelm the tenuous adjustments that have been achieved. The adolescent no longer knows himself, his body seems strange to him, his body image and his reality sense are altered, and in consequence he may show concern about his own sanity (Fraiberg, 1955). He wonders who and what he is in terms of the significant people around him.

SEXUAL MATURATION

As if this were not enough, "the demon sex rears its ugly head," and the adolescent must struggle with this, often alone, unaided, uncounselled. For physiological reasons, the instinctual sex drive is suddenly, tremendously heightened, and the adolescent is often aghast with fear and shame at his own potentialities. He has little recourse but to struggle experimentally through the period as best he can; his culture is disapproving and his mores prohibit satisfactory expression of his needs and desires. He dreads to meet the challenge of sexual maturity. He is disturbed by erotic sensations which are strange and new. He fears he cannot attract members of the opposite sex. It is a trying period, and how can he explain it to himself, or begin to understand what is happening to him? He defends himself against this new surge of instincts mainly by ego restriction, and he avoids neurotic anxiety by concentration on limited goals with circumscribed laws. As Erikson says, "There is no doubt that this adolescent in his most intimate feelings is detached from his genitals; they have been called 'private' all along, and this not in the sense that they were his private property, but rather that they were too private even for him to touch. He has been threatened —early and almost casually—with the loss of his genitals; and in accord with the general ego restriction which is his favorite defense mechanism, he has detached himself from them. Of this he is, of course, unconscious. Vigorous exercise helps to keep his body image intact and permits him to live out his intrusiveness in the goal-mindedness of sports" (Erikson, 1950, p. 268).

To try to understand ourselves what is happening to such a person, it might be easier if for the moment we put aside a consideration of the early adolescent and turn instead to the adult. We might then get some idea of where this process of development is heading and some hint of what we might look for when we turn back to the adolescent.

By the time sexual maturity has been completed, somewhere between 18 and 21 years in most cases, we find that the sexual excitations which once gave satisfaction to the child now contain a disagreeable component and heighten rather than relieve tension. Thus they come to be merely a forepleasure which impels to further activity. The sexual object, which has come to be a member of the opposite sex, wins greater definition; and the sources of excitation have become more localized anatomically in the genitals (Jones, 1910). Three things have happened to bring this about (Jones, 1922). First of all, the sexual desire is no longer inhibited in respect to the sexual goal. This means merely that the adult knows what he wants, sexually, and goes about achieving it directly, without having to repress his sexual energies or otherwise divert them into substitute channels. The second change is that the sexual desire is now directed to strangers, or at least to people outside the small family unit. This was not the case in infancy, for the child knew only his immediate family and could not direct his drive elsewhere. And finally, in the adult the capacity to love has grown stronger at the expense of the desire to be loved. The adult is more actively engaged in loving someone else ('tu-ism' as Wittels [1949] called it), while the infant is a mere passive recipient of the love of others.

Now how are these changes brought about? What happens to redirect the sexual impulses into their appropriate channels, outside the family and onto someone else? Psychoanalytic studies have shown that the adolescent makes use of his experiences in infancy to get him over the hurdles of his own age. The sexual development of early childhood is recapitulated and repeated in condensed form, and the Oedipus complex is reactivated (Nunberg, 1955).

Infantile sexuality was only minimally in evidence during the relative equilibrium of the latency period. In place of continuing advancement of sexuality, it was the ego and object relationships which were greatly developed and expanded. But the biologic intensification of the instinctual urges at the time of puberty presents a new challenge to this ego, which must adapt itself to and somehow come to accept sexuality. This is not simple in societies such as ours where legitimate sexual expression is deferred for so inordinate a period (Fenichel, 1945; Schneiders, 1960). The task of adaptation is complicated by several factors: 1) the newly intensified instincts threaten to overwhelm the ego since genital primacy is not yet established and there is no satisfactory outlet as yet; 2) the instinctual demands are similar to the experiences of the period of infantile sexuality and of the Oedipus complex; therefore, the conflicts of these times also reappear; 3) fear of the new forms of the drive encourage the individual to regress to older, more familiar forms of infantile sexuality; and 4) the relative equilibrium of the latency period has stabilized certain attitudes which are hostile to the instincts; thus the ego has definite reactions to external and internal demands which were not present in childhood (Fenichel, 1945).

The adolescent, then, is a house divided against itself, with conflicts between the newly strengthened instincts and the ego defenses against them. Because of cultural conditioning, the child came to recognize his sexual impulses as dangerous; at puberty, he returns to just that point in his sexual development where he had abandoned it earlier, and the fears and guilts connected with the Oedipus complex reappear in the form of hostility to his own instincts and a generalized asceticism whose point seems to be not only the suppression of sexuality but of everything pleasant as well.

The conflicts for a time center consciously about autoeroticism. Sooner or later, the increased sexual drive of puberty finds expression in masturbatory activity. Masturbation is absent only in those cases where intimidation and suppression of infantile autoeroticism has been severe (Fenichel, 1945; Nunberg, 1955). The fears and guilt feelings which in infancy were associated with the Oedipal phantasies are now displaced onto the act of masturbation; in consequence of the guilt he feels about masturbation, the adolescent at this point is mainly involved in a struggle to give it up. Different personalities approach the conflict in different ways. On the one hand, some may side with the drive and try to fight the anxiety and the prohibiting parents by rebellious, defiant, antagonistic behavior. On the other hand, and this is more common, many will side with the anxiety and with the parents, and these fight instinctual temptations and rebellious tendencies. We see this in increased intellectual, scientific and philosophical interests, which can best be understood as attempts to control feelings and think about anything but sex (Freud, 1937). Often the adolescent takes both forms of reaction, successively or even simultaneously, and it is of utmost importance to him whether he fails or succeeds in his struggle. If he fails, feelings of inferiority, depression, self-devaluation and self-abasement ensue; if he succeeds, self-esteem is raised, ambition is heightened and, in extreme cases, even megalomania can be seen (Lampl-DeGroot, 1950).

At this point, certain features of other infantile stages are seen. In the oral area, for instance, the person becomes argumentative or complaining; he goes through food fads and at other times eats barely enough to keep a bird alive. He becomes rude and almost intolerable in conversation. He starts to smoke and may develop the habit of grinding his teeth. Certain holdovers from the anal stage come into prominence at about this time. The nice gentle lad of 10 changes into the rough, untidy boy of 13; he is extravagant, obstinate, with a tendency to procrastination and a passion for collecting. And finally, elements of the phallic phase are seen in the characteristics of bumptiousness, conceit, cocksureness, or as the reverse, as self-depreciation, uncertainty and lack of confidence.

This period passes gradually into the homosexual phase. Some adolescents who have conflicts about masturbation fight their consciences by proving to themselves that they are no worse than others; they gather together with other adolescents of their own sex to swap stories about sexuality, or even for common sexual experiences such as mutual masturbation or group masturbation.

It is probably because of social factors that adolescents frequently prefer to meet in homosexual gatherings. Probably because, in our culture, childhood and adolescent heterosexual play is taboo while close friendship with others of one's own sex is approved, homo-erotic attachments appear to be part of the normal course of development at this time of life. By meeting in homosexual groups the adolescent avoids the exciting presence of the other sex and at the same time avoids being alone; thus he may find the reassurance he is looking for. But these gatherings in and of themselves become sexually stimulating, and the friendships that were founded in the hope of avoiding sexual relationships assume a more or less obvious homosexual character (Fenichel, 1945). Occasional homosexual experiences between adolescents should not be looked upon as abnormal so long as they seem to be temporary and do not result in definite blocking at this level.

Finally, the stage of heterosexuality is reached; by this age the social and cultural taboos have relaxed to permit freer expression of attraction to members of the opposite sex, and courtship is culturally approved. The normal adolescent should have the strength to weather the storms of this period of sexual development.

> Puberty is overcome, that is, sexuality is worked into the personality, when the capacity for full orgasm is attained. Disturbances in this sphere, rooted in previous respressions, serve as the basis for neurosis. Persons afraid of the definiteness of adulthood, that is to say, the definiteness of their instinctual demands which they feel they must accept when growing up, resent growing up and prolong their puberty (Fenichel, 1945, p. 113).

Most adolescents do, in fact, battle their way through; some, however, force themselves on the attention of others by their oppositional, defiant behavior, while others withdraw or otherwise show signs of emotional disturbance (Wilson, 1949; Zachry, 1949). The chief danger signals of this period include preoccupation with physical development, anxiety over the sexual role the adolescent feels he must adopt, hostility, excessive shyness, antisocial behavior, sudden or gradual loss of interest in the environment, excessive feelings of inadequacy and excessive feelings of guilt and failure in school (Schonfeld, 1951).

By the time late adolescence is reached, we can see signs of failing, of emotional upheaval, actual psychotic or neurotic signs in almost all who will eventually become maladjusted adults. Puberty is protracted in those who have difficulty in adapting themselves to reality—in some asocial types, for example. If there are difficulties in overcoming the Oedipus complex, the component instincts, or in establishing genital primacy, there may result all sorts of disturbances—fixation on homosexuality, perversions, impotence, etc. (Nunberg, 1955). In the time remaining, I should like to undertake a brief consideration of some of these.

MASTURBATION

It is recognized that all children masturbate during the infantile period, most do during adolescence, and some do during the latency period (Lampl-DeGroot, 1950). Masturbation, then, can be considered psychologically normal during childhood, and as a major avenue for the discharge of instinctual tension. Under present cultural conditions, masturbation can also be considered psychologically normal* during adolescence, and to some extent even in adulthood when gratification of a physical and emotional relationship with a member of the opposite sex is not possible (Fenichel, 1945; Lampl-DeGroot, 1950).

Kinsey (1948) finds that masturbation occurs in 92 percent of American males, and these figures are in line with other surveys and estimates both in this country and in Europe. Von Gagern (1955) cites: Rohleder: 85-96 percent; Meirowsky: 71-88 percent; Mano: ô5 percent; Markuse: 93 percent; Deutsch (Hungary): 96 percent; Duck: 91 percent; Dukes (England): 90-95 percent; Scarley (United States): 95 percent; Brockman (United States): theology students, 99 percent; Hirschfeld and Hahn: 96 percent; Joung (United States): 100 percent; Bergler, (United States): 100 percent. Schneiders (1960) cites: Ramsey: 98 percent; both Willoughby and Fry ca. 100 percent; Hamilton: 91 percent; Exner: 79 percent.

As to age of onset: Kinsey (1948) finds the peak at 10-12 years, but most other writers would put it somewhat later (cited in Von Gagern [1955]: Prick and Calon: 12-15; Harvey: 12-18; Meirowsky: 14-15; Hirschfeld: 12-14; Ramsey: 8-15).

Masturbation accounts for the first ejaculation in 68 percent of males, the remainder experience first ejaculation with nocturnal emission or with coitus. There is a significant variation in incidence dependent upon educational level; those who finish high school and those who go on to college show a higher incidence of masturbation than those who do not go beyond grade school (96 percent vs. 89 percent [Kinsey, 1948]).

Although the average frequency of masturbation in adolescence is over two ejaculations per week (2.4 to be exact), there are wide variations: 17 percent have frequencies of 6-7 per week, and the group with the highest frequency averages 23 per week in early adolescence, dropping to 15 per week by the age of 20, 6 per week

---

* The term "normal" as used herein is meant to refer to that which is usual, typical, and/or common as inferred from whatever empirical observations are available and without reference to whether or not what is so termed complies or conflicts with the natural or moral law. The term "normal," then, is used somewhat in a statistical sense to refer to what is found in a majority of cases, and specifically to indicate behavior which in itself is not considered pathognomonic of severe psychiatric or emotional disorder.

by age 50, and once every two weeks by age 60. Masturbatory frequency is lowest in Orthodox Jews and devout Roman Catholics, and tends to be highest in inactive Protestants.

Those adolescents who do not masturbate during puberty show regularly in analysis an especially deep repression of infantile masturbation, threats about which have overwhelmed them with guilt and fear; such patients, incidentally, have a poor prognosis in psychotherapy.

While masturbation can be considered normal in certain situations, this is not to say that it is a simple alternative equivalent to proper sex relations, nor do we mean to imply that it can be put on the same level with involuntary nocturnal emissions as a form of natural activity (Edelston, 1956; Von Gagern, 1955). We must recognize that masturbation is not a wholly adequate substitute—in contrast to sexual gratification with a love object, masturbation gives no feeling except for the self, physical pleasure becomes an end in itself, and the senses become dulled and sated—giving rise to a hunger for stimulation which seeks ever new ways of gratification but never leads to complete satisfaction (Edelston, 1956; Kanner, 1935; Nunberg, 1955; Von Gagern, 1955). The easy access to satisfaction leads to an overdevelopment of phantasy life and an independence from the real object, with a resultant flight from reality into egocentricity and a moving away from object relationships.

Certainly sexual gratification is important to the individual, yet the healthy person can tolerate a temporary lack within certain limits and can find substitute gratification along the line of sublimation; it is only the disturbed, neurotic patient who is unable to tolerate any diminution in or postponement of gratification without becoming depressed, and such patients use masturbation to prevent potential depression and to remove already existing depression (Abraham, 1916). The conflicts which the adolescent has over his masturbatory activity are often solved by reaction formations; if he is successful, these contribute to the formation of valuable character traits; if unsuccessful, he must find substitutes for masturbation, or the masturbation itself becomes a neurotic symptom (Nunberg, 1955). Thus the control and inhibition of instinctual impulses, at least within certain limits, may well be salutary for the development of character and personality. "It is victory over impulses, rather than surrender to them, that leads to personal integration" (Schneiders, 1960, p. 111).

Probably the most important consequence of masturbation is the guilt which typically accompanies it, and the struggle to defend oneself against it which may last for years and adsorb onto itself all the energy of the psychic system. And it is surprising to note how very incompletely the adolescent can be reassured about the dangers of masturbation to which he ascribes almost every conceivable ill—pimples, insanity, stooped shoulders, weakness, loss of manly vigor, weak eyes, ulcers, impotence, feeblemindedness, cancer, to name only a few. Freud tended to the view that neurasthenia could follow upon excessive masturbation; it is nowadays felt that it would be more correct to say that neurasthenia is an outcome of insufficient orgasm—that is if anxieties and guilt disturb the satisfactory character of the masturbation (Fenichel, 1945). Neurasthenia manifests itself as retentive spastic symptoms (indicative of an attempt to block the physical and emotional discharge), such as muscular and vasomotor spasm, constipation, headache, fatiguability, hypersensitivity to light and sound; and/or as explosive involuntary emergency discharges, such as sweating, diarrhea, irritability, and inability to concentrate (Fenichel, 1945; Ferenczi, 1912).

It appears, then, that harmful physical consequences may possibly follow masturbation, but that these effects and the likelihood of their occurrence have been greatly exaggerated, and that the chief harmful consequence is in the psychic sphere and pertains to the feeling of guilt over masturbation. When one deals with the adolescent in conflict about the practice, however, he is soon aware that the young boy is unable to accept this benign approach. Instead, he has a deep need to believe that masturbation is a terrible thing and he strongly resists enlightenment about its harmlessness. This is because the conscious masturbatory phantasies are distorted derivatives of unconscious Oedipus phantasies, and if the adolescent did believe that masturbation is harmless he would have to resurrect these phantasies and would have to face the Oedipal desires which are responsible for the guilt (Fenichel, 1945). It is of some interest to note that the Hebrews indicated their recognition of this fact in the story of Onan, in the Bible, who masturbated instead of having intercourse with the dead brother's wife, as he should have according to the levirate law. "If we understand that the spilling of semen on the earth is to be taken symbolically as earth equals mother, then the whole episode means intercourse with mother, for which transgression one is killed by God (father)" (Nunberg, 1955).

Whatever the full explanation, guilt is almost universally present in masturbating adolescents, and conflicts over it do give rise to certain disturbances. Phobic avoidances are frequent and here the object feared may symbolize a temptation to masturbate—as in fears of falling asleep, fears of being alone, fears of touching first the genitals and later any object, fears of dirt, or the object may symbolize a punishment for having committed the act, as in fears of going crazy and of being repulsive or ugly.

Defenses against masturbation and substitutes for the masturbatory phantasies may also be expressed by conversion symptoms—spasms, rhythmical contractions and sensory disturbances of all sorts. Daydreaming is often undertaken as a way to keep one's thoughts off sexuality; in some, this is further elaborated to the point of obsessive interest in certain fields. In similar manner, tics, undoing actions, rituals, ceremonials, stealing (i.e., secretly doing something which is forbidden) and gambling are frequently explicable as substitutes for masturbation and/or as defenses against it.

Characterologically, several types of disturbance may occur as a result of masturbatory conflicts (Lampl-DeGroot, 1950). In boys with a negative Oedipus—that is, with the father as the sexual object—castration is a prerequisite of the passive desires. Thus masturbation and its accompanying phantasies must be completely inhibited. Usually such inhibition spreads to paralyze the entire personality, the submissive tendencies are reinforced and the individual ends up a completely dependent, infantile personality.

If there has been too strong a prohibition of masturbatory activity, this may be suppressed, but opposition will then be manifested in everything else toward the significant adults in the adolescent's life. Such an individual wants the environment always to be the opposite of what it is and manifests a generally disenchanted attitude toward life, often with outbursts of impulsivity, acting out and even delinquency.

When the adolescent is able to win the struggle against masturbation on his own, there is a tendency to megalomania or at least a lack of self-criticism, overbearing behavior, over-estimation of the self, and consequent difficulty in adjusting to the real world. Failure in the battle, however, leads to pronounced self-accusations and self-torment, marked inferiority feelings, and compulsive masturbation which may paralyze all other activities. Finally, the adolescent may achieve partial success in his struggle, with periodic breakthrough of masturbatory activity; then the picture is one of vacillation between megalomanic and inferiority phantasies.

HOMOSEXUALITY

Overt homosexuality is perhaps the most common sexual disturbance in the male. Kinsey's (1948) statistics indicate that about 40 percent of all American males consciously remember at least one homosexual experience leading to ejaculation, and in the majority of cases this does not represent so-called accidental homosexuality, which occurs with great frequency in situations where there are no women—such as at sea, or in prisons. We are then led to ask in the non-accidental cases, why does the individual choose a member of his own sex as his sexual object? We shall not give much time here to a consideration of this question, since it will be discussed in a later session, but in brief we can see three major factors leading to homosexuality. The first is related to traumatization at the sight of the female genitalia leading to marked intensification of castration fears; such individuals may turn to homosexuality so that their sexual partner will always have a penis. Another cause is a fixation on a man in early childhood, such as when there was no mother figure in the family group. The third, and probably most common factor, is defending oneself against the mother by identifying with her and subsequently projecting the subject's person onto another boy—a narcissistic type of object choice, in other words.

SEXUAL PERVERSIONS

Normally, the object of the sexual impulses is the other sex, and the aim of sexual activity is genital union with that person—but this is not always stable, and object and aim are not always welded together (Nunberg, 1955). A deviation in sexual aim constitutes a perversion that within certain limits is normal (as when it is used as part of forepleasure); the deviation becomes a true perversion when it is the exclusive form of sexual activity.

Fetishism. This perversion is almost exclusively confined to men, and evidence of it in almost all cases is apparent during the adolescent period. When we use the term fetishism we refer to the individual's need for some particular object to be present before he can achieve orgasm. This object may be a part of the body of his sexual partner other than the genitals, or it may be some other object such as shoes or earrings. I once treated a fur-coat fetishist whose partner had to wear a long fur coat before he could have intercourse with her. Other examples are men who must be able to see their sexual partner's feet while they are having intercourse, or the sex partner must have long hair, or something of the sort. This is seen, though to a lesser degree, in many relatively normal people, who must have certain conditions before they can function effectively—the lights have to be on, or off, etc. Fetishism also includes the widespread symptom of sexual interest in women's underwear.

In all these cases, the problem goes back to the fear of people without a penis. Shoes, long earrings, long hair—these symbolize the penis; in the fur coat fetishist, the fur symbolized pubic hair, long enough and thick enough so that the patient felt it could conceal a penis. Fetishism, then, is an attempt to deny that there is anyone who does not possess a penis.

Exhibitionism and Voyeurism. These perversions, again, are founded on castration anxiety. The exhibitionist is unconsciously saying to his audience: "Please be afraid of my penis, then you will show me that I really have one. Show me you are afraid of me and I'll not have to be afraid of you. I show you what I wish you would show me; then I can believe that everyone has a penis." Similarly, the voyeur is afraid of adult sexuality himself, because he fears that in intercourse he would lose his penis. So he must watch others having intercourse and otherwise take a passive role without running the risk of losing his penis.

REFERENCES

Abraham, K. The first pregenital stage of the libido (1916). In *Selected papers on psychoanalysis.* London: Hogarth, 1948. Pp. 248-279.

Edelston, H. *Problems of adolescents.* New York: Philosophical Library, 1956.

Erikson, E. H. *Childhood and society.* New York: Norton, 1950.

Fenichel, O. *The psychoanalytic theory of neurosis.* New York: Norton, 1945.

Ferenczi, S. On onanism (1912). In *Sex and psychoanalysis.* New York: Basic Books, 1950. Pp. 185-192.

Fraiberg, Selma. Some considerations in the introduction to therapy in puberty. In Ruth S. Eissler, *et al.* (Eds.) *Psychoanalytical study of the child.* Vol. X. New York: International Universities, 1955. Pp. 264-286.

Freud, Anna. *The ego and the mechanisms of defense.* London: Hogarth, 1937.

Jones, E. Freud's psychology (1910). In *Papers on psychoanalysis* (5th ed.) London: Balliere, Tindall and Cox, 1948.

Jones, E. Some problems of adolescence (1922). In *Papers on psychoanalysis.* (5th ed.) London: Balliere, Tindall and Cox, 1948.

Kanner, L. *Child psychiatry.* Springfield, Ill.: Thomas, 1935.

Kinsey, A. C., Pomeroy, W. B., & Martin, C. E. *Sexual behavior in the human male.* Philadelphia: Saunders, 1948.

Lampl-DeGroot, Jeanne. On masturbation and its influence on general development. In Ruth S. Eissler *et al.* (Eds.) *Psychoanalytical study of the child.* Vol. V. New York: International Universities, 1950. Pp. 153-174.

Moodie, W. The adolescent boy. *Practitioner,* 1949, *162,* 263-268.

Nunberg, H. *Principles of psychoanalysis.* New York: International Universities, 1955.

Schneiders, A. A. Personality development and adjustment in adolescence. Milwaukee: Bruce, 1960.

Schonfeld, W. A. Pediatrician's role in management of personality problems of adolescents. *Amer. J. Dis. Child.,* 1951, *81,* 762-770.

Von Gagern, F., *The problem of onanism.* Westminster, Md.: Newman, 1955.

Wilson, H. Mental disorders in adolescence. *Practitioner,* 1949, *162,* 305-312.

Wittels, F. The ego of the adolescent. In K. R. Eissler (Ed.) *Searchlights on delinquency.* New York: International Universities, 1949. Pp. 256-262.

Zachry, Caroline B. Adolescence. In V. C. Branham & S. B. Kutash (Eds.), *Encyclopedia of criminology.* New York: Philosophical Library, 1949.

Homosexuality: Genetic
and Dynamic Factors

PAUL G. ECKER

*Paul Gerard Ecker received his M.D. degree
from the School of Medicine of Western Re-
serve University in 1944. His residency training
in internal medicine was taken at the Peter Bent
Brigham Hospital in Boston. He combined this
training with a simultaneous teaching fellow-
ship at the Harvard Medical School. His psychiatric residency was at the New York State Psychiatric Institute at Columbia, subsequent to
which he held a teaching position at Columbia
Medical School. Two years were spent in research at the Rockefeller Institute. Subsequent
to his work in New York, Dr. Ecker served as
Chief of the Functional Disease Service at the
Hospital of the University of Pennsylvania, and
this was the position which he held at the time
of the 1957 Pastoral Psychology Institute. At
the present time, Dr. Ecker is engaged in private psychiatric practice in Philadelphia, and is
an instructor in Psychoanalysis at the Institute
of the Philadelphia Association for Psychoanalysis.*

Homosexuality has a long history in the annals of recorded civilization. According to the code of Hammurabi it was known in As-
syria. Egyptian mythology attributed homosexuality to the gods

Horus and Set, according to references in the Fayum papyrus, and it seems from the available evidence that the Egyptians did not regard homosexuality as reprehensible (Ellis, 1942). In Greece, during its period of greatest cultural and intellectual ascendancy, homosexuality was not only regarded as beneficial, but bordered on the status of being idealized, for among the Dorians it was felt that an older man propagated his virtue in the youth he loved. That homosexuality was equally widespread in ancient Rome is well attested in many works by writers of the time, notably in the Satyricon of Petronius.

By the time of the caliphate of Harun al Rashid (786-809) the institution of the *ghilman* had been established to provide for the practice of homosexuality at the court in Baghdad. The virtues of these "beardless young boys" were extolled by the poets at the time. The institution was extended in the Arab Moslem world by Harun's son, the caliph al-Amin following the Persian precedent (Hitti, 1943, p. 109).

In the twelfth century, Anselm gave instruction in the manner of dealing with the sodomist, and stated: "This sin has been so public that hardly anyone has blushed for it, and therefore many have plunged into it without realizing its gravity" (Ellis, 1942, p. 40). The Catholic Church commented on homosexuality at the Council of Paris and later at the Council of Rome in the early part of the 13th Century, when the death penalty was levied against sodomy. It has been often alleged that many architects of the Renaissance in Italy were known homosexuals.

The records of the courts in London recount the history of a woman known as "Mother Clap" who was charged at the Old Bailey in 1726 "with keeping a sodomitical house." At her trial, she was condemned to pay a fine, to stand in the pillory, and to undergo imprisonment for two years. The punishment for sodomy at that time, when completely effected, was death. The history of Oscar Wilde in the 19th century is well known.

Studies of primitive societies regularly indicate homosexual practices, whether the groups studied were in the East or in the West. From what has been said, it is obvious that homosexuality has been recognized among all peoples throughout the records of civilization (Ellis, 1942, p. 8).

INCIDENCE OF HOMOSEXUALITY

There are no adequate statistics available concerning the incidence of homosexuality. In general, the available studies tend to indicate a higher prevalence than is commonly realized. Earlier studies such as those of Havelock Ellis in England and Magnus Hirshfeld in Germany, revealed an incidence varying between two and five percent. Havelock Ellis stated: "I am still led to the conclusion that there must be a distinct percentage which may be sometimes slightly over two percent" (Ellis, 1942, p. 64). His estimates were based largely on information which was supplied to him by correspondents. Kinsey quotes Hirshfeld's study of 3,000 students at the Charlottenburg Institute of Technology and 5,721 metal workers in Berlin, where 94 percent of the males are described as being exclusively heterosexual, 2.3 percent solely homosexual, and the remainder as having both homosexual and heterosexual experience. Later on, Hirshfeld did an even more elaborate study involving 23,771 persons from whom he was able to separate 525 cases considered to be truly homosexual, for an incidence of approximately 2.2 percent.

More recently in Kinsey's study of the male population, 27.1 percent of the youngest unmarried group are reported to have had some homosexual activity to the point of orgasm. The incidence among single males rises in successive age groups, and reaches a maximum of 38.7 percent between the ages of 36 and 40. Any sampling of the population to determine the incidence of homosexuality immediately encounters several obvious difficulties. There is the manifest reluctance of many people who have had overt homosexual experience to reveal the fact because of the shame that they feel. On the other hand, there is another segment of the population who, having had homosexual experience with much undercurrent conflict, are inclined to discuss the problem with great frankness and openness. Consequently if one relies solely on volunteers in such a statistical study, as Kinsey points out, it is impossible to ascertain the true prevalence of homosexuality in the general population, and whether or not this incidence, determined on the basis of histories taken from volunteers, represents an undue or unrealistic proportion (Kinsey, 1948, pp. 610-666). Kinsey attempts a strict biological definition, based solely on the history of any physical contact with a member of the same sex ending in orgasm, but this definition is necessarily limited. In the sense of this review, it is necessary to emphasize that a single, isolated homosexual experience does not constitute homosexuality, nor should the history of homosexual play in childhood or early adolescence be construed as diagnostic of homosexuality in the individual concerned.

A survey of available data from the Selective Service during the last war of the rate of rejection at induction centers, points to an incidence of about one percent of homosexuals. To this should be added the numbers of those who were subsequently discharged for homosexual activity while they were in service. It may well eventually turn out that the incidence of 2.2 percent of Ellis and Hirshfeld may represent the true incidence of active, continuing, dominant homosexuality in the population at large.

Turning now to the question of the incidence of homosexuality in the female, Kinsey gives the figure of 25 percent of his sample as having had recognized erotic responses at some time in their lives to other females by the age of 30 years. Of his total sample, 19 percent had had actual homosexual contact by the age of 40, with an incidence of 24 percent among the women who had never been married, 3 percent in the married group, and 9 percent as the incidence in previously married females. A half to two-thirds of this group with a history of sexual contact with members of their own sex achieved orgasm in at least some of these contacts (Kinsey, 1953, pp. 453-455). Kinsey states that these figures are probably higher than would be expected in the United States population as a whole. Kinsey's figure of 4 percent for the unmarried group between the ages of 46 and 50, continually engaged in homosexual relations, may be very close to fact. It seems clear from the statistics that there were a fair number of histories in which the female homosexual partners lived together and maintained constant sexual relationships for many years. Kinsey had the impression that such long-term homosexual relations among males are far less frequent, and it is obvious that little thought is given in our society to the fact that two women may live together for many years without sexual relations being suspected, as might be the case in a similar relationship between men. Kinsey's figures pointed to a higher incidence of overt homosexual contact among women in the higher educational levels, the incidence paralleling the level of education (Kinsey, 1953).

Kinsey's statistics on the incidence of female homosexuality are probably open to even more serious question than are the statistics for the incidence of introversion in the male. It is commonly accepted among psychoanalysts that the incidence of overt homosexuality in women is probably far higher than in men (Freud, 1931, pp. 252-272).

THE CONCEPT OF HOMOSEXUALITY

Let us turn now to some consideration of the concept of homosexuality. Homosexuality is but one of the general class of human behavioral disorders known as perversion. The term "homosexuality" has the common meaning of a persistent physical attraction to members of the same sex. In the first instance, the distinction should be drawn between homosexual experience and persistent homosexuality, for it is a well-known fact that isolated episodes of homosexual play in children are by no means uncommon and do not, per se, lead to persistent homosexuality. In fact, isolated homosexual experience in childhood is likely to prove to be of such frequency as data is accumulated as to lead one to suspect that it represents a normal phase in the development of the child. This review will deal essentially with the problem of persistent, overt homosexuality.

Freud, in his *Three Essays on the Theory of Sexuality,* distinguished three classes of homosexuals, the first being the absolute invert, the individual whose sexual objects are exclusively of his (or her) own sex, who never experiences attraction to members of the opposite sex toward whom an active aversion is felt. Freud recognized as a second group the amphigenic homosexual, or bisexual individual, in whom the quality of exclusiveness was absent. Thirdly, he recognized a class of contingent homosexuals—that is, those individuals who would resort to homosexuality in the absence of a normal, heterosexual outlet; individuals capable of taking as their sexual object someone of their own sex and deriving satisfaction from the relationship (Freud, 1905, p. 14).

Examples of contingent homosexuality, a not uncommon problem in prisons and the armed services during the war, were the sporadic outbursts of overt homosexuality in certain individuals who found themselves under stress, separated from heterosexual contact, and thrown together with members of their own sex under conditions of close physical proximity for long periods of time. Lawrence of Arabia (1938) graphically described the homosexuality among his troops in the desert in World War I. Many of these individuals returned to their communities, married, and settled down to have no further homosexual activity during their lifetime. Such individuals should obviously not properly be classed as true homosexuals, nor should the individual who has had an isolated, single homosexual experience—out of curiosity, or under the influence of alcohol— for in such individuals, the essential preference of sexual object is not for members of their own sex.

Turning our attention now to the problem of the other two classes of invert, the absolute and the amphigenic, several questions arise. Freud asked whether homosexuality was in any sense innate, that is, constitutionally determined. In answer it can be said that to date, there is no biological evidence for any physiological difference between the homosexual and heterosexual individual. The careful endocrine assays of Perloff (1949) have failed to reveal any significant difference in the ratio of male to female hormones in the homosexual, when compared to the heterosexual individual.

Continuing with his observations on the possibility that homosexuality is an innate characteristic, Freud states: ". . . we must ask in what respect it is innate, unless we are to accept the crude explanation that everyone is born with a sexual instinct attached to a particular sexual object" (Freud, 1905, p. 19). He goes on to say:

> By studying sexual excitations other than those that are manifestly displayed, it has been found that all human beings are capable of making a homosexual object choice and have in fact made one in their unconscious. . . . Psychoanalysis considers that a choice of object independently of its sex,—freedom to range equally over male and female objects—is the original basis from which, as a result of restriction in one direction or another, both the normal and inverted types develop (Freud, 1905, p. 23).

He continues in his study of inversion:

> Experience of the cases that are considered abnormal has shown us that in them the sexual instinct and the sexual object are merely soldered together—a fact which we have been in danger of overlooking in con-

sequence of the uniformity of the normal picture, where the object appears to form part and parcel of the instinct. We are thus warned to loosen the bond which exists in our thoughts between instinct and object. It seems probable that the sexual instinct is in the first instance independent of its object; nor is its origin likely to be due to its object's attraction (Freud, 1905, p. 26).

Freud also recognized that homosexuality was probably not simply acquired as the result of certain sexual experiences in early childhood alone, for, he reflected, and again I quote:

Many people are subjected to the same sexual influences (e.g., to seduction or mutual masturbation, which may occur in early youth) without becoming inverted or without remaining so permanently. We are therefore forced to a suspicion that the choice between innate and acquired is not an exclusive one or that it does not cover all the issues involved in inversion (Freud, 1905, p. 18).

Cases of hermaphroditism are, of course, well known in the medical profession, and it is striking that although these individuals have the physical characteristics of both the sexes, they seldom, if ever, are bisexual from a psychological standpoint. Again to quote Freud: "The truth must therefore be recognized that inversion and somatic hermaphroditism are on the whole independent of each other" (Freud, 1905, p. 20). From this, it is apparent that a distinction must be drawn between bisexuality on a purely physical basis, and inversion in the psychological sense, for it is the thesis of modern analytic psychiatry that it is the *interaction* between the constitutional make-up of the individual and his early life experience which finally determines at puberty the direction which his adult sexual life will take.

Freud delimited perversion not only in terms of the object of sexual attraction, but also in terms of the sexual aim, that is, the deviation in terms of the pathway of gratification taken by the individual. In other words, he recognized that certain individuals found gratification only in certain inhibited forms of sexuality in terms of their relationship to the sexual object and not in terms of heterosexual union in the usual physical sense. He thus further classified perversions as follows when he said: "Perversions are sexual activities which either (a) extend, in an anatomical sense, beyond the regions of the body that are designed for sexual union, or (b) linger over the immediate relations to the sexual object which should only be traversed rapidly on the path towards the final sexual aim" (Freud, 1905, p. 28).

He went on to distinguish between the so-called masculine and feminine traits, which he defined in terms of activity and passivity. Freud recognized clearly the difficulties inherent in the attempt to arrive at a strict definition of masculine and feminine, and felt that this antithesis could best be understood from a psychological standpoint in terms of activity and passivity, with the equivalence of masculinity with activity and femininity with passivity. From a schematic standpoint it can be seen that certain homosexuals in their relationships behave in a predominantly active or passive manner, depending upon the specific constellations of their conflicts. It is interesting from a clinical standpoint that the relative dominance of either the active or passive aims in the given homosexual is associated with some rather typical patterns of behavior. In this respect, the dominantly active male homosexual is more likely to be an amphigenic invert who may possibly marry, often to mask his homosexuality. On the other hand, the dominantly passive male homosexual with deep feminine identification is far less likely to marry and may have virtually no physical contact with women during his lifetime.

The converse appears in respect to the female homosexual. The active (masculine) female homosexual is usually an absolute invert who seldom, if ever, has relations with men and is often extremely jealous of her partner, whose feminine attributes she values so highly. She is far less likely to marry than is her passive, feminine counterpart. The latter often falls into the class of amphigenic invert and may marry, her homosexual activity being oftentimes sporadic and transient.

Of course, it is also seen that certain individuals in one type of situation will play the active or masculine role, and in another the passive, or feminine role. Nunberg pointed clearly to the presence of both active and passive instinctual aims in the sexual life of both men and women, as forming the basis of bisexuality from a psychological standpoint (Nunberg, 1949, p. 52). That this distinction between activity and passivity is never total or absolute is abundantly evident.

GENETICS AND DYNAMICS OF HOMOSEXUALITY

Male Homosexuality. Turning now to the interplay of factors which from a psychological standpoint are decisive for the development of homosexuality in the male, one must recognize the aspects of fear of the woman and rejection of the woman by the homosexual man. This basic attitude exists, despite the observation that in some instances homosexual men are capable of being friendly with women, and often are manifestly masculine, able and aggressive individuals —at times, highly talented.

One factor appears as a specific determinant in the problem of homosexuality. The recognition of the physical difference between the male and female gives rise to the castration complex (Freud, 1908b, pp. 59-75; Freud, 1909, pp. 149-289). Of course, castration anxiety is not limited to the homosexual individual, for it is also found in the histories of heterosexual men (Fenichel, 1945). Psychoanalysis points to the fact that homosexual men are actually aroused by women, but this arousal is repressed and displaced onto men. In this sense it is understandable that some homosexuals value very highly feminine dress and feminine traits in their partners, even to the point of selecting transvestites as objects, i.e., men in women's clothing.

Furthermore, the relationship to the mother may be of decisive importance. Fear of and/or disappointment in the relationship to the mother may lead to an identification with her. In other words, the individual becomes like the person whom he either fears or has lost. The homosexual man may then behave like the object with whom he has identified, and turn to men for love.

On the other hand some homosexuals are raised by a possessive, unconsciously seductive mother. Such women often deny and unconsciously condone manifest homosexuality in their sons and are intensely jealous of any attention paid by the son to other women. Ferenczi (1950, chap. 12) delimited the various paths which may be taken by the individual subsequent to his identification with the mother. This mechanism may be apparent in the male homosexual who has been raised by a rejecting, controlling, or aggressively hostile mother, who provoked fear in the child which was dealt with by the defense mechanism described by Anna Freud (1948), namely, identification with the aggressor.

Another type of the homosexual's conflicts are dictated in particular by his narcissistic needs. Out of his identification with the mother, he then proceeds to love individuals oftentimes younger than himself toward whom he behaves as he wishes his mother had behaved toward him. He is, in effect, loving himself. His emotions are centered in his love objects whom he regards as a reflection of himself and thus, for example, he may search only for young adolescent boys. This same factor is found as a determinant in the perversion of pedophilia in which there is frank sexual attraction toward small children. The individual treats these children either in the way that he wished to have been treated himself, or in its exact opposite.

Case I: Illustrative of this latter pattern of homosexuality was a middle-aged man remanded for treatment by the court, having been arrested and sentenced on two occasions for sodomy. The patient was a pleasant, well-mannered, obviously intelligent person, thoroughly masculine in his appearance. There was no gross evidence of emotional disturbance. His homosexual activity commenced with his seduction by an uncle when he was eight years of age. At puberty, he began to take an active part in homosexual practices with the uncle on a continuing basis and later became involved with other individuals. Typically, this patient sought out and seduced adolescent boys between the ages of 12 and 15 who had had no prior homosexual experience. He always played the active part in the relationship. His masturbatory fantasies were limited to images of himself having intercourse with young boys.

This individual had had episodic relations with women on occasion through the years, but little satisfaction existed for him in these relationships, which were always transient and brief. He admitted to difficulty in being able to relate to women in any close, emotional way, and yet recognized quite readily that he was temperamentally far more like his mother than like his father. His father was described as a gruff, stern, temperamental individual, whose irascible outbursts had always frightened him. It was of considerable interest in this history that the patient became involved with these young men in settings which almost invariably resulted in his arrest. On the two occasions when he was arrested and sentenced, he was found in a public place with the parents of the boy nearby. This suggests, of course, a considerable degree of unconscious guilt, with the obvious need to assuage this guilt in his need to suffer punishment. On the other hand, in another pattern following the identification with the mother, the individual experiences the wish for

sexual gratification in the manner in which the mother experiences this
in relationship to the father. In other words, the father thus becomes
the object of the homosexual's love, who then strives to submit to males
who serve as surrogates for the father. In this case, the passive submission to the father may mask a deeper, unconscious aggression serving
the end of robbing the father of his strength. Actual or fantasied physical
fear of the father in childhood may be a determinant in this type of
homosexuality (Freud, 1908a, pp. 45-50).

Case II: An example of this latter type of homosexuality was a patient
referred for psychiatric help following his third syphilitic reinfection
which he had contacted incident to his homosexual practices. He was a
36-year-old white, single laborer. His homosexual practices involved his
seeking contact with disreputable, dirty, infected individuals in the
poorest sections of the community. He would then submit to these individuals in the passive, feminine position, leaving them thereafter with
a feeling of revulsion and disgust, and intense feelings of shame. He
recalled at puberty a homosexual relationship with a man older than
himself, who left to enter service. He became quite disturbed at that
time and expressed ideas that the world was full of women disguised as
men. He felt persecuted, and expressed the idea that he was the sole key
to everything in the world: the epicenter, the source of condemnation
and salvation. Regressive fantasies were present in his desire to return
to the womb, with thoughts of being born again. Finally he expressed
the delusion that everything was a gigantic plot, organized by women
in an attempt to persecute him, and that Hitler was a woman.

In this example, overt homosexuality is seen to be part of a major
mental disturbance and may in this instance subsume the function of
maintaining a tenuous contact with reality. It is obvious in such a
situation that great care in clinical judgment has to be exercised in
disturbing the balance of the individual concerned in attempts to
deal with the homosexuality therapeutically.

Numerous other factors may contribute to the development of
homosexuality. For example, early homosexual experiences with sib-
lings may mask a primary deeper hatred of an older or younger
brother (Fenichel, 1945). In general, the probability of homosexuality in the male is increased in direct proportion to the degree
of identification with the mother which exists in the individual. On
the other hand, the absence of the mother early in life, and longing
for the early relationship with the father who may have been the
only loved object in childhood may also be a specific determinant.
Freud, in questioning the extent of homosexuality in ancient Greece,

pointed out that the young boys were raised and educated by male slaves (Freud, 1905).

Female Homosexuality. The paradigm of homosexuality in women is the mother-child relationship. As Helene Deutsch (1944) has said, the female homosexual may identify herself with the active mother, and as such find her greatest pleasure in searching out younger women toward whom she can play the maternal role. Conversely, certain types of female homosexuals will find in the older partner an unconscious equivalent for the longed-for mother. In essence homosexuality in the woman constitutes a regression in that it is a turning away from the man (father) back to the earlier relationship with the mother.

One type of homosexual woman plays an active, masculine role in the relationship, which may also include male attire to the point of transvestitism. Such women tend to behave as the man in the relationship to another woman, with their greatest emphasis on giving pleasure to their more feminine partners. Such young girls as they may choose as love objects may serve as representatives of themselves, and they then treat these loved objects as they had been or wished to have been treated themselves by the father (Fenichel, 1945). The aspect of narcissism in this instance parallels the similar case in the male homosexual, where the individual essentially loves himself in his love for his partner.

Certain female homosexuals may harbor sadistic fantasies concerning the sexual relationship, with fears of immolation or actual death. These fantasies may have been engendered by overtly sadistic behavior on the part of the father in early childhood. Thus the masculine identification and denial of any feminine attributes in herself subsumes a counterphobic function, in which the individual no longer experiences any risk of anxiety which might be engendered by a relationship to a man. Furthermore, this masculine identification, leading to a predominantly active type of (masculine) homosexuality in the woman may mask feelings of aggression and revenge toward the father.

Case III: The patient in this instance was a plainly dressed, attractive young woman in her middle 20's, brought to treatment by members of her family who had learned of her perversion. This young woman had been raised in a somewhat strict, Catholic environment, with a warmly affectionate, alcoholic, irresponsible father, who was at times punitive and who left the home about the time the girl was seven years of age. She then moved into her mother's bed, where she remained throughout her high school years. This patient never consciously experienced any physical attraction to men. Several aspects of her behavior in the homosexual setting are of significant interest. Her predilections were toward young, feminine, "soft" women, whom she felt great pleasure gratifying sexually. She was quite disinterested in any attention paid to her and played what appeared to be the masculine role in the relationship. From a dynamic standpoint, she appeared to have identified with her father in treating the young women as she was for a time treated by her father. In treatment she very quickly began to see the parallel in her sexual attraction to women and the frank erotic responses which she experienced in the years in which she had slept in her mother's bed. Among the determinants in this girl's homosexuality was the profound ambivalence she harbored toward the at-once-loved and threatening father whose loss she had taken so keenly.

Turning our attention now to the more dominantly passive kind of female homosexual, the tendency to passive submission in the relationship to another woman may reflect the unconscious desire to be loved by the mother. Other determinants are found in the fantasies centered in the castration complex in women, and in the fear of violation. These fears concerning the sexual act may so disturb the capacity for sexual enjoyment that gratification is possible only when there is a physical absence of the penis in the loved object. Feelings of guilt or archaic fears of the loss of the love of the mother, based either on past reality or fantasy, may act as other determinants in the passive submission to mother surrogates in homosexual relationships.

Case IV: The patient in this instance was a 50-year-old white, married mother of one daughter who had had a long history of overtly homosexual relationships with women her age or somewhat younger than herself. In these relationships she consistently played the role of the dominant, aggressive partner. She did not appear to be in any way manifestly masculine in her dress or in her mannerisms. She had been married for many years to a man whom she described as a passive and inadequate person. The relationship to him had been, at best, a tenuous one, the patient having worked at a job which kept her away from home through the late afternoons and the evenings so that the amount of contact between her and her husband was minimal.

She had been raised by an overly hostile, aggressive, domineering mother, whose preference was obviously for her sons. Her father was a meek, compliant, passive individual who rarely expressed himself. The patient tended to play the active masculine role in her relationships with other women. Her behavior clearly exemplified an identification with the hostile, rejecting mother and her attempt to give sexual gratification to other women was, in essence, what she would liked to have experienced in her relationship to her mother. Her homosexuality with its turning away from men also reflected the disdain and resentment she felt toward all men, in particular, her husband. This in turn appeared to be a compensation for at once the deeper feelings of inferiority and jealousy felt in relationship to her brothers and a long-standing resentment of the father for his unwillingness or inability to assume a dominant, masculine position in the family circle.

SUMMARY

Psychoanalysis regards mental illness as the expression of intra-psychic conflict. In this sense illness represents a lack of resolution of infantile conflicts and a relative failure in the specific modes of resolution of intra-psychic conflict. These conflicts occur under the pressure of either internal or external events, with the formation of symptoms which are regarded as compromises or, in other words, as further necessary but less efficient attempts at adjustment. To these basic contributory features must be added the factors of the biological determinants coming from heredity and the constitutional make-up of the individual.

The perversion of homosexuality can well be regarded as a symptom, an expression of an unresolved, neurotic conflict—the roots of which are the phantasy residues of repressed, unresolved, infantile conflict. As such, homosexuality may represent, in certain cases, the only possible avenue of defense against psychosis. The factor of polydeterminism in terms of unconscious conflict presented by these patients is a problem of great interest to this group.

Few homosexuals, if any, are actually at peace with their perversions, the pathway of gratification being unstable and incomplete, and the degree of gratification in the perversion always limited. The factor of unconscious guilt looms large in many of these individuals, who are often confused, frightened and socially outcast. The perversion, at best, is self-destructive in that it typifies an almost constant masochistic experience. Thus, these people remain incapable, by and large, of forming satisfactory and durable human relationships.

It is necessary to emphasize in any discussion of the genetic and dynamic factors in homosexuality, that what has been presented up to this point represents an over-simplification of the problem. It is merely an attempt to present, in a somewhat schematic fashion, some of the elements which have been recognized in certain cases as being of decisive importance in the development of homosexuality. However, one must guard against over-simplification, and recognize that the various factors which have been outlined here must be seen in the setting and context of the total personality of the individual. They are in a sense defenses which ward off deeper, unconscious drives which might give rise to either fear or intense feelings of guilt. All factors here enumerated may play a part in any given case, with a relative dominance of one or the other within the warp of the given individual's psychological constellation. Without ignoring the possibility of as yet unrecognized constitutional determinants in this process, the growing body of psychiatric evidence gathered in studies of these individuals point more and more clearly to a psychological nature for the complexes of which homosexuality is the expression.

PSYCHIATRIC TREATMENT

With respect to the problems inherent in the treatment of homosexuality, the psychiatrist is in the first instance faced with a diagnostic problem involving an appraisal of the total personality of the homosexual individual. Many considerations are relevant to such an appraisal. For example, it may be that the presenting perversion of homosexuality is the only area of neurotic conflict immediately apparent in the total personality. On the other hand, the homosexuality may be associated with or incident to other disorders such as chronic alcoholism, psychopathy or schizophrenia. In the latter cases, it is immediately evidenced that the problem in treatment may be very complex indeed, or even impossible. It behooves the psychiatrist, insofar as he is able, to arrive at an estimate of the assets in the personality, as well as an appraisal of the patient's determination to get well and to effect a change. The prognosis depends first and foremost on the latter consideration. In some individuals it is possible to mobilize this sense of determination to get well, as is the case when the patient is moved to seek help out of consideration for those close to him. Prognosis may be quite favorable in those individuals in whom there is a considerable degree of neurotic suffering with feelings of anxiety and guilt about their homosexuality. On the other hand, the individual who seems completely at peace with his perversion and is satisfied and gratified by it and in whom there is little motivation to treatment, may prove impossible to deal with in the psychotherapeutic situation.

From a therapeutic standpoint, parallels can be drawn from the treatment of homosexuality to the treatment of other impulse disorders, such as chronic alcoholism and drug addiction. In the very fact that the symptom does provide the individual with a certain degree of tangible gratification, the patient may be quite unwilling to surrender this satisfaction in order to achieve what is regarded as an illusion, that is, a greater gratification in normal heterosexuality. From what has already been said, it will be appreciated that, not only is there gratification for the individual in his homosexuality at an instinctual level, but furthermore, in terms of his total psychic economy the perversion protects him from a greater danger, that is, it subsumes the function of denial as well as reassurance against an activity or a situation which is fearful. His fear may be so great that he will be unwilling, or unable, to renounce the perversion in favor of the treatment. Characteristically, many homosexual patients are impulsive and have poor frustration tolerance. They expect their needs to be gratified immediately, and they are unable to tolerate delay.

Assuming then, a sincere desire on the part of the patient for help, coupled with some determination to effect changes in their personalities, and assuming sufficient disturbance accompanying the presenting symptom of homosexuality, the prognosis for analytic therapy is probably better than is usually thought by most people.

It is probably true that the prognosis is best in those individuals who seem to be suffering the most intensely because of their complaint. Concerning the treatment itself, psychoanalysis offers the best possibility for cure. Deeper, analytically directed psychotherapy must ultimately be directed to the mobilization of the unconscious conflicts in the individual, coupled with the working through of the resistances and the defense mechanisms, which have been erected in the personality to bind anxiety and to maintain repression. Ultimately and ideally, there must be a mobilization in the treatment situation of the infantile conflict which lays the basis for the development of the homosexuality as it emerged in the context of the whole personality. These, then, are some of the considerations which inhere in the problems of treatment of the homosexual.

REFERENCES

Bonaparte, Marie. *Female sexuality*. New York: International Universities Press, 1953.

Deutsch, Helene, *Psychology of women*. Vol. I. New York: Grune & Stratton, 1944.

Ellis, H. *Studies in the psychology of sex*. Vol. I. New York: Random House, 1942.

Fenichel, O. *The psychoanalytic theory of neurosis*. New York: Norton, 1945.

Ferenczi, S. *Sex in psychoanalysis*. New York: Basic Books, 1950.

Freud, Anna. *The ego and the mechanisms of defense*. New York: International Universities, 1948.

Freud, S. *Three essays on the theory of sexuality* (1905). London: Imago, 1949.

Freud, S. Character and anal erotism (1908). In *Collected papers*. Vol. II. London: Hogarth, 1924. Pp. 45-50. (a)

Freud, S. On the sexual theories of children (1908). In *Collected papers*. Vol. II. London: Hogarth, 1924. Pp. 59-75 (b)

Freud, S. A phobia in a five-year-oll boy (1909). In *Collected papers*. Vol. III. London: Hogarth, 1925. Pp. 149-289.

Freud, S. The psychogenesis of a case of homosexuality in a woman (1920). In *Collected papers*. Vol. II. London: Hogarth, 1924, Pp. 202-231.

Freud, S. Female sexuality (1931). In *Collected papers*. Vol. V. London: Hogarth, 1942. Pp. 252-272.

Hitti, P. K. *The Arabs*. Princeton, N. J.: Princeton Univer., 1943.

Kinsey, A. C., Pomeroy, W. B., & Martin, C. E. *Sexual behavior in the human male*. Philadelphia: Saunders, 1948.

Kinsey, A. C., Pomeroy, W. B., & Martin, C. E. *Sexual behavior in the human female*. Philadelphia: Saunders, 1953.

Lawrence, T. E. *Seven pillars of wisdom*. Garden City, N. Y.: Doubleday, 1935.

Nunberg, H. *Problem of bisexuality as reflected in circumcision*. London: Imago, 1949.

Perloff, W. H. The role of hormones in human sexuality. *Psychosom. Med.*, 1949, *11*, 133-139.

Homosexuality: Pastoral Notes

JOHN C. FORD, S.J.

Father John C. Ford, S.J., is Professor of Moral Theology at the Catholic University of America and he has degrees from Boston College (A.B., A.M., LL.B.), from Weston College (S.T.L.), and from the Gregorian University (S.T.D.). Prior to assuming his present post at the Catholic University of America, Father Ford was Professor of Moral Theology successively at the Gregorian University, Rome, and at Weston College, Weston, Massachusetts. A renowned theologian, Father Ford's publications include, in addition to numerous articles in theological journals, the following books: Depth psychology, morality and alcoholism *(1951);* Man takes a drink *(1954); and with Father Gerald Kelly, S.J.,* Contemporary moral theology, Vol. I: Questions in fundamental moral theology *(1958). Father Ford has made a distinguished effort to relate the findings of modern psychology and psychiatry to Catholic moral principles, and the three books mentioned above, as well as many of his other writings, testify to this fruitful and abiding interest.*

Since other speakers in the Institute are dealing explicitly with pastoral problems and procedures in dealing with homosexuals, I will make only brief reference to them, and then comment on two related matters: the Mattachine Society, Inc., and the recommendations (in England) of the Roman Catholic Advisory Committee on Prostitution and Homosexual Offenses and the Existing Law.

The Invert, by Anomaly* is an excellent book to give the priest an understanding of the male homosexual's mentality, and to help homosexuals to understand themselves. It is written from a Catholic point of view by a man who learned to live a useful Christian life in spite of his crippling psychological handicap. It is one of the few books which can be handed to the homosexual himself in order to help him in the very difficult job of coming to terms with life, love and eternity.

Advising marriage to a male who is truly homosexual could hardly ever be the prudent thing to do. Furthermore, in my opinion, it would be gravely sinful for a true homosexual to contract marriage without first making a frank disclosure of this basic unsuitability for normal married life. Apparently, many female homosexuals are able to adjust rather well to the requirements of matrimony. Consequently the above remarks do not apply to them to the same degree.

Advising priesthood or religious life to homosexuals involves various practical dangers. However, the mere fact that the sexual instinct is deviated as to its object, so that the individual has a sexual attraction for his own sex and not for the opposite sex, should not, in my opinion, be an absolute indication of unsuitability for religious or priestly life. The ability to practice continence, proved by actual success over a long period of time, plus the ability to adjust to the social and spiritual requirements in a particular religious order, are much more important, in my opinion, than the fact of a deviated instinct. It would be somewhat anomalous to make sexual attraction for the opposite sex an absolute requirement for a life in which one makes a vow of chastity, excluding the indulgence of any sexual attractions whatever.

Advising psychiatric treatment. A priest will do well to keep the following points in mind when advising a homosexual to seek psychiatric help. First, he should not raise false hopes in the mind of his consultant by giving him the impression that psychiatry will be the answer to his problems. As far as I can judge, psychiatrists and psychoanalysts have rather poor success in actually changing back

* Published by Balliere, Tindall & Cox, London, 1948, but available through the Newman Bookshop, Westminster, Md.

to normal the deviated instinct of the homosexual. And the treatment may be very expensive. The psychiatrist's aid, however, can be very valuable in helping the individual to live with himself and with a world which regards him with so much hostility and so little sympathy and understanding. Secondly, a psychiatrist or psychoanalyst should not be recommended unless one has the assurance beforehand that his principles and practices do not offend against Catholic morality. The psychiatrist need not be a Catholic in order to fulfill this requirement. On the other hand, the mere fact that the psychiatrist is known as a Catholic does not always give sufficient assurance. This remark is not made in disparagement of the high moral ideals of the psychiatric profession in general. It is merely a practical recognition of the fact that many psychiatrists have moral standards which differ from ours in important respects.

The Cross of Christ takes many forms in the life of Christians. In the present state of our knowledge many homosexuals can find salvation only by accepting the cross of psychological suffering which God allows them to bear. It is the task of the priest to help them to bear it; to give them a practical plan of life; to try to dispel the harsh attitudes of the public which make the lot of the homosexual so much more difficult. Sympathy, understanding, and Christian charity are not the rule where homosexuals are concerned. Many people who should know better still assume ignorantly that the homosexual's attraction for his own sex is a proof of his willful depravity.

THE MATTACHINE SOCIETY, INC.

This is an organization of homosexuals founded in 1950, with a small membership at present (perhaps about one hundred members), with headquarters in San Francisco and branches in Los Angeles, Denver, Chicago, Washington and New York. The name Mattachine had its origin in medieval Southern Europe. "The Mattachines were court jesters, teachers, fools—in the original sense of the word. They lived and moved in circles of the nobility. They dared to speak the truth in the face of stern authority, regardless of the consequences. And they were men of wisdom."

The aims and principles of the organization are set forth as follows in *Mattachine Society Today,* an explanatory brochure issued by their national headquarters*:

To sponsor projects of education:

1. Education of the general public so as to give them a better understanding concerning sex variation, so that all persons may be accepted as individuals for their own worth and not blindly condemned for their emotional make-up; to correct general misconceptions, bigotries, and prejudices resulting from lack of accurate information regarding sex variants.
2. Education of variants themselves so that they may better understand not only the causes and conditions of variation, but formulate an adjustment and pattern behavior that is acceptable to society in general and compatible with recognized institutions of a moral and civilized society with respect for the sanctity of home, church and state.

To aid the variant through integration:

1. Since variants desire to be accepted by society, it behooves them to assume community responsibility. They should, as individuals, actively affiliate with community endeavors, such as civic and welfare organizations, religious activities, and citizenship responsibilities, instead of attempting to withdraw into an invert society of their own. For only as they make positive contributions to the general welfare can they expect acceptance and full assimilation into the communities in which they live.
2. The long-term aid is not only to support well-adjusted variants with full integration into society, but to give social aid to maladjusted homosexuals for their own welfare as well as that of the community.

To conduct a program of social action:

1. To secure the active cooperation and support of existing institutions such as psychology departments of universities, state and city welfare groups, mental hygiene departments, and law-enforcement agencies in pursuing the programs of education and integration.
2. To contact legislators regarding both existing discriminatory statutes and proposed revisions and additions to the criminal code in keeping with the findings of leading psychiatrists and scientific research organizations, so that laws may be promulgated with respect to a realistic attitude toward the behavior of human beings.
3. To eliminate widespread discrimination in the fields of employment, in the professions and in society, as well as to attain per-

* Suite 309, 693 Mission Street, San Francisco 5, Calif.

sonal social acceptance among the respectable members of any community.

4. To dispel the idea that the sex variant is unique, "queer" or unusual, but is instead a human being with the same capacities of feeling, thinking, and accomplishment as any other human being.

General Aims:

1. To accomplish this program in a law-abiding manner. The Society is not seeking to overthrow or destroy any of society's existing institutions, laws, or mores, but to aid the assimilation of variants as constructive, valuable and responsible citizens. Standard and accepted democratic processes are to be relied upon as the technique for accomplishing this program.

2. The Society opposes indecent public behavior, and particularly excoriates those who would contribute to the delinquency of minors and those who attempt to use force or violence upon any other person whatsoever.

3. The Mattachine Society is a non-sectarian organization and is not affiliated with any political organization. It is, however, unalterably opposed to Communists and Communist activity and will not tolerate the use of its name or organization by or for any Communist group or front.

The members of the Mattachine Society take an impressive pledge to uphold the aims and principles of the organization, to guard absolutely the anonymity of all members, to conduct themselves in such a manner as to reflect credit on the Society, and so forth.

The organization publishes a monthly magazine *Mattachine Review* at its national headquarters. Some of the local chapters also publish monthly Newsletters for their members. Apparently the Mattachines are all male homosexuals. There is also a society of female homosexuals, called Daughters of Bilitis, who publish a monthly magazine called *The Ladder.**

It is too early to evaluate thoroughly the work of the Mattachines. I have seen only a little of their literature. Although its aims and principles may be acceptable as stated, it is hard to avoid the suspicion that they condone, and wish society to condone, sexual relations, at least in private, between consenting males who are of age. There is an article in *Mattachine Review* bearing the title: "No Need to Despair," by Rev. Davis Stern (1957), who is introduced by the editor as a Catholic priest. This article is, to say the least, fundamentally misleading and gravely inaccurate as to the Cath-

* P.O. Box 2183, San Francisco 26, Calif.

olic position on the morality of homosexual acts. An article in the *Washington Newsletter** for July 1957 takes a dim view of the recent Supreme Court rulings in the obscenity cases. Is it not rather tactless for a homosexual group that is anxious to make friends and influence people to put itself in the position of defending the rights of dealers in obscenity? Articles like these will make suspect the aims and principles of the organization, and will impede rather than promote legal reforms in the handling of homosexual offences.

THE CATHOLIC ADVISORY COMMITTEE IN ENGLAND

In England there is dissatisfaction with the existing laws governing prostitution and homosexual offences. At the request of the government the Cardinal Archbishop of Westminster commissioned a Catholic Advisory Committee to draw up some recommendations. Their report was made part of an article which appeared in the *Dublin Review* bearing the title: "Homosexuality, Prostitution and the Law" (Roman Catholic Advisory Committee, 1956). The report contains three sections, "Catholic Teaching on Homosexual Offences," "The Nature of Sex Inversion" and "Summary of Conclusions and Recommendations." The following parts of this last section are of special interest here:

I. The existing law does not effectively distinguish between sin, which is a matter of private morals, and crime, which is an offence against the State, having anti-social consequences. . . .

II. Under the existing law criminal proceedings against adult male persons in respect of consensual homosexual acts in private (whether of the full offence of sodomy or of gross indecency) inevitably fall upon a small minority of offenders and often upon those least deserving of punishment.

III. The Committee recommends that the criminal law be amended so as to exclude consensual acts done in private by adult males and to retain to the full extent penal sanctions to restrain
(a) offences against minors;
(b) offences against public decency;
(c) the exploitation of vice for the purpose of gain.

IV. . . . the Committee . . . recommended that for the present purpose male persons should be deemed adult at the age of 21.

V. The Committee has reached the conclusions (a) that imprisonment is largely ineffectual to reorientate persons with homosexual

* P.O. Box 8815, Washington 3, D. C.

tendencies and usually has deleterious effects upon them, and (b) that a satisfactory solution of the problem is unlikely to be found in places of confinement exclusively reserved for homosexuals. Accordingly, no positive recommendation is made with regard to methods of detention.

VI. The Committee regards with abhorrence arrangements understood to obtain in Denmark whereby homosexuals condemned to imprisonment may obtain release by voluntarily submitting to castration.

VII. The Committee accepts the propriety of the use for good cause under medical supervision of drugs to suppress sexual desire and activity, with the consent of the patient. Such treatment is permissible where serious pathological conditions obtain and when other remedies have proved ineffectual.

These recommendations were adopted unanimously by the Committee of seven distinguished Catholics, among whom there were three priests, one of them a professor of moral theology. They are of interest in this country because we have similar problems. Our laws against homosexual offenders differ from state to state, but some of them are very harsh, e.g. twenty years in state prison for an act of sodomy. There are also serious abuses in the apprehension of offenders. Members of the vice squad have been known at times to entice the suspect, to solicit him and then arrest him. And there is little evidence that present penal procedures are really corrective or rehabilitative.

The English Catholic Committee's report was discussed at the regional meeting of the American Catholic Theological Society in Washington, D.C., on March 20, 1957, and was touched on again, briefly, at the national meeting in Philadelphia, June 25, 1957.

With regard to repealing statutes which provide penalties for homosexual acts in private between adult, consenting males, various opinions were expressed. One view was against repeal because the state has obligation to support the natural moral law. Legislation of this kind re-invigorates the public conscience, and the state should take a stand even on private acts of immorality. On the other hand, the state certainly cannot enforce the entire moral law. Someone referred to a passage in St. Thomas according to which the state is not competent to make simple fornication a crime. The question is which moral violations should also be made crimes, and what is the wisdom and effectiveness of a given criminal statute.

The further point was made that to repeal these laws would give practical encouragement to homosexuality. Homosexuals, for example the Mattachines, would argue: it is legal, therefore it is permissible. Organized efforts to give positive legal sanction to homosexual relationships are not unheard of.

It does not immediately follow that because repeal is advisable in England it would also be advisable here. Our laws are by no means uniform in the various states, nor are social conditions similar. The practical effects of repeal might be very different here from what they would be in England, and repeal might be advisable in some parts of this country and not in others. In my opinion it would be premature to jump to the conclusion that these statutes should be repealed outright. We need a careful study of existing legislation, followed by a practical weighing of the advantages and disadvantages of outright repeal as against modifications of the law and correction of abuses in its administration.

The whole matter of homosexuality is of deep pastoral concern to us as priests of Christ, because here in the United States millions of people are involved in it. Pathetically they call themselves gay. In actual fact they are deeply unhappy, and often desperately in need of our help.

REFERENCES

Roman Catholic Advisory Committee on Prostitution and Homosexual Offenses and the Existing Law. Homosexuality, prostitution, and the law. *Dublin Rev.*, 1956, *230*, 57-65.
Stern, D. No need to despair. *Mattachine Rev.*, 1957, *3*, No. 2, 16-17.

Homosexuality: Pastoral Counseling

GEORGE HAGMAIER, C.S.P.

Father George Hagmaier, C.S.P., is Associate Director of the Paulist Institute for Religion in American Life, located in New York, and Instructor in Pastoral Psychology at the Paulist House of Graduate Studies in Boston. His A.B. degree is from Santa Clara University, California, his M.A. from St. Paul's College, Washington, D.C., and his Ph.D. from Teachers College, Columbia University. He is the first priest to have been awarded the doctorate by the Department of Marriage and Family Life at Teachers College, Columbia. Father Hagmaier has contributed numerous magazine and journal articles, particularly in the areas of pastoral counseling and of religion and mental health. He is a frequent and widely-known lecturer, and is the author, jointly with Father Robert W. Gleason, S.J., of Counseling the Catholic *(1959). Father Hagmaier has become one of the most consistent contributors to the Pastoral Psychology series, having given papers in two subsequent Institutes in addition to the one presented here.*

Most priests approach the counseling of a homosexual problem with mixed feelings. Fear, mistrust, feelings of inadequacy, and just plain ignorance make the prospect an unsettling one. The priest is often as disposed as the next man to accept the stereotype which society has

177

identified as "the homosexual type." Willful depravity, seduction of the innocent, preoccupation with effeminacy, perversion of morality —these, and similar associations, have prompted many a priest to give short shrift to a puzzled, struggling, unhappy soul who has dared to reveal the psychological and moral burden which he has heretofore carried alone.

Homosexual problems are much more common than the public imagines. Due to the stigma which society at present places upon the homosexual, accurate statistics are difficult to obtain. Five per cent of the total population is an estimate which appears in a number of presumably reliable studies. Other samplings give far higher rates. One might speculate that there are anywhere from 100,000 to nearly half a million homosexuals in New York City (Kinsey, 1948). While some of these figures may be exaggerated, it is almost universally agreed that this form of sexual deviation is a real and present problem. The tragic reception which many a homosexual has received from an uninformed, ineffectual, and sometimes even hostile priest at least partially explains why so many of these unfortunates leave the Church in frustrated rebellion or deep despair. It is characteristic of the homosexual to feel that society has abandoned him, as indeed it has. It is easy for him to conclude, then, that the Church has abandoned him too. For this reason I feel that a vast number of inverts never even approach a priest with their problem. We must not be fooled into thinking that this problem is relatively rare because we do not meet it often in the confessional or in the parlor.

Happily, social attitudes are changing somewhat. "Homosexuality" is not quite the dirty word it used to be. In certain circles at least, it can be talked about quietly and dispassionately. With continued enlightenment of the public, some of the more repulsive, distorted, and judgmental interpretations of the problem will disappear. The parish priest, by informing himself on this subject, can join society in reevaluating this much misunderstood affliction, can contribute substantially to preventative educational techniques, and can help individual deviates in his flock to live chaste, productive, and happy lives.

HOMOSEXUALITY, AN INDIVIDUAL PROBLEM

There are many conflicting opinions as to the nature and treatment of homosexual tendencies. It is a great temptation for most of us, in our threefold confessional role of judge, doctor, and teacher, to jump to quick conclusions, arrive at pat diagnoses, and hand out ready-made solutions. We must, first and foremost, train ourselves to tread cautiously and speak prudently in cases of homosexuality. In these matters, perhaps more so than in many another, it is better to say nothing than to say the wrong thing. The admonition of our moral theology to avoid prying into sexual details and motives without sufficient reason is never more in force than here. The priest-counselor must, above all else, be convinced that there are few cut-and-dried solutions to this problem. Homosexuality is an emotional, intellectual, volitional, moral, compulsive concoction uniquely peculiar to *this* man or woman. It is admittedly one of the most difficult psychiatric challenges. We must begin humbly in the face of such complexity, realize our limitations, and regardless of our sympathetic interest and readiness to help, we must stay clear of amateur probing and speculation for which we are not trained.

The average priest, in his role as confessor or counselor, should be skilled and informed enough to make an elementary diagnosis. This is a matter of necessity, not prerogative, for in many cases an individual with a homosexual problem will speak only to a priest. It is important, therefore, that the priest should know that the person who engages in homosexual activity is not necessarily a homosexual. To label him as such, to prescribe directives aimed at the solution of a homosexual problem, or to suggest psychiatric remedies might be quite out of place and positively harmful. Let me mention a few typical examples.

A panicky young mother brought her two sons, aged six and seven, to the rectory one afternoon. She insisted that the priest hear their confessions at once, and sobbed that she wanted to bring up her children "pure and decent." It seems that she had found her sons with a number of neighborhood pals of the same age running around the room with their trousers off. The mother was unaware that exploratory interest in their own and others' bodies is an innocent and widespread characteristic of young children in both the pre-school and latency periods. Adults, and especially parents, are often much too quick to assume their young children are seeking gratifications which parallel adult stimulation. This is not so. When children demonstrate this normal curiosity, it is more often the parents who need counseling than the children. The mother mentioned above, for example, needed reassurance that her young sons were not irretrievably on the road to depravity.

Considerable evidence indicates that many boys toward the end of the latency period and on into the early years of adolescence engage in at least occasional sex play of a homosexual nature. Again, while we do not condone such activity, we must be careful not to assume that such experimentation leads to the formation of a homosexual personality. In the vast majority of cases it does not. Boys at this age are often preoccupied with the absorbing curiosity about the size, shape, and function of their own and others' genitalia. One author has described this period as that of "sloppy adolescence where sex is vague, curiosity compelling and exciting." Many boys seem to solve this curiosity among themselves in a singularly direct way, yet without any pathologically homosexual involvements. Again, revelations of such experiences must be received with the greatest delicacy. It is here that adequate and sympathetic education can play a vital role in removing undue fear and guilt regarding sex. By directing the child's interests into healthy channels, encouraging reverence and self-control in the youth's acceptance of his new-found powers, the priest-counselor can help resolve oedipal conflicts which might otherwise prove troublesome. He can avoid harsh and threatening confessional tactics; he can point out that such youthful experimentation is essentially an infantile phenomenon; he can help the boy take pride in his new manhood and encourage him to exercise, with God's grace, that self-mastery which must be part of the psychological equipment of every self-reliant adult.

Although somewhat more suspect, even an occasional homosexual experience in late adolescence or early adulthood need not mean that the individual who performs them is a homosexual. The satisfaction of a latent curiosity, the haphazard release of sexual tension, the complete absence of heterosexual outlets, are all possibilities which do not necessarily assume an inverted personality. Many of the findings of the Kinsey report are certainly open to question, but the remarkably large number of men who are reported to have had homosexual experience before the age of 35, without any apparent need to continue such overt activity, seems at least in part to support this viewpoint.

When we come to consider the *de facto* homosexual, we are confronted again with a bewildering variety of types, symptoms, and motivations. There is the bisexual who is capable of both homosexual and heterosexual stimulation. There is the latent homosexual who may go for years, and often for a lifetime, without a single overt experience; indeed, he may never be aware of the nature of his deviation. The true, overt homosexual has been categorized by the experts into innumerable categories. Dr. George Henry and Dr. Albert Gross (1938) have, for example, distinguished three homosexual types: the fairy, the hoodlum, and the orderly (including the Madison Avenue type). In his classes, Dr. Marcel Frym, the famed West Coast criminologist, scorns such an arbitrary division. He feels there are as many types as there are homosexuals, and that each case must be evaluated and treated as the problem of a unique personality. We have, in addition, homosexuals who are "active" and "passive"; homosexuals who maintain an exclusive relationship for long periods of time, and others who establish only relatively transient liaisons. There are often overtones of sadism, masochism, voyeurism, fetishism, transvestitism, exhibitionism, etc.

I stress these details because I want to demonstrate, even without mentioning the psychological and environmental beginnings of this disorder, how diverse and complex a problem it is. When this conviction hits home, the priest-counselor is much less disposed to make quick judgments, propose facile solutions, or pronounce hasty condemnations. If the counselor has a profound respect for the intricacies of human nature, he will be far more capable of holding his tongue in case of doubt, and bearing with Christ-like patience the apparent failure of the moment.

WHAT TO DO WITH THE PROBLEM

The average parish priest, when confronted in the confessional or the parlor with a parishioner who admits to homosexuality, is baffled and often helpless. What can he do?

All too many of our priests need to be better informed on psychological matters in general, and on this problem in particular. Part of the solution lies in more adequate seminary preparation. Fortunately, many of our theological students are today getting excellent courses in pastoral psychology and counseling. Meantime, priests who are already caught up in the myriad and time-consuming activities of parochial life can attend clergy conferences and pastoral workshops.

The ordained priest can also keep abreast of the latest psychological information by a judicious reading of pertinent periodicals and books. The bibliography at the end of this paper lists just a few of the many current writings on this subject.

Secondly, the parish priest should make a special effort to acquaint himself with the community agencies in his locality, both public and private, which may be of help to him. Psychiatric clinics, Catholic Charity agencies, and individual doctors and psychologists can be of tremendous help to the busy shepherd of souls. He should also take pains to discover any priests or clergymen in his area who have had special training in psychological counseling. Finally, the regular parish priest must not overlook his own possibilities as a counselor. By a careful cultivation of the virtue of prudence, he will learn to be at least a good listener, and, with some experience, will be able to draw upon his rich treasure of spiritual truths in an effective, consoling, and encouraging way.

Perhaps this is the place to say a word or two of caution about the referral of a homosexual problem to the medical profession, a psychologist, or another priest.

Early in his appointment to a new parish, the priest should carefully investigate the psychiatrists and psychologists in his area to whom he might with reasonable assurance refer parishioners or penitents with mental and emotional problems. These professional people need not necessarily be Catholics; in fact a non-Catholic is often the most competent professional available. It seems, however, that some theories regarding the origin and treatment of homosexual problems cannot help but violate the moral teaching of the Church on this matter. Some doctors and psychologists hold to the rigid determinism of human behavior. If a homosexual is "born this way," fate intends that he seek and enjoy perverse sexual gratification. Psychologists and psychiatrists of this school have only one aim, namely, to help the deviate adjust without guilt to his overt homosexual experiences. They will often encourage the individual to seek companions of his own kind, and they attempt to explain away the gnawings of conscience which bedevil even the most confirmed profligates.

One possible way of checking a psychiatrist's or a psychologist's philosophy in this matter is to ask him if he can agree, at least in principal, to the following points:

1. Almighty God, in His plan of nature, intended that human-kind

be heterosexually orientated. The homosexual, regardless of the origin of his tendency, is afflicted with a disorder of nature.

2. The homosexual must make every effort to avoid those persons and places which will lead him to a deliberate participation in overt homosexual activity.

3. The ultimate, ideal goal of therapy must be the heterosexual adjustment of the individual.

These seem to me to be the principles which the therapist of a Catholic patient must accept, at least in theory. Having stated them, we must point out some qualifications. While homosexuality is a distortion of nature, it is in many cases a distortion which, practically speaking, cannot be undone. Whether the psychic processes of the true invert are organically determined, or fixed by the early environment, or develop from an interaction of both we do not yet know. In the psychiatric area, psychoanalysis is at present the only technique which claims to cure this aberration in the true sense of the word. Analysis is obviously time consuming, very expensive, and still in the process of evaluating its own successes. It is certainly for the few. Thus, though there are hopes for new solutions in the future, we must face the inescapable fact that the great majority of today's inverts will have to live with their alien tendencies to the end of their lives.

UNDERSTANDING THE INVERT

The true invert (we are not speaking here of the bisexual) was either born so, or made so very early in his development. As an adult he faces life as one who is psychologically handicapped. It is a medical error and a moral injustice to call him depraved or perverted. Both these words imply a deliberate *turning away* from a healthy and normal state to a degraded one. The true invert has never had this choice. He has not turned away from anything. Heterosexual affection has never been a reality for him. He has known only one attraction—an attraction to his own sex. He is no different from a child born blind, or with one leg shorter than the other. We can hope and pray and work for a cure, but the medical challenge in this psychiatric area seems as great as the task which would restore sight to sightless eyes.

Having said all this, let me emphasize that the positive and universal rule of the Catholic Church permitting directly voluntary sexual expression only in marriage, applies to the homosexual as it does to everyone else. In that remarkable book, *The Invert* (which should be on every priest's shelf), the author points out again and again a persistent parallel between the normal and the abnormal in this regard. The homosexual can expect to practice self-control and continence with the same spiritual helps as the heterosexually-orientated woman or man who is besieged with temptation.

> Among the normal are saints and profligates. Between those who have achieved sanctity and those who have chosen vice will be found the larger number. Struggling sinners, whose faltering progress is marked by many a pitiful tumble. Among inverts there are saints and profligates, and between the extremes many who are struggling in a more or less successful attempt to follow the dictates of conscience and direction of authority (Anomoly, 1948, p. 84).

It must be remembered, however, that the invert has a difficult time avoiding stimulatory situations. A typical unmarried person has at least the capacity for normal sexual expression, and may actively and hopefully work toward wedlock within acceptable social dating patterns. The confirmed homosexual can never entertain the prospect of a legitimate outlet for his drives. To suggest that he seek his recreation and relaxation in female company is unrealistic—such attempts will usually lead only to more anxiety, tension, and frustration. Yet he must live in a "man's world" which is often unescapably attractive to him. He will often find himself in contact with persons and situations that may constitute an occasion of sin for him. But alternative consequences—namely complete withdrawal and isolation from accepted social circles—are so much more damaging that exposure to certain risks is justified. Habitual fear and flight responses to normal social situations can create severe psychological and moral problems. This is important for the spiritual guide to know. The uninformed confessor has a tendency to demand that the invert avoid every contact which might possibly be a source of stimulation for him, e.g., swimming, sports, stag society, artistic circles, male friendships. In many cases such involvements help to sublimate a more basic urge for physical contact. To stifle these outlets could very well precipitate the penitent into more frequent and more overt homosexual activity. In other words, the invert should be encouraged to participate in all the social activities which bring him satisfaction, unless he feels certain that a person or place is an inevitable source of seduction.

It is important, too, to help the distressed and guilt-ridden penitent understand that there is a significant difference between acted out, overt homosexual behavior, and the compulsive, involuntary imaginings and desires which are so often a large part of the fantasy life of the invert. He must be helped to see that in certain situations such fantasies are bound to become more persistent and vivid, and that as long as he does not consent to them or act on them he is blameless.

In rare instances an overt homosexual experience may be the only outlet which prevents a seriously disturbed individual from crumbling into a psychotic. Such compulsive behavior is almost certain to be largely free from responsibility. In such cases, should a confessor be aware of them, it would be extremely unwise to emphasize the heinousness of these actions. However, such a judgment should never be made without the expert opinion of a consulting psychiatrist. In most cases a confessor might safely presume that his homosexual penitent will benefit from the same spiritual advice that he would give to others whose temptations are of a heterosexual nature. We will have more to say of this in the final section of this chapter.

Occasionally a priest will meet a homosexual problem through a referral from the courts. It is a tragic fact that in many states— probably most—the legal procedure and penal custom is both harsh and unfair to the homosexual. Only a small proportion of offenders —usually the most pathetic and compulsive of the lot—are apprehended and imprisoned. Prison itself is not only ineffective but more often than not contributes positively to the delinquency of the young deviate. It is contaminating rather than rehabilitative. A revision of the laws in this regard should be of special concern to the priest, the representative of all his people and a public figure, who more than many, is capable of bringing about more realistic public opinion and legal changes salutary for the common good. Those interested in reading further on the inadequacies of our present penal code in reference to the homosexual should consult the Report of the Roman Catholic Advisory Committee on Prostitution and Homosexual Offenses and the Existing Law (1956) published in the *Dublin Review*. Here are a few key sentences:

> The existing law does not effectively distinguish between sin, which is a matter of private morals, and crime, which is an offense against the State, having anti-social consequences. . . . Under the existing law criminal proceedings against adult male persons in respect of consensual homosexual acts in private (whether of the full offense of

sodomy or of gross indecency) inevitably fall upon a small minority of offenders and often upon those least deserving of punishment. . . . It is accordingly recommended that the criminal law should be amended in order to restrict penal sanctions for homosexual offenses as follows, namely to prevent (a) the corruption of youth, (b) offenses against public decency, (c) the exploitation of vice for the purpose of gain. It should be clearly stated that penal sanctions are not justified for the purpose of attempting to restrain sins against sexual morality committed in private by responsible adults. They should be discontinued because (a) they are ineffectual, (b) they are inequitable in their incidence, (c) they involve severities disproportionate to the offense committed, (d) they undoubtedly give scope for blackmail and other forms of corruption.

Chief Magistrate John M. Murtagh of New York heartily concurs with the substance of this report and has incorporated it into his book on prostitution, *Cast the First Stone* (Murtagh & Harris, 1957). He feels very strongly that many present juridical and penal procedures are most unfair, inadequate, and detrimental to public as well as private good.

THE PRIEST AS A COUNSELOR

The foregoing observations have emphasized the danger and futility of the untrained clergyman attempting psychological counseling. Without special study and experience, any probings into the whys and wherefores of this deeply-rooted disorder can only lead to confusion and distress. The average priest must sternly repulse his natural tendency to investigate the bizarre, and to probe into the unconscious.

The homosexual should be protected from the guidance techniques of two types of priests. He should be kept away from the confessor who has no patience with human weakness, and who speaks of homosexuality in cynical, often vulgar jargon. (Interestingly enough, such a priest will often be something of a "woman hater" as well, reflecting a crude, disdainful, unsympathetic attitude toward everything sexual.) The other type of cleric who should be dissuaded from counseling in this area is the "boyologist," the youth-enthusiast who is obviously reaping intense and unusual emotional satisfaction from his avocation. Such dedicated and absorbed involvement is almost always quite innocent and praiseworthy. But the capacity for identification called for in such absorbed relationships puts too many emotional blocks in the way of effective and objective airing of delicate homosexual problems.

The phenomenon of transference (at work in any one-to-one counseling relationship) can completely befuddle and mislead the well-meaning but inadequately informed counselor and counselee. Perhaps we should bluntly state that this tendency to probe for detailed and confidential material is a particularly attractive device for the occasional priest who may, in perfectly good faith, be sublimating certain latent homosexual characteristics of his own.

Although the average priest must shy away from protracted depth therapy of any kind, he can still be tremendously effective as a supportive counselor. As a matter of fact he is more often than not the most practical and effective referral source. At present there are not nearly enough professional agencies and experts to whom we can send people with homosexual problems who might come to us. It remains then for us to exercise, in the most informed, judicious, and Christ-like manner those techniques which can give at least a modicum of help and reassurance to the penitents who seek our aid.

What are some of the qualities which the effective counselor can bring to this work? Of chief importance are the attitudes and feelings which the priest himself entertains in regard to the problems of his penitents. Can he accept the homosexual as another person with a problem? Or is he filled with stereotypes, biases, revulsion and impatience in the face of such an aberration. "I have no absolution for the likes of you," thunders a priest to a homosexual penitent. This approach can do nothing but harm. If the priest is persuaded that the tendencies of the invert are evil in themselves, and that a fall from grace constitutes the unpardonable sin, then there is no good to be gained, even in the sacramental relationship.

The counselor of the homosexual must be personally and fervently convinced that, in the eyes of God, the homosexual is as capable of fruitful, chaste, yes, holy living as the heterosexually-oriented person. Such a counselor must be deeply persuaded that the homosexual can, through psychological help and sacramental guidance, avoid inevitable occasions of sin, and refrain from voluntary overt activity.

One of the chief reasons why the homosexual seems to find it difficult to sublimate his lower tendencies into healthy and acceptable behavior is because society as a whole has made him, at least in his own mind, an outcast and a derelict. The average homosexual, either through hostility or despair, feels himself abandoned by his fellow men. Society finds it much easier to tolerate the masturbator, the fornicator, the adulterer, and the birth-controller. The homosexual often has no other consolations but the inadequate and fleeting solace of his own pathetic sexual practices.

The priest-counselor can help the homosexual to regain a conviction of his own worth. By stirring up new hope in the real possibilities of a chaste life, the homosexual can also strengthen his faith in the bounty of God's grace and his own ability to cooperate with it, and can thereby stir up a new and deep supernatural charity which can prompt him to lead a useful, altruistic, and devoted life in the service of God and of his neighbors.

Whenever possible, the homosexual who is consistently involved in overt activity should be referred for psychological help. More often than not the cooperation of an understanding confessor is desired and appreciated by the therapist. I have tried to avoid any discussion of dynamic psychological phenomena in this paper. Something, however, should be said about the function of guilt and fear in the behavior of the homosexual, because the attitude and response of the priest can be a very helpful or hindering factor in his treatment.

Regardless of whether the penitent is receiving therapy or not, the priest cannot go wrong in helping to minimize undue fear and guilt which is part of the psychological equipment of most homosexuals. To stress the concepts of mortal sin, damnation, the foulness of the occasions of sin, and like matters is more likely than not to increase the number of falls. A *mere* feeling of guilt helps to strengthen the obsessive-compulsive mechanism which is so much a part of the homosexual character. A constant preoccupation with the fact that one has done or desired something wrong generates excessive feelings of fear or retribution, and of punishment. Time and again we see that a purely negative fear—whether it be the religionist's fear of God, or the atheist's fear of fate—is an insufficient deterrent to undesirable moral behavior. The confessor, therefore, should be careful not to instill more fear in an already frightened human being. The paranoic element, so common in the homosexual, tends to distort and exaggerate further these threats of punishment. Very often punishment is precisely what the homosexual is unconsciously seeking as a palliative for the dreadful desires and drives he fears within himself.

The priest must above all show the mercy of Christ to his troubled penitent. He must not be punishing or rejecting; he must not show amazement or disgust. He must assure the homosexual that he is not evil. He must help him to accept the fact that something is wrong, that there is a block to natural desires for which the invert is often not responsible. He must convince his discouraged penitent that God loves him as much, and perhaps more, than the heterosexually oriented folk around him. He must persuade him that this tendency can be lived with in a life of tranquil self-control and sublimation most pleasing to God and most meritorious for him who practices it. When the homosexual slips and falls, the priest can face this failure with the same patience, tolerance and readiness to help which he brings to the masturbation and petting problems of his other penitents. A true representative of his compassionate Lord, the priest can commend the struggling homosexual to the grace of the Church in a seventy-times-seven fold extension of Heaven's mercy.

PRACTICAL INFORMATION

Let me close this paper with a few random suggestions that have been found useful by Catholic counselors who deal with homosexual problems. These comments may be particularly helpful for those counselors who are at least temporarily unable to find a professional referral for a homosexual client. The priest-counselor should be aware that egoism and selfishness are usually characteristics of the confirmed homosexual. He needs great patience, and must be prepared for many disappointments inherent in the counseling relationship.

The untrained counselor should avoid long and frequent personal interviews with a true invert. He can be most effective as a kind and understanding confessor, though he might find that an occasional word of encouragement in the parlor is not out of place.

The danger of presuming that only homosexuals engage in homosexual activity must be understood. This is especially true of adolescent experimentation. The priest can do much damage by implying outright or subtly that an individual has all the earmarks of a deviate. This is especially true of the adolescents who regard sex play among themselves as signs of masculinity and virility. To identify their behavior with the effeminate perversions which they fear and despise may mark them emotionally for life.

Occasionally, the priest may be influential in effecting some change in an incipient homosexual's environment. The evidence of a too-exclusive feminine upbringing; the presence of an overdominant mother and a too-submissive father; the problem of overly stern parents; puritanical or stimulatory attitudes toward sex in the home; poor relationships between mother and father or parents and children —these are some situations which can occasionally be eased by the prudent and the gentle suggestions of an interested counselor. Occasionally too, the priest may help find a new job, new recreational interests, and even new living quarters for a young person with homosexual tendencies.

This paper is concerned chiefly with the counseling of the *male* homosexual, since the large majority of cases the priest will meet will be of this sex. This is a curious circumstance, since there is solid evidence to show that the incidence of homosexuality is considered higher in the female. Since public expression of affection between women—kissing, hugging, fondling, rooming together, etc.—is much more socially acceptable in our culture, latent forms of lesbianism do not carry the same sort of stigma as similar relationships between males evoke. Also, the apparent slowness of many women to reach orgasm would suggest that many of these interchanges are not stimulating enough to generate guilt or arouse misgivings.

If it is certain that the male homosexual is a true invert, then the counselor should dissuade him from attempting marriage. The counseling of a bisexual is more complicated, but there is more chance of his marriage successfully diverting homosexual tendencies into heterosexual channels. Female inverts are able to perform the marital act and raise children without as many difficulties. There seems to be somewhat less danger of such marriages ending quite so disastrously as the marriages of true male inverts. In any case, the opinion of a qualified psychologist or psychiatrist should be obtained.

The confessor should avoid speculating about the degree of responsibility involved in the overt homosexual activity of his penitents. As Dr. Rudolph Allers has pointed out, we cannot know anything about the true nature of "allegedly irresponsible impulses unless we know all we can find out about the total personality" (Allers, 1939, p. 219). If at all possible, we should avoid discussing the subject with the penitent. Certainly we should not tell him that he is not responsible. On the other hand, we cannot actually determine his guilt either. There are certain cases, for example, where the penitent must be treated as insane, even though he is completely lucid and in control of his will in all other aspects of his behavior. Father John F.

Harvey, O.S.F.S., in his article, "Homosexuality as a Pastoral Problem," suggests that this type of homosexual is analagous to the full-fledged alcoholic, and should be similarly handled (Harvey, 1955).

In dealing with young people, spiritual advisers should be careful to avoid instilling an excessive sense of guilt about matters sexual, particularly those of a heterosexual nature. One must always remember that fear of the opposite sex, much more so than an attraction to one's own, is the hallmark of the homosexual. For example, petting and dating practices of the bisexual must sometimes be viewed as attempts to risk and test a genuine heterosexual relationship, which could be for him a tremendously threatening and bewildering undertaking.

The invert must seek in works of love and service an outlet for his zeal and energy. The priest can encourage such sublimation by providing opportunities for works of mercy and personal sacrifice.

A sense of humor, on the part of the counselor and counselee, can help tremendously. The author of *The Invert,* for example, suggests in a letter that he quotes that we "take the passing amorous adventures of sentimental youth with a certain gaiety and lightness of touch to avoid sexual obsession" (Anomoly, 1948, p. 110).

The priest can help his penitent to focus his perspective so that his whole life is not clouded and colored by this one problem. The invert can be helped to develop and exult in the many positive talents he is sure to have. In doing so, he can actually minimize the obsession with sexuality which can so poison the mind with guilt and fear and helplessness that all other creative and compensating activity becomes stifled or sterile.

We have already indicated how reluctant an adviser should be to suggest that a homosexual abandon his normal social contacts. The counselor should, for similar reasons, be slow to presume that certain occupations are likely to mean trouble. Teachers, social workers, athletic directors, scout leaders, etc., who have been involved in actual sexual activity with their charges should, of course, be dissuaded from continuing in such positions. And pastors must exercise prudent vigilance in screening applicants for these parish posts. On the other hand, such occupations can be desirable and healthy outlets for those who have no problems with overt seductive behavior. As long as the worker is honest with himself and his confessor, the dangers of remaining in any job where deviate tendencies are being effectively sublimated are largely imaginary. It is quite possible, too, for a penitent to be so emotionally constituted that he has difficulties only in his private, off-the-job hours which never involve his vocational contacts, tempting as they might appear.

Both the counselor and his client must be deeply convinced that grace is an indispensable help to the dawning of adequate self-knowledge through which the cause of inner conflict is gradually revealed. The homosexual penitent must be fully convinced that chastity is a supernatural gift which requires an action of the will to achieve, and a firm dedication to an ascetical ideal. Earnest, placid prayer for such healing grace should be the persistent recommendation of the clerical counselor.

On the other hand, we must not fall into the error of pan-religionism. *Gratia perficit naturam* is never more apt than here. There is no magic quality to the genuine reformation of any life. Both the counselor and the penitent must be resigned to a long period of patient struggle. We can safely say that where the invert honestly faces up to his problem, avoids the avoidable occasion of sin, has the determination to get well psychologically and spiritually, prays constantly for the grace of God, confesses and receives communion frequently, formulates a plan of ascetical striving in the world, and cooperates closely with priest and psychiatrist—then he can validly hope for a fruitful, meritorious, and happy life.

REFERENCES

Allers, R. Irresistible impulses. *Amer. Eccl. Rev.*, 1939, *100,* 208-219.

Anomoly. *The invert and his social adjustment.* London: Balliere, Tindall and Cox, 1948.

Bergler, E. *Homosexuality: disease or way of life.* New York: Hill and Wang, 1956.

Flood, P. (O.S.B.), (Ed.) *New problems in medical ethics.* Vol. I. Westminster, Md.: Newman, 1953.

Harvey, J. F. (O.S.F.S.), Homosexuality as a pastoral problem. *Theol. Stud.,* 1955, *16,* 86-108.

Henry, G. W., & Gross, A. A. Social factors in the case histories of 100 underprivileged homosexuals. *Ment. Hyg.,* 1938, *22,* 591-611.

Henry, G. W. Pastoral counseling for homosexuals. *Pastoral Psychol.,* 1951, *2,* No. 18, 33-39.

Henry, G. W. *All the sexes.* New York: Rinehart, 1955.

Kinsey, A. C., Pomeroy, W. B., & Martin, C. E. *Sexual behavior in the human male.* Philadelphia: Saunders, 1948.

Murtagh, J. J., & Harris, Sara, *Cast the first stone.* New York: McGraw-Hill, 1957.

Odenwald, R. Counseling the homosexual. *The Priest,* 1953, *9,* 940-944.

Roman Catholic Advisory Committee on Prostitution and Homosexual Offenses and the Existing Law. Homosexuality, prostitution, and the law. *Dublin Rev.,* 1956, *230,* 57-65.

Homosexuality: Moral Aspects

ROBERT W. GLEASON, S.J.

Father Robert W. Gleason, S.J., of the Department of Theology and Religious Education at Fordham University, received his A.B., M.A., and Ph.D. degrees from Fordham University. He is also the holder of an S.T.L. degree from Woodstock College, Maryland, and an S.T.D. from the Gregorian University in Rome. Father Gleason joined the Fordham University faculty in 1955, and in 1958 he was named Chairman of the Department of Theology. Father Gleason is a member of the Catholic Theological Society, the Catholic Philosophical Association, and other learned societies. His major fields of interest are ascetical theology and pastoral psychology. Besides contributing numerous articles for philosophical and ecclesiastical journals in these and allied fields, Father Gleason is the author of a recent series of books in theology, including the following: The World to Come (*1958*), Christ and the Christian (*1959*), To Live is Christ (*1961*), *and* Grace (*1962*).

The objective disconformity of homosexuality to the moral law consists in the fact that the sexual appetite and affections are directed to persons of the same sex. The homosexual personality, while normal from a physical point of view, is entirely oriented to his or her own sex and not susceptible to the emotional and sexual attraction of the opposite sex. Those persons who do not manifest this fundamental orientation to their own sex, but practice homosexual acts as a substitute or variation should rather be called pseudo-homosexuals.

The moralist's problem with homosexuality is with the subjective rather than the objective morality. As always, subjective morality is more difficult to evaluate than objective because of the many concrete situational, individual, and cultural factors that enter into any judgment concerning subjective morality. All that we can do here is simply point out a few general principles by which the moralist tries to come to a judgment of responsibility.

It must be noted first that the *condition* of homosexuality cannot itself be imputed to the sincere penitent. Even though this state may have arisen as a result of repeated deliberate acts on the part of the penitent (a fact which will be disputed by most psychologists), if the penitent has sincerely repented of these lapses his present state may be declared involuntary. It will sometimes be of help to a penitent of this type if it is explained to him that his present condition cannot be imputed to him as a sin. Secondly, one can note that those spontaneous affections and desires which arise from the sincere penitent's habitual dispositions are no more free or sinful than are the spontaneous desires of his normal companion. Nor will it always be possible for him to repress them positively. The best that he can do is to avoid their causes and divert his attention to other objects when these affections become conscious. In doing so he will follow more or less classic rules for those whose sexual desires have a normal object. He may contemn those that arise spontaneously and involuntarily. He should be inspired with the desire to free himself from this abnormality and taught to avoid the occasions of sin for him.

SPECIAL PROBLEMS OF THE HOMOSEXUAL

Because of the unusual situation in which the homosexual finds himself, attracted to that sex with which social organization forces him to have most contact, one should be careful to avoid giving him the impression that he must isolate himself from his own sex on the grounds that some of its members may be an occasion of sin for him. It is well to remember also that this type of penitent may more often be in necessary occasions of sin that his normal counterpart, simply because he cannot reorganize society to permit him to live with the cultural and social barriers that ordinary mores set up between the sexes. This fact may make one more lenient in judging the homosexual in certain situations.

The fact that the homosexual's sex life is *abnormal* does not mean that his attractions and desires are *insuperable*. The qualitative abnormality does not of itself by the very fact of its existence destroy imputability. On the contrary the homosexual is to be judged according to the usual principles that determine responsibility. Because an act is qualitatively abnormal does not automatically mean that its agent is deprived of that use of reason and liberty required for responsibility.

However, the principles that determine responsibility should be applied to the homosexual as principles and not materially imposed upon him as concrete advice exactly paralleling the advice given to his normal counterpart. The statement, for example, that the homosexual has no more difficulty controlling his impulses than does the normal man must be accepted with definite reserves, or it will lead to a most unrealistic appraisal of the penitent's situation. The homosexual is under many non-sexual pressures which aggravate his sexual tensions and push him in the direction of the false securities of his pathetic love affairs. He lives in constant fear of blackmail, which the normal man does not, even if he indulges in sexual activity outside marriage. He is economically exposed in that few employers care to retain homosexual employees if their secret is discovered. He has constantly to suspect his own friendships and normal social dealings with men. This secrecy, loneliness, and insecurity aggravate the temptation to have at least one chosen companion with whom he can be wholly open. Since society approves of his accepting attitudes, occupations, and social conduct which are foreign to him, his life is rather more reflex than the normal man's. He has the difficult task of structuring his own ideals for himself according to patterns which he must in many cases determine for himself, since society has not elaborated a rule of conduct governing the details of his confusing situation. In what measure should he apply materially to himself the rules of morality governing those acts which incite *per se* to venereal pleasure? Shall he, for example, avoid all such occasions as nude swimming with men? The moralist would answer this question rapidly for the normal man with regard to women. It is perhaps less easy to decide in the case of homosexuals. One must beware of advice which will further complicate their social situation, bringing on new tensions which will seek release in sexual activity.

It must be recognized however that the homosexual personality is invariably a psychologically disturbed and frequently a neurotic personality and that his judgments of value will often be distorted by his disturbed condition.

THE SUBJECTIVE GUILT OF THE HOMOSEXUAL

It is admitted by everyone today that sexuality is by no means confined to genital impulses; sexuality irradiates the entire personality and promotes a general orientation of the entire affective life so that the whole of life and personality is marked by its influences. Since the elements of sexuality are subject to a psychosexual evolution the normal personality will be one whose development has passed through the various stages of psychosexual evolution. The child's affective and sexual interests must be guided past the stage of concentration upon himself to an heterosexual and altruistic stage. Only the man whose evolution is accomplished in a fortunate manner will have that general attitude toward others and moral conduct which is really adult. The homosexual personality lacks this perfect adulthood of the sexual instinct, in its widest sense. His entire affective orientation is disturbed. Because it is disturbed his judgments of value will reflect this disturbance in greater or lesser degree. To think that one can reorientate the genital activities of such a person without affecting first a general re-education of his entire personality structure is an illusion. His sexuality must be re-educated, but as I have said, sexuality is by no means confined to the genital sphere. Without this general re-education it is very doubtful if such a disturbed personality will ever have the psychical equilibrium and energy needed to bring his moral life into accord with the objective laws which foster his genuine development as spirit. To bring one's activity into accord with objective morality one needs knowledge and one needs freedom. A defect in either will ordinarily imply some lessening of responsibility. The reaction of the neurotic character to his moral problem will not infrequently be: "I know that what I am doing is objectively wrong; I am aware of this and troubled by it, but it is stronger than I, and I am unable to do otherwise."

Such a penitent as this registers both *feelings* of guilt and a tendency to exculpate himself on the grounds of lack of freedom. In approaching this case the confessor must avoid two extremes. One extreme is immediately to absolve the penitent from all responsibility as though freedom were automatically and totally obliterated by the neurotic condition of the penitent. Such an attitude doubtless would end in moral nihilism. Objective moral laws exist which are universally binding, founded upon immutable natures and essences.

At times the invert will experience a relatively high degree of freedom from those psychological conflicts which limit his power to choose. There are periods of his life, periods even of the same day which vary considerably with regard to freedom. It would be doing the penitent a great disservice to suppose that the mechanisms which inhibit his freedom work always at equal intensity. Hence general statements about his lack of moral guilt are completely out of place and should never be given to him.

On the other hand the moralist must avoid an objectivist frame of mind which tends automatically to equate objective disconformity to the moral law with subjective guilt. Factors of the subjective, existential, concrete, situational order and psychological mechanisms must be taken into consideration and usually these factors cannot be established by the confessor unless he is working in collaboration with the psychiatrist.

What is attracting the attention of moralists today is especially the case of those penitents who claim to lead a rather vigorous interior life on most points, who express a rather determined aspiration to obey God's law in its entirety but who encounter within themselves a difficulty which they express as an impossibility, in the matter, e.g. of their homosexual desires. It appears to them that the disequilibrium that they experience within themselves is due to causes outside, at least in part, the domain of their responsibility. They claim an inability to execute in the real order the fundamental aspirations of their spirit to God. Doubtless in such cases we must recall that our characters and our moral worth are to be judged by our deepest attitudes as well as by our external acts.

We are called by God not only to act well but to *be good*. We must take into consideration of the invert's guilt the whole fundamental orientation of his life. Is it to God or to self? In the strata of motivation that are not directly translatable in act does he manifest a desire to serve God, practice virtue and lead a good life? Is his moral life in other matters conformed to the laws of God and the Church? Does he make use of the religious helps offered to him in the sacraments, prayer, and the advice given him by his confessor? If so, one may judge that he is sincerely trying to help himself and this fact should make the confessor more lenient in judging the occasional fall which may occur.

NEED OF VALUATIONAL APPRECIATION OF WRONGDOING

In order to found adequate responsibility for grave sin our knowledge should proceed, not only from an abstract, juridical understanding of the moral disvalue in question, but also from some type of interior comprehension of the law and the value it embodies. It is recognized today by moralists that the clear knowledge required for mortal sin is not always satisfied by a purely conceptual knowledge even when this is explicit. The fact that the law of God and the Church forbids this particular action may be quite clear to the invert at the moment of his temptation without giving him the requisite valuational appreciation of the good involved in this law. If this value-aspect of the law, its inner goodness, its inner suavity and beauty is separated from the majesty of law the moral knowledge that results may be schematic, theoretical, notional, but in the sense of Newman, unreal. In that case, not only does the good-for-me aspect of the value recede to the periphery of consciousness, but the inner goodness in itself, the importance of the value in itself tends to be obscured in the mind of the subject, and the remaining conceptual knowledge may be insufficient to found grave responsibility.

This affective valuation will be found lacking in many homosexuals with respect to their particular situation. And of course liberty is dependent upon knowlege. But even when theoretical knowledge is adequate for responsibility it can happen that the individual describes himself as blinded and chained when called upon to pass over to practical action. This indeed seems to be the case with many inverts. Here we must recognize that traditional moral theology admits that an individual, because of conditioning and habit, may indeed be incapable at a precise moment in his history, of observing objectively this or that commandment.

Thus even when valuational knowledge is actually had, the individual may experience such neurotic pressures that his liberty does not retain that degree of energy required for grave sin. The emotional drives upsetting his spiritual equilibrium may be such as to exert an almost hypnotic effect upon his will, giving an air of unreality to the good embodied in the moral law. Even with valuational knowledge present the tangle of neurotic pressures and emotions to which he is subject may, as it were, anesthetize the appeal of the good for the moment. Realizing this may help the confessor to understand that the penitent is not entirely insincere when he describes himself as irresistibly drawn by the object of his sin. It should also be noted that the will, even if its decision is free, does not have despotic control over the external faculties. Thus it is possible that there will exist, even in the sincere penitent, a considerable gap between objective and subjective morality. He has, however, always the obligation of striving to close this gap in his life between objective and subjective morality. The gap which may exist in a particular case between the order of intention and the order of execution does not dispense the subject from effort.

HOMOSEXUALITY ONLY SECONDARILY A MORAL PROBLEM

If one group of extremists seems to feel that any responsibility is out of the question in the case of inverts, it is another extreme to think that the action of grace will cure all psychical defects. Grace is not given for that purpose in the usual scheme of things. Its function is not to cure the malfunctioning of nature in the order of psychology. In the degree that a particular nature is subject to a natural psychological imbalance grace meets with obstacles in restoring that nature to objective conformity to the moral law. In the ordinary course of events we should not expect grace to perform miracles in the natural order or to ensure clinical cures. Grace is given for interior, subjective, spiritual success in our dialogue life with God, and will not ordinarily remove the clinical obstacles to objective success in the moral life.

It is undeniable that there exist unfortunate psychisms which dispose their owners ill for objective conformity to the moral law. There are types who probably never will know the lucidity in judgments of value that the normal man knows. But if we avoid confusing sanctity with objective moral perfection we will not despair of these types, among which seem to be the invert.

In forming any moral judgment of the subjective guilt of this class of neurotic personalities, it is obvious that the confessor and the psychiatrist must work in common. The problem of homosexuality is primarily a problem for the psychiatrist and only secondarily a moral problem. Insofar as it is a moral problem it lies particularly in the domain of those principles which seek to establish subjective responsibility. The confessor who approaches this problem should then be aware of the researches of modern psychology and the assistance that this science offers to him in determining the presence or absence of moral knowledge and moral freedom. The real is always complex and it is quite impossible, in dealing with this class of penitents, to lay down simple rules of thumb for determining the extent and degree of subjective responsibility. Nor may the penitent always be believed completely when he testifies against himself. Many of them are unaware of the conditions required for freedom and confuse freedom from external force with psychical freedom. Moreover they do not usually evaluate justly the non-sexual neurotic pressures to which they are subject living as they do in a society which considers them as outcasts and thus aggravates their sexual tensions.

The universal moral law governing these cases is as intrinsigent, as binding as in any other cases. But the Christian conception of morality has never been one of mechanical conformism, of objectified legalism. The experience of generations of spiritual directors and confessors is there as a rich traditional source of understanding of the complexity and limits of human freedom. It should not be neglected in favor of some neatly codified rule of thumb capable of an automatic application to all individuals.

THE PRIEST AND THE HOMOSEXUAL

In his pastoral work the confessor and the counselor has an excellent opportunity to encourage the homosexual to seek that medical treatment which we hope will restore to him the freedom needed for accomplishing objectively the demands of a Christian moral life. The counselor should avoid holding up too glowing a promise for future recovery since prognosis, especially in the case of older and habitual inverts of overt activity, is quite poor. Since the homosexual is already in a difficult social position the counselor must do what he can to encourage him to make some positive contribution to the community in which he lives and should avoid a censorious, accusatory, rejecting attitude. Above all he must stimulate the penitent to seek the requisite help and must do what he can to see to it that human needs in the nonsexual area are satisfied, so that further tensions are not built up in the penitent by frustrations of a purely social order. Anything that contributes to the human equilibrium of the penitent will have its effects on the moral order. The entire personality needs reorganization and usually the treatment will be long since areas of the personality have to be explored that are not immediately accessible to the therapist. Moreover many homosexuals will feel that no real change is either possible or especially desirable. Their attitude is usually pessimistic, fatalistic. Here the priest-counselor may play an important role in stimulating a desire for recovery and treatment.

If the counselor or confessor can take the time to explain the differing roles of the natural and the supernatural in effecting a cure, and if the priest does not lead the penitent to a magical conception of the sacraments' efficacy, much good can be done by the sacraments. The quantitative aspect of the case may be helped by reception of the sacraments and the number of overt acts diminished. The attitude of the confessor or counselor should remain encouraging and should stress that the penitent must extend the area of his self-control gradually, with the combined natural and supernatural helps.

The penitent must be helped to gain insight into his own situation and for this he needs as complete a picture as possible of the factors that may contribute to that situation. Besides an understanding of the role of sex and love in human life he should be brought to realize, in a very general fashion, the mechanisms that effect his freedom and the principles that determine his responsibility. This will usually be done by collaboration of priest and therapist. The priest must stress that whatever the appearances to the contrary may be, interior, spiritual victory lies ahead for the penitent who cooperates with God's grace. The dogmatic truths concerning both the distribution and the efficacy of grace may be stressed with advantage, providing always that the penitent is not led to some magical idea of grace as a substitute for human effort or for therapy.

To present grace in such a fashion will only cause rebellion and loss of faith for the invert will reply to these magical promises with a cold denial based upon experience. A counselor should not ordinarily undertake the direction of a homosexual personality without collaboration with a therapist. Nor should he take it upon himself to promise cures or to determine the limits of recovery possible. In some cases the best that will be achieved is a relatively successful adjustment to a non-sexual social life with no overt acts. If the priest-counselor realizes this ahead of time he will save all concerned much distress. The necessity of regular and consistent direction for this type of penitent should not need to be stressed. It is obvious.

REFERENCES

Duhamel, J. (S.J.), & Hayden, J. (O.S.B.), Theological and psychiatric aspects of habitual sin. *Proc. Annu. Conv. Cath. Theol. Soc. Amer.*, 1956, *11*, 130-167.

Flood, P. (O.S.B.) (Ed.), *New problems in medical ethics.* Vol. I. Westminster, Md.: Newman, 1953.

Ford, J. C. (S.J.), & Kelly, G. (S.J.), Psychiatry and moral responsibility. *Theol. Stud.*, 1954, *15*, 59-67.

Harvey, J. F. (O.S.F.S.), Homosexuality as a pastoral problem. *Theol. Stud.*, 1955, *16*, 86-108.

Mailloux, N. (O.P.), Psychic determinism, freedom, and personality development. In J. A. Gasson (S.J.) & Magda Arnold (Eds.), *The human person.* New York: Ronald, 1954. Pp. 264-280.

Moore, T. V. (O.S.B.), The pathogenesis and treatment of homosexual disorders. *J. Pers.*, 1945, *14*, 46-83.

Autosexuality: Compulsive Masturbation

PAUL G. ECKER

*Paul Gerard Ecker received his M.D. degree
from the School of Medicine of Western Re-
serve University in 1944. His residency training
in internal medicine was taken at the Peter Bent
Brigham Hospital in Boston. He combined this
training with a simultaneous teaching fellow-
ship at the Harvard Medical School. His psychiatric residency was at the New York State Psychiatric Institute at Columbia, subsequent to
which he held a teaching position at Columbia
Medical School. Two years were spent in research at the Rockefeller Institute. Subsequent
to his work in New York, Dr. Ecker served as
Chief of the Functional Disease Service at the
Hospital of the University of Pennsylvania, and
this was the position which he held at the time
of the 1957 Pastoral Psychology Institute. At
the present time, Dr. Ecker is engaged in private psychiatric practice in Philadelphia, and is
an instructor in Psychoanalysis at the Institute
of the Philadelphia Association for Psychoanalysis.*

It is a commonly accepted fact that masturbation is often in evidence from earliest infancy, and is to be regularly noted in the
fourth to sixth years, incident to the period Freud delimited as the
phallic phase in psychosexual development. It is seen as an essentially normal infantile, sexual activity. Only later on do masturba-

tory activities become associated with phantasies relating to objects. It may be that infantile masturbation serves as a means of learning in order to gradually achieve mastery over sexual excitation. By the fourth to fifth year, analysis reveals that masturbation is regularly accompanied by active phantasy. In the period of latency, from 6 to 12, sexual activity is usually nil; the sexually active child in this stage is neurotic.

The onset of puberty, with its attendant biological upheaval and upsurgence of sexuality, is usually accompanied by an upsurge in masturbatory activity. Inhibition of masturbation at adolescence may be indicative of overwhelming fear or guilt, possibly due to a particularly intense repression of infantile masturbation. Conscience, of course, plays an important role. However, masturbation, as such, is to be regarded as essentially non-neurotic sexual activity either on the part of the child or the adolescent at puberty. When it appears in excess, it is indicative of pathology.

Persistence of masturbation or habitual masturbation in later life may subsume the function of preference by an adult for autoerotic activity to normal heterosexual intercourse, or it may be an attempt to relieve sexual tension denied any other outlet because of neurotic inhibition. Compulsive masturbation usually is the expression of neurotic conflict. As such, it is the symptom rather than the cause of neurosis.

The same considerations apply in arriving at an appraisal, from a diagnostic standpoint, of what may be regarded as the symptom of compulsive masturbation. The latter may be found to be the presenting symptom or complaint in a variety of mental states— from a very benign to the most malignant forms of mental disorder.

In the first instance, the symptoms may serve as a simple pathway for the discharge of anxiety. The patient may experience diffuse feelings of tension arising from some unconscious source which he then discharges in the masturbatory act. Compulsive masturbation may be a pathway for the discharge of aggressive impulses as, for example, when it takes the form of angry, punishing defiance of the parental authority. Compulsive masturbation is often found associated with adolescent depression, with its attendant feelings of loneliness and isolation which are resolved, for the moment at least, in the sensations produced in the act. Another type of compulsive masturbatory pattern is found in the individual who feels great guilt over some unconscious phantasies and who punishes himself in his compulsive masturbatory activities. As such, the masturbation may take on the character of a masochistic experience, with self-punishment as its aim.

As was said before, at puberty there is a usual resurgence of masturbatory activity, which parallels the activity of the child in the phallic phase of development. One has to see that in certain individuals this flooding of impulses, both sexual and aggressive, appearing at this age may be potentially threatening to the total personality organization of the individual. As such, the masturbation may provide a pathway of discharge and, at the same time, an attempt to master the conflict. Furthermore, it should be stressed that common as masturbation is, particularly among adolescents, it may be in the given instance the symptom of severe neurotic disorder or major emotional disturbance bordering upon psychosis, and that in these individuals great caution should be exercised in the manner of handling the problem.

From a therapeutic standpoint, the problem of compulsive masturbation remains the same as it does for most disorders. The psychiatrist must evaluate the symptoms in the context of the neurotic conflict and this, in turn, in terms of the total personality of the individual concerned. Psychotherapy or psychoanalysis is the treatment of choice, provided a proper diagnostic evaluation of the case is first developed. Insofar as the compulsive masturbation is simply symptomatic of a mild adolescent upheaval, encouragement and reassurance, coupled with patience, support and understanding, oftentimes suffice to help the individual through this most difficult phase of his growth and development. Insofar as the compulsive masturbation is symptomatic of a more malignant type of mental disorder, proper psychiatric and medical evaluation of the individual is indicated. The patient should be referred for this kind of treatment.

It is necessary that great care be exercised in estimating the depth and the extent of conflicts centered around masturbation, and threats and unrealistic fear may only reinforce a pre-existing conflict to the point that the individual's psychic balance is completely disturbed. In recent years, two such instances have been noted in my own practice.

The first of these cases was that of a married mother of two children who on two occasions was admitted to the hospital in a totally dissociated state within 24 hours after having made her confession. Her guilt over masturbation became so intense that her flight from the impulse was into psychosis. Needless to say, this mother who functioned with reasonable adequacy in her household, was unable to achieve adequate gratification sexually in relationship to her husband because of neurotic inhibition in her sexual life, which found its earliest origin in a deeply repressed conflict having as its center her infantile masturbatory phantasies.

Another type of difficulty was presented by a fifteen-year-old student who was referred for treatment incident to an almost complete adolescent disorganization in his personality. From having been an honor student, a star member of the football team, outgoing in his relations with his classmates and teachers, he became profoundly disturbed and almost completely organized at a compulsive level. His every action was determined along ritualistic lines; he refused to wash himself, stopped school and refused any contact with his peers, either male or female. His entire existence bespoke an attempt to control the impulse to masturbate. He refused to look at magazines, posters, or even roadside signs. He stopped attending even the best of movies, his scrupulosity revealing itself in completely unrealistic proportions. Fortunately, an understanding priest having recognized the depth of his disturbance, materially allayed his guilt and reinforced the attempts of the therapist to deal with this boy's difficulties.

Autosexuality: Habitual Masturbation

ROBERT J. CAMPBELL

Robert Jean Campbell, III, M.D., is Chief of the Out-Patient Psychiatric Service at St. Vincent's Hospital; Instructor in Psychiatry at Columbia University College of Physicians and Surgeons; and Adjunct Associate Professor, Fordham University Graduate School. Prior to assuming his post at St. Vincent's Hospital, Dr. Campbell was Senior Clinical Psychiatrist at the New York State Psychiatric Institute. After graduating from the University of Wisconsin, Dr. Campbell received his M.D. degree from Columbia University. He is a Diplomate, American Board of Psychiatry and Neurology, a contributor to various medical journals, and is currently editor of Hinsie & Campbell's Psychiatric Dictionary *(1960). The 1957 Pastoral Psychology Institute was the first to which Dr. Campbell contributed, but since then he has become the series most consistent contributor, having participated in each of the three subsequent Institutes.*

Perhaps it might be wise to acquire a little historical prospective with reference to the proposals made for the treatment of habitual masturbation, for in this way at least we shall know what to avoid. The first specific reference to treatment was made by Becker in England in 1710. He proposed two ways: Force the patient into marriage or frighten him into giving up the habit! Next there was

Tissot, in France in 1769. He advised frequent baths, frequent exercises, and methods assuring a good night's sleep. The individual should have a routine mapped out for him to keep him distracted from sex. Tissot also suggested one interesting thing: Look out for loneliness on the part of the individual and try to correct this deficiency in family or community life. This same author also emphasized the fearful consequences of masturbation, and thought this was the best method of prevention. An Englishman, Vogel, in 1786, suggested the reading of long religious tracts! He also advised the client to avoid alcohol because it tends to excite sexual desires for which the only adequate method of relief is masturbation. He also advised some frightening mechanical measures, even including infibulation, or sewing up of the genital organs. And there were other methods proposed for the treatment of habitual masturbation: bleeding, castration, circumcision, cauterization, etc. More recently, emphasis has been on education: providing the person with more knowledge about sex and reality, on the theory that forewarned is forearmed. There are obviously various methods of developing conscience, and impressing the individual with the value of self-control and the value of mortification. But these procedures are more in your province than in mine!

In the treatment of habitual masturbation, you might first consider if it might be only a relatively temporary problem best handled on a counseling level. I think it would be most helpful in the treatment of habitual masturbation to find out what it is the masturbator is expressing. We have discussed masturbation as a form of sexual behavior which appears with great frequency. Such masturbation, from the psychological point of view, is part and parcel of what seems to be usual development, and will tend to be limited to a particular period, or periods, of life.

There will be cases other than these relatively temporary ones. I might point out that what we consider as habitual masturbation is genital self-stimulation which continues with such frequency as to make one wonder if the individual is capable of deriving satisfaction from his activity. If it does not give him a certain amount of satisfaction (or if there are frequent indications of no satisfaction) we are led to believe there is a lack of capacity for enjoyment, and we would do well to search for possible causative factors in other, non-sexual, parts of his life. One which occurs with great frequency is monotony. Obviously this is a relatively simple cause which can be eliminated. Another factor is family background. The child who is deprived of love and affection will often show an increase in masturbatory activity. Sometimes, masturbation is due to faulty training, so that the individual experiences a lack of self-confidence, a lack of feeling of value as an individual. This type of person needs education.

We find habitual masturbators among those who react to frustration and disappointment with depression, most typically among psychiatric patients. By such persons, masturbation is used to remove existing depression or to ward off future and threatening depression. Threatened disappointments or discouragement will turn such a person to habitual masturbation. Reverses in life may do so, if the child is not secure, if he is trying to gain affection, or if there is an unsatisfied need for love. Too much love is as bad as too little love, such as being pampered by love and affection, too much devotion, or too much of what appears to be love.

Another source of difficulty in patients who are habitual masturbators is loneliness. Masturbation is frequently used as a means of withdrawing from reality, and keeping away from threatening interpersonal relationships. Neurotic inhibitions and shyness in relation to the opposite sex are frequently found in habitual masturbators. It is wise also to remember that masturbation can be used as a discharge for sexual wishes of any kind. We find many people who are potential perverts who show a trend toward habitual masturbation. It is only through masturbation that they can satisfy their other sexual impulses. For it is much easier to obtain their sexual object in imagination, in order to secure what they feel is a "higher pleasure" related to their perverse phantasies. Masturbation is also used in expression of other drives and other activities, and many patients attempt to use the genital apparatus as substitute gratification for non-genital needs.

There are three major areas to look to in attempting to determine the basis for habitual masturbation. The first is the sexual area itself. The sexual response is used by others as a way of asserting independence. This is not so dangerous psychologically as the person who uses masturbation to get away from objective reality. The third use of sex is as an expression of aggression, which cannot be openly expressed in weak, insecure individuals, who use masturbation as a means of opposition and defiance. In such patients, conflicts typically center about hostility, about aggression as a means to force satisfaction, about anticipated punishment for aggressivity, and by some, "dangerous" masturbation is used as a substitute for punishment.

The symptom of habitual masturbation is often seen in grossly disturbed, psychotic patients. Very often the compulsive neurotic too will use habitual masturbation as a way of ending his doubts and indecision. After you have gained some idea from the person as to what the problem might be, I would advise you to say to him, "Well, the problem is that something else is wrong." The individual is using masturbation to express something else.

Three points are important in treatment. In the first place, never take the direct attack, for this will center the attention of the individual on the habit, instead of excluding it from the pattern of reaction. Then he will use it more frequently to express anything that comes up. Secondly, you might forewarn him that the problem is not going to be solved at once, particularly not in young patients. Neither priests nor psychiatrists have all the answers, and the patient should be forewarned of this, so that he does not draw away from treatment or even religion should counseling efforts not bring immediate relief. Finally the individual who complains of masturbation in the first place has a certain degree of shame. We know his feeling of guilt. One must be aware of this and take the kind, sympathetic approach or you will drive the individual away from you. It is only a stable, consistent approach which will give results.

One problem that comes up frequently with the adolescent masturbator is that the aims of psychoanalysis and puberty are to some extent antagonistic. In adolescence, the aim is to cover up impulses and desires so as to fit in with and be accepted by the adult world, whereas in analytically oriented psychotherapy the aim is to uncover and expose the impulses giving rise to conflicts. The ego will strain to maintain its integrity, and we can therefore anticipate that resistance will be high, especially in the beginning. Avoid too early interpretation with the adolescent. Feel your way before you open up any new phase for analysis and consideration. When referral to a psychiatrist seems indicated, don't do it in such a way that he feels you are disgusted or discouraged with him, but rather convince him this is part of your treatment approach.

There is one big area of importance which time allows little more than mention of—counter-transference—feelings aroused in the therapist in response to the patient. We see this, for example, in people who are over-severe. Perhaps they have problems, and are trying completely to eliminate in others what they fear in themselves. Sometimes these are problems we have completely well-controlled, ordinarily, but they may be brought into the open by one particular case. One should suspect that counter-transference is out of hand when he finds himself negatively disposed toward the patient and is tempted to judge, moralize and berate rather than trying to understand what it is which makes the patient choose this symptom as an expression of his conflicts.

Autosexuality: Moral Aspects*

JOHN C. FORD, S.J.

Father John C. Ford, S.J., is Professor of Moral Theology at the Catholic University of America and he has degrees from Boston College (A.B., A.M., LL.B.), from Weston College (S.T.L.), and from the Gregorian University (S.T.D.). Prior to assuming his present post at the Catholic University of America, Father Ford was Professor of Moral Theology successively at the Gregorian University, Rome, and at Weston College, Weston, Massachusetts. A renowned theologian, Father Ford's publications include, in addition to numerous articles in theological journals, the following books: Depth psychology, morality and alcoholism *(1951),* Man takes a drink *(1954), and with Father Gerald Kelly, S.J.,* Contemporary moral theology: Vol. I: Questions in fundamental moral theology *(1958). Father Ford has made a distinguished effort to relate the findings of modern psychology and psychiatry to Catholic moral principles, and the three books mentioned above, as well as many of his other writings, testify to this fruitful and abiding interest.*

It is not my purpose here to discuss the objective morality of masturbation. Objectively the act of masturbation is a grave viola-

* Parts of this paper were adapted prior to publication from the book by John C. Ford, S.J. and Gerald Kelly, S.J. *Contemporary Moral Problems* Volume I: *Questions in Fundamental Moral Theology*. Westminster, Md., Newman, 1958. It is here reproduced with the permission of the publisher.

tion of the natural law. And although there are many problems in establishing this as a universal rule by arguments from reason, nevertheless, for the Catholic theologian there is no practical problem, because the teaching of the Church is clear. I do not intend to discuss it further, therefore, but will take for granted this proposition: Every act of masturbation is objectively a mortal sin.

The moral aspects of masturbation which I propose to discuss are concerned with the subjective responsibility of the habitual or compulsive masturbator. Habits and compulsions diminish imputability. In pastoral practice confessors and counselors have to make some kind of practical judgment or practical estimate as to the presence or absence of subjective grave guilt.

The conclusion of my remarks will be this: Subjective impediments and disabilities excuse from subjective mortal guilt much more frequently than we have been accustomed to admit in the past. But we do not possess accurate criteria by which to measure subjective responsibility, and in the present state of our knowledge it is not justifiable to make sweeping, general presumptions of nonresponsibility for large classes of penitents. Each individual case must be studied on its own merits, and after taking the time and the trouble to make this study, the human, fallible confessor or counselor should give his advice in accordance with it.

And so the question on which we seek more light is this: When can we judge emotional stress in these cases to be so great that it diminishes freedom below the point where grave imputability is possible? We cannot hope to solve this problem. But we should like to clarify it, and move in the direction of solving it. But real progress in this direction will require more profound studies, in the philosophy of liberty, the psychology of will and emotion, and the theology of grace.

DEGREES OF FREEDOM AND THE DISTINCTION BETWEEN PHILOSOPHICAL FREEDOM AND PSYCHOLOGICAL FREEDOM

In moral theology we speak of semi-deliberate acts, and of imperfectly voluntary acts. These expressions mean that the acts referred to, though they are human acts, and are objectively mortal sins, are so lacking in deliberation or so imperfectly consented to that subjectively they cannot be more than venial sins. The inescapable implication of this doctrine is that there are degrees of freedom, or at least degrees of imputability in human conduct.

This scale of imputability ranges all the way from the minimum that is compatible at all with the concept of a free, human act, up through all the degrees of venial culpability, across the threshold of mortal sin, through all the indefinite gradations of mortal guilt, to the highest point of the very limit of human malice. The two critical points on this scale are the point at the very bottom which distinguishes a free *actus humanus* from a non-free *actus hominis,* and the point, surely very much higher on the scale, that distinguishes mortal guilt from venial guilt.

To put the matter fancifully, if one were given marks on malice and culpability where bad actions are concerned, or on virtue and merit where good acts are concerned, or on degrees of freedom where both are concerned, the marks might range all the way from one percent to ninety-nine percent. Zero percent would mean no human act at all; and I avoid speaking of one hundred percent because it seems more appropriate to angels or devils than to men. Still speaking fancifully, what is the passing mark for mortal sin? Certainly not ninety-nine percent freedom. The full deliberation and consent of the moralists does not demand that much. Is it ninety percent? Seventy-five percent? Sixty percent? Who can say? Some would put it higher, others lower. Only God knows the exact answer.

Although it is an indubitable fact that there are indefinitely numerous degrees of freedom, the idea of speaking of degrees of freedom at all is very confusing, and the word freedom itself is equivocal. The reason is that moralists and theologians seem to use the word freedom (as I have done) in two very different meanings. I am going to call these two meanings philosophical freedom and psychological freedom. The first does not admit of degrees, the second does.

By philosophical freedom is meant the *libertas indifferentiae* which we attribute to the human will in scholastic philosophy. It is the kind of freedom that is required in order to have a human act. It presupposes advertence and rational deliberation, and has its metaphysical roots in the power of the intellect to make objectively indifferent judgments. There have been bitter theological controversies about its relation to grace and to God's concursus with human acts. Even in defining it, theologians have difficulty in prescinding from these disputes.

But I believe that the following description of free will in the philosophical sense would be admitted by theologians of all schools. It is the power, given certain prerequisites of knowledge and motivation, of saying yes or no freely to a proposed action, or of choosing freely between two alternative courses of action. "Freely" does not mean easily or without reluctance, although sometimes free choices are easily made. *"Freely" means that at the time the choice was made the man could have made the opposite choice—even if with difficulty or repugnance.*

Is it not obvious that freedom thus understood does not admit of degrees? We can say of an action either: "He was able not to have done it," or: "He was not able not to have done it." It must be either the one or the other. It cannot be a little of each. There is nothing in-between. The absolute physical power of choice, the freedom of the will from internal coaction *stat in indivisibili.*

By psychological freedom is meant freedom from obstacles and pressures which make the exercise of philosophical freedom difficult. I am calling it psychological for want of a better word, and because it is the kind of freedom psychologists often speak about. Most if not all of the impediments to human acts discussed by moralists in fundamental moral treatises are obstacles to this freedom. Freedom in this sense, then, obviously does admit of degrees; it is by its very nature not absolute but relative. The fewer or weaker the obstacles, the greater the freedom and facility with which the will can choose and direct the execution of bodily activities.

It is unfortunate that the one phrase "freedom of the will" should be used to describe these two widely different things, but we frequently use the one phrase to describe them both. When we say that passion interferes with freedom, sometimes we mean the kind of passion that prevents all deliberation and makes philosophical freedom impossible, so that there is no human act at all. At other times we mean the degree of passion that leaves the fundamental act essentially intact, but creates greater or lesser obstacles to the exercise of freedom, thus diminishing imputability—and sometimes diminishing it below the point where mortal guilt is possible.

To me it seems clear that for mortal sin both kinds of freedom are essential, the absolute, physical freedom which is the philosophical "liberty of indifference," and the relative, psychological freedom from obstacles and difficulties, *a sufficient degree of which* is required before a human act can be *gravely* imputable.

This distinction makes it possible for us to state with greater accuracy what our problem is. Supposing that the prerequisites of philosophical freedom are present, and that a person is acting freely in the philosophical sense, how can we discover what is meant by sufficient psychological freedom for mortal guilt? Our interest is directed to cases of severe emotional stress, of so-called irresistible impulses, of obsessions and compulsive urges. Our special interest is severe or compulsive habits of masturbation. On the scale of psychological freedom what is the passing mark for grave imputability? What follows will certainly not solve this problem, but will supply, it is hoped, some data that will throw light on the problem and keep us from putting that mark too high or too low.

SOME THEOLOGICAL GUIDEPOSTS WHICH KEEP US FROM SETTING THE MARK TOO HIGH

The following three considerations will guard us against the extreme of making sweeping presumptions of non-responsibility: 1) Catholic teaching and practice take it for granted that normal individuals are capable of committing mortal sin; 2) Catholic tradition takes it for granted that mortal sins frequently take place in the world; 3) the doctrine of grace.

(1) The idea that normal individuals are capable of mortal sin is implicit in the way in which the sacrament of penance is administered under the guidance of supreme ecclesiastical authority. It is implicit in the idea that normal men are capable of committing an ecclesiastical crime, and that normal men are capable of that degree of human responsibility which is necessary for matrimonial consent. Recent Papal statements have made it very clear that even under a considerable amount of emotional stress a human being can still be responsible, and gravely responsible, for his acts.

(2) Sometimes one hears exaggerated statements to the effect that a formal mortal sin is almost impossible to commit, or that a formal mortal sin hardly ever takes place in actuality. To hold such propositions would be to contradict experience and the ordinary

preaching and practice of the Church. Much of the Catholic teaching and practice in moral matters clearly supposes not only that formal mortal sin exists but that it is by no means a rarity. It may well be that the number of merely material mortal sins is very large, and that in modern times we are more and more aware of this fact, but this does not reduce the number of formal sins to a negligible number.

(3) If it seems harsh to hold that there are so many sins, yet we must remember that they are really avoidable with the help of God's grace, and that God never refuses this grace. Perhaps if one were to consider merely the natural psychology of man one would have to take a pessimistic view of his interior powers of self-control and self-determination. But we have the assurance from revelation that God's grace is sufficient for us and that He will not allow us to be tempted beyond our strength.

However, we should not interpret the phrase, "My grace is sufficient for thee," to mean that God promises to preserve everyone even from material mortal sin. It means that He gives sufficient grace to make it possible to avoid formal mortal sin. We are in a mysterious realm here in which often enough we simply do not know when human helps are in vain and only the divine help of grace can avail. But in doing battle against the *mysterium iniquitatis,* the tragedy that afflicts mankind, medicinal grace and mental hygiene do not exclude one another. The man of faith relies on all the help there is, both natural and supernatural.

SOME PSYCHOLOGICAL GUIDEPOSTS WHICH KEEP US FROM SETTING THE MARK TOO LOW

Let us center our discussion around two questions which are sometimes put to penitents (and very usefully) in order to elicit from them information about their subjective dispositions at the time an objectively mortal sin was committed. "Did you realize fully that it was a grave sin?" And "Could you have resisted it?"

The first question: "Did you realize fully it was a grave sin?" has to do with sufficient advertence and deliberation. It is like the "right and wrong" test of criminal law. Is it universally true that in the presence of sufficient advertence, there always follows automatically sufficient consent of the will? Moralists, canonists and scholastic philosophers have hesitated to admit that with the use of reason unimpaired, with intellectual perception intact, the will can be anything but sufficiently free. They appeal to St. Thomas: "To whatever extent reason remains free and not subjected to passion, to that extent the movement of the will which remains does not tend with necessity toward the object to which passion inclines" (Summa Theologica, I, IIae, qu. 10, a.3).

Apparently, however, scholastic psychologists today would not consider that given the mere cognition of the right and wrong of an act the subsequent choice of the will is necessarily free. Let me offer one or two considerations which incline me to believe that the advertence test, though it may be a criterion of philosophical freedom, is not apodictical as far as grave imputability is concerned.

The first of these considerations is the distinction between conceptual cognition and evaluative cognition, which has its principal application in practical judgments such as the judgments of conscience, and decisions in practical affairs. Conceptual cognition expresses, they tell us, what the object is; evaluative cognition appraises the value the object has. The normal adult, making everyday judgments in practical matters, perceives both in the same act of cognition. But there are cases, more or less pathological, in which, according to the psychologists, conceptual cognition is present without evaluative cognition. If this takes place one could have full conceptual advertence but still might not have sufficient advertence for grave culpability. Since the evaluation referred to may depend on emotional as well as on intellectual factors, this opinion leaves room for emotional interference with full consent even though the abstract or conceptual operation is intact.

In the case of ingrained habits like that of masturbation, this evaluative cognition of the grave sinfulness of an act may be habitually present in this individual, but under the influence of habit and passion (or of the unconscious) the evaluative cognition recedes into the background of consciousness. The person knows that this is a gravely sinful act (conceptual cognition) and there is actual advertence to that conceptual cognition; however, the impediments to freedom rob that knowledge of its reality and implications (evaluative cognition). Hence, despite sufficient conceptual knowledge that the act is a mortal sin, freedom and imputability should be measured not in proportion to that knowledge but rather in proportion to the evaluative knowledge which has been greatly disturbed or totally, though temporarily, suppressed.

Another tentative consideration is based on an analogy between the dependence of the intellect on the phantasm and the dependence of the will on the emotions. In scholastic psychology continual stress is laid on the extrinsic dependence of the intellect on the phantasm, or imagination. It is emphasized that a disturbance of the phantasm can result in a disturbance of reason—even a complete disturbance. The authors are at great pains to account for and theorize about the mysterious process by which the phantasm exercises its causality on the intellect, bridging the gap between the material and the spiritual.

When the spiritual will, following upon the deliberation of the intellect, elicits an act which is philosophically free, may there not be an analogous dependence on the emotions as far as its psychological freedom is concerned? In other words may not the internal act of choice itself depend to some extent, that is, for its psychological freedom, on healthy emotional functioning, just as the intellect depends on the healthy functioning of the phantasm? The result would be that passion, emotion, and concupiscence could have their effect on the will more directly, and not merely through the operations of the intellect. The mystery would not be greater in the case of emotion acting on will than in the case of phantasm acting on intellect. The emotions and the will are both rooted in the same fundamental principle of operation *radicantur in eadem anima*. Perhaps this or some other philosophical principle could be used in an attempt to solve the mystery. But whatever the explanation, there seems to be no insuperable philosophical objection to making the attempt.

Furthermore, when the spiritual will, enlightened by the deliberation of the intellect, makes its choice and commands an external act of the body, is there not still an analogous dependence of the free will on the emotions, on the sense appetites and instincts? Is there not here, also, a bridge to be crossed, from the spiritual act of the will to the material acts of bodily execution? Is there any philosophical objection to the assertion that emotional pathology can block that crossing, even though the intellectual operation of deliberation remains essentially unimpaired?

In this view emotional disturbance could destroy freedom not

only by blinding the intellect beforehand and preventing deliberation, but also during and after the act of the will, in the sense that
it could diminish psychological freedom or even effectively block
the execution of the free will's commands, thus depriving the individual of the power of disposing of his activities.

The second question: "Could you have resisted the temptation?"
has to do with sufficient consent of the will, and is another way of
asking whether the person acted from a so-called "irresistible impulse."

The phrase "irresistible impulse" is particularly unfortunate for
the purposes of the moralist. Apart from the confusing connotations
of criminal court usage, the word "impulse" means primarily a
spontaneous movement of passion such as occurs in a sudden erup-
tion of intense anger, or a sexual outburst, also sudden and overpowering. In these impulses there is no question of deliberation, or
at least no question of the kind of deliberation required for grave
guilt; and so there is no great problem to be solved. The case we
wish to explore is concerned rather with a continuing fascination,
or attraction, or temptation, which may almost obsess the mind, but
which does not usually exclude all advertence to the malice of the
act. The word urge describes it more accurately than the word
impulse.

As for the word "irresistible," that is misleading, too, as regards our purpose. For an urge may be resistible as far as philosophical freedom is concerned, and yet be so inhibitory of psychological freedom that the person's acts are no longer gravely imputable
to him.

The moralist's chief concern is not to find out whether a persistent
urge was irresistible or not in the absolute sense, which precludes a
human act entirely, but to find out whether it was so intense that
even though philosophical liberty was not destroyed the possibility
of mortal guilt was. Consequently the word "compulsive," though
not entirely satisfactory, is closer to our real meaning. It does not
have an absolute connotation. Compulsions admit of degrees. They
affect the mind with greater or lesser force and with greater or lesser
frequency. I prefer, therefore, the term "compulsive urge" to the
term "irresistible impulse." But in using it to describe the morbid
attraction, or compelling fascination with which the mind of the
habitual masturbator dwells on the thought of self-abuse for some

time before the act takes place, I do not intend to prejudge the question of his moral responsibility. It merely describes an event in which his resistance *de facto* gives way to the "compelling" force of passion.

In order that the will can make a free choice with liberty of indifference, there must be an appearance of good in both alternatives. In this sense there must be present to the mind motives in each direction. On the other hand it is stated that the will is necessitated only when presented with infinite good. This would seem to mean that even with an enormous disparity of motive the will would remain philosophically free. Whether this is true or not, the same thing is not true of the degree of psychological freedom requisite for grave human imputability. Lindworsky remarks, much to the point: "We . . . call the will free if, at least within certain limits of value, it can consciously strive or not strive for a value, or if in view of two equal, or at least not too dissimilar values, it can deliberately choose the one or the other" (Lindworsky, 1929, p. 70). It would seem that in order to have the degree of freedom necessary to commit mortal sin there must not be too great a disparity in the attraction of the values represented to the mind. In the case of monoideistic narrowing of consciousness and of pathological fascination with the object of sense desire, such disparity often exists.

The psychological considerations, then, which I have advanced to keep us from asserting too readily that there is grave subjective guilt in cases of habitual or compulsive masturbation are these: First, that mere conceptual advertence to the grave objective malice of the act is not conclusive evidence that the subsequent act is gravely imputable. The question "Did you realize fully it was a mortal sin?" is not an apodictical criterion of grave guilt. Secondly, the fact that a temptation could have been resisted indicates indeed that the act was a human act, performed with philosophical freedom, but it does not necessarily indicate that there was sufficient psychological freedom for grave imputability.

When a confessor is exploring the conscience of a penitent the two questions just discussed can be very useful. Criticism of these questions is by no means meant to deny that they are frequently useful. But it is important to note that affirmative answers to these questions do not indicate conclusively that mortal sin has taken place, while intelligent negative answers to them can indicate clearly that mortal sin has not taken place.

In making a judgment of grave guilt the confessor will have to rely first of all on the enlightened testimony of the penitent's own conscience. God judges men on the basis of their conscious motives and decisions. It may be that the unconscious is playing a significant role in this penitent's conduct, but the confessor is a poor judge of that. Even psychiatrists will disagree vigorously on the significance of unconscious factors in a given case. Some recent theological authors attribute a great deal of influence to the dynamic unconscious, but others warn us not to conclude too hastily to psychoanalytical explanations, because hidden insincerities, habits, and other psychological factors of the conscious mind may be to blame. At any rate the confessor must rely principally on the conscious data supplied by the penitent himself. But I added the phrase "the testimony of the *enlightened* conscience" of the penitent, because so many penitents are ignorant or confused and are poor witnesses to their own inner experience.

There are some further considerations, or criteria, which when present should lead the confessor to judge leniently the question of mortal guilt in individual cases. When several of them are present together there is all the more reason for asserting that there is no grave culpability.

(1) The first of these is a history of mental or emotional illness, nervous breakdowns, etc. With penitents who have been, and still more who are presently under psychiatric or neurological care there is often a strong reason for doubting grave guilt.

(2) The fact that there is a severe habit, that is one of long duration and inveterate frequency, but which the penitent is seriously trying to overcome, is itself an argument for lenient judgment. Some persons are much more prone than others to form enslaving habits, whether physiological or psychological. They are spoken of as addictive personalities. Some quickly develop habituation or addiction to drugs or alcohol or almost anything of a sense-satisfying kind. Some seem to be peculiarly susceptible to the formation of

compulsive, repetitious patterns of behavior. Such habits can be more or less pathological; and it is the psychiatrist who is to judge of pathology. But when these habits do occur there is good reason for asserting that grave guilt is absent.

(3) The intensity of sexual passion when thoroughly aroused can be overpowering. It often precludes not merely grave guilt, but any human act at all during the moments when it is at its height. The scholastic theologians of the Middle Ages disputed as to the reasons which would justify or excuse the marriage act, not because they considered it something evil in itself, but because they took it for granted that man was deprived temporarily of the use of reason during the act. *"Ratio absorbetur in congressu sexuali"* they said. Such a deliberate deprivation of the use of reason required a justifying cause, which they found in the *tria bona* of matrimony. It is not to be thought that in every act of self-abuse passion is so intense; but if a person has resisted and refused consent up to the point where passion is very intense, or orgasm is almost at hand, he should be presumed not to be gravely responsible for what thereupon takes place.

(4) The narrowing of consciousness to one all-absorbing fascinating object of desire can exclude any realistic appraisal of the alternatives to that desire, and thus reduce psychological liberty beyond the point where mortal guilt is possible.

(5) A sudden onslaught of passion that takes one unawares will hardly leave the opportunity for sufficient deliberation and consent.

(6) Senseless, unsatisfying, frequent repetitions of the act of self-abuse within a short time are a sign of pathological impulse and an indication of greatly reduced responsibility.

(7) The indulgence of fantastic or weird ideas during the struggle with temptation, for example: "This is another person, not I, who is doing this," or "The natural law is different for me," or "I am dreaming that I am doing this," etc.,—all these and similar confabulations and irrational defenses show that a person is not himself, and are arguments against grave culpability.

Perhaps most important of all in helping the confessor to make his judgment is a knowledge of the general state of the penitent's soul. If a penitent is making serious efforts to lead a life pleasing to God; if he is sincerely trying to overcome this habit and avoid the individual acts; if he avoids the occasions that are avoidable, frequents the sacraments and is constant in prayer; and especially if on the individual occasions when temptation comes he does not yield except after a long struggle or a hard one—the confessor should be lenient in judging the case.

A confessor or spiritual guide cannot form a prudent judgment about the state of the penitent's soul unless he takes the time and the trouble to do so. If penitents are rushed in and out of the confessional they may receive valid absolution, but the confessor will fail in his office not only as a teacher, father, and physician, but, in these difficult cases, in his essential role of judge. Many of these cases can be dealt with much more effectively by the spiritual counselor outside the confessional. When the confessor or spiritual father has taken the trouble to understand the penitent's case well enough to make a prudent judgment about it, he should then help him to know the true state of his soul, whatever it is.

He should tell him the truth as he sees it. His judgment is a human and imperfect one, but Our Lord has instituted the sacrament of penance in such a way that He wants to make use of our human, fallible judgments in applying the grace of the sacrament to the soul of the sinner. Let the confessor tell the penitent the truth. Not the unexplained truth: "You committed mortal sin," or "You did not commit mortal sin"; but the truth with kindness and tact, the truth with appropriate instruction, advice and encouragement. For no matter what the truth is as to the mortal guilt of the penitent, there is still work to be done: the eradication of the bad habit. Nothing will serve as a better foundation for helping the penitent to understand himself and accomplish this task than the truth about the state of his soul. Only on this basis can the confessor or spiritual father cooperate effectively in his restoration.

Consequently, if the priest is convinced that the penitent has sinned mortally he should tell him so, with kindness and with encouragement for the future; trying to bring him to a better disposition of sincerity and fervor in his Christian life, in accordance with the usual pastoral practice for dealing with sinners.

If he remains doubtful about the grave subjective guilt but believes it is really probable that the penitent has not committed mortal sin, again he should tell him the truth as he sees it; that probably there was not grave sin, and probably there was. Even this will be very encouraging to a penitent who has been sincerely trying. Furthermore, it will keep him trying, when a lapse occurs in the future. Too often these penitents, after failing once, conclude that they have already sinned mortally when this point is actually doubtful. They then give up, say: "What's the use?" and make no effort to avoid further falls before the next confession, thus making the habit all the more ingrained. Telling them the truth as far as it can be discovered will be the best spur to continued resistance against temptation, besides being the best basis for collaboration in eradicating the habit.

Finally, if the confessor or spiritual father is convinced that the penitent has not been guilty of mortal sin he should tell him this also; again with kindness and encouragement, but being careful not to lull the penitent into a false sense of security. He should not allow the penitent to think that because the acts already performed were not gravely guilty that this automatically absolves him from all responsibility for them. It would be worse to allow him to think he has no responsibility for the future. Besides being false (since in the great majority of cases we are speaking about, the acts seem to have been free human acts and therefore at least venially guilty ones), this can be very demoralizing to the penitent. It may leave him with the impression that he is "not right" mentally, or that he is just an irresponsible person. Worst of all it might leave him under the impression that he is the helpless victim of his own passions, with neither the obligation nor the ability to do anything about his habit.

If a person is emotionally sick, it is not bad tactics to tell him so, as long as you tell him at the same time that he can do something about his sickness and that you will help him to do it. It is not bad tactics to tell this type of penitent, so many of whom are confused and overburdened with exaggerated, hopeless feelings of neurotic guilt, that he is not mortally guilty when this is the truth as you see it. It is not bad tactics to explain to him that he is suffering from a more or less pathological obstacle to liberty, if you tell him at the same time that he can get rid of the obstacle and that he should get rid of it and that you will help him to get rid of it.

In other words, with this type of penitent, who is sincerely trying to please God, it is often very helpful to treat his problem, for practical purposes, as a psychological one rather than a moral one.

In this way one may discover the psychological source of the difficulty. At least one may correct the habit even though failing to find the source. By reducing the disproportionate feelings of guilt and tension, and by dealing with the difficulty in the calm objective light of scientific discussion, it is often possible to bring the penitent to a clearer understanding of himself and his problem.

Sometimes there comes to light a hidden fear. The penitent is subconsciously fearful of sex and of this manifestation of sex. He is so afraid it will happen, he becomes convinced it will happen, and it does.

At other times there is discovered a latent insincerity. There are some personalities who get into the habit of masturbation through a sort of interior compromise. On the one hand they want to avoid mortal sin and the unpleasant consequences of having to admit that they committed mortal sin. On the other hand they desire the satisfaction that comes with sex acts, not with a really deliberate desire of the will but at least with bodily desire. In themselves these two things are incompatible, but they are made compatible by a sort of subconscious compromise, as a result of which the act is always committed with enough mental hesitation to enable the person to say: "I am not really acting with full freedom."

When such hidden insincerities are brought to light the problem can be met head on and dealt with straightforwardly. It sometimes yields to this approach. The same thing is also true of other simple factors of psychological experience, which do not require the highly specialized knowledge and technique of the psychiatrist, or the deep probings of the psychoanalyst. But there is needed the help of a spiritual counselor who will take the time and the trouble to understand the individual case, who will have the courage to pass judgment on it, and the patience to keep working with it.

CONCLUSION

All theologians are agreed that for formal grave culpability there is required not only liberty of indifference, which I have referred to as philosophical liberty, but also a certain degree of the liberty from obstacles and pressures which I have referred to as psychological liberty. This is implicit in the common teaching that objectively grave sins become only venially sinful *ob imperfectionem actus* in certain circumstances.

Our problem was to investigate the question: What degree of psychological freedom is required?—and not to put the mark so high as to negate the fundamental moral responsibility of the average man and woman, and not to put the mark so low that the avoidance of grave sin becomes practically impossible for very many persons in very many situations of emotional stress—especially in the familiar case of severe or compulsive habits of masturbation. The problem is obscure and baffling. Frequently we can only admit our ignorance. It would seem, however, that given the traditional conceptions of sufficient deliberation and sufficient consent, and given the psychological knowledge we now have as to emotional and instinctive obstacles to human acts, we are staying well within the bounds of the theological requirements when we conclude that we should judge much more leniently than we have in the past a great many individual cases of human misconduct and frailty. Competent Catholic moral theologians who have written recently on self-abuse agree with this conclusion. "Though man may be more reasonable than the psychiatrists believe, he is less so than the philosophers think." We are still waiting for more profound studies in the philosophy of liberty, the psychology of will and emotion, and the theology of Divine grace.

REFERENCES

Angermair, R. Moral and theological notes on the problem of self-abuse. Printed as an appendix to F. Von Gagern, *The problem of onanism.* Westminster, Md.: Newman, 1955. Pp. 115-119.

Duhamel, J. S. (S.J.), Theological and psychiatric aspects of habitual sin: I, Theological aspects. *Proc. Annu. Conv. Cath. Theol. Soc. Amer.,* 1956, *11*, 130-149.

Fleckenstein, H. The moral and religious guilt of the act of self-abuse. Printed as an appendix to F. Von Gagern, *The problem of onanism.* Westminster, Md.: Newman, 1955. Pp. 129-135.

Flood, P. (O.S.B.) (Ed.), *New problems in medical ethics.* Vol. I. Westminster, Md.: Newman, 1953. An entire issue of Cahiers Laennec (Vol. 10, 1950) was devoted to the series of articles on masturbation which appears in the above collection as Sexual Problems of the Adolescent.

Ford, J. C. (S.J.), & Kelly, G. (S.J.), *Contemporary moral problems.* Vol. I: *Questions in fundamental moral theology.* Westminster, Md.: Newman, 1958.

Hayden, J. (O.S.B.), Theological and psychiatric aspects of habitual sin: II, Psychiatric aspects. *Proc. Annu. Conv. Cath. Theol. Soc. Amer.,* 1956, *11,* 150-163.

Lindworsky, J. (S.J.), *The training of the will.* Milwaukee: Bruce, 1929.

Snoeck, A. (S.J.), Masturbation and grave sin. In P. Flood (O.S.B.) (Ed.), *New problems in medical ethics.* Vol. I. Westminster, Md.: Newman, 1953. Pp. 35-44.

Von Gagern, F. *The problem of onanism.* Westminster, Md.: Newman, 1955.

Sex Education: Role of the Parent

ALEXANDER A. SCHNEIDERS

*Alexander A. Schneiders has been a central
figure in the series of Fordham University Pastoral Psychology Institutes from the beginning.
He served as Chairman of the Institute Committee for the first four Institutes and has been
a contributor in all five. His own undergraduate
degree is from Creighton University in Omaha
and his master's and doctoral degrees are from
Georgetown University. From 1939 to 1944,
Dr. Schneiders was Director of Student Per-
sonnel at Loyola University in Chicago, and
from 1945 to 1953 he was Chairman of the
Department of Psychology at the University of
Detroit. He served as Professor of Psychology
and Director of Psychological Services at Fordham University from 1953 to 1961. He is the
author of numerous journal articles and the following books (among others):* Personal adjustment and mental health *(1955), and* Personality
development and adjustment in adolescence
(1960), and his most recent book The anarchy
of feeling *(1963). At the present time, Dr.
Schneiders is Professor of Psychology in the
School of Education at Boston College.*

Despite the tremendous growth of liberalism and precocity in
matters of sex during the past three or four decades, under the influence of movies, psychoanalysis, feminine emancipation, and a

host of kindred factors, we are still faced with certain basic and troublesome facts regarding sex and sex behavior. There is, first of all, the fact that sexual liberalism has brought an increase rather than a decrease in the magnitude of the sex problem. This means that sex education is more necessary than ever. Secondly, despite the tremendous emphasis on sex education in recent years, there is no concrete evidence that we have made the strides in this area that the massive efforts for adequate sex instruction would lead us to expect. This may mean that, by liberalizing the program of sex education, we have been heading in the wrong direction. Thirdly, all the evidence would seem to indicate that we have made little headway in inducing parents to accept the responsibility for the sex education of their children; nor have we been able to settle in our own minds the decision regarding the role of other agencies than the parents in the business of sex education. All of this means that the problem of sex education is just as acute, and in some respects more acute, than it was several decades ago. These facts constitute some of the issues around which this discussion is organized.

THE SPECIFIC PROBLEM OF THE PARENTS' ROLE IN SEX EDUCATION

While almost everyone is agreed that the primary responsibility for the sex education of children and youth rests with the parents, there are certain lines of evidence that indicate clearly that this is more of a pious assumption than a realistic attitude. Study after study has shown that the vast majority of parents do not accept this responsibility and are quite willing and even anxious to turn the whole business over to someone else. For example, in his study of 2,000 Catholic boys, Fleege found that whereas 54.9 percent reported companions as the source of first information, only 17.4 percent reported the father and 15.4 percent reported the mother as the source of first information on sex. Companions, street experiences, books, magazines, and priests outranked parents as the sources of first information. When the boys were asked to rate the parents' contribution to sex education, 82 percent reported none, 13 percent little, 4 percent fair, and 1 percent used the term adequate (Fleege, 1945, p. 272).

In a recent survey of 1400 senior students in the high schools of Milwaukee, to determine the source and extent of their sex knowledge and the role of the parent in sex instruction, it was found that 58 percent of the 619 boys and 781 girls received sex information outside the home. Common sources of information were street corners, movies, radio, sexy books, and experience. Of the 1400 students, 810 were left to themselves and compelled to find out about sex on their own (O'Brien, 1953, p. 13). As one writer remarks: "If parents don't do their job, we are left in a decidedly awkward position in our protests against transferring responsibility to the schools" (O'Brien, 1953, p. 14). Confirmation of these findings comes from another source in a questionnaire sent to 500 pastors in which the following questions were asked: "Is it your impression that parents give the necessary sex instruction early enough to their children? If not, why not?" In response to the first question, 320 of the 363 who replied answered "No." As one of the pastors observed, "You will render a much needed service if you will do something that will make parents bestir themselves" (O'Brien, 1953, p. 21). In answer to the question why parents do not give necessary instruction, the following reasons were assigned: 1) parents do not know how to impart such instruction; 2) they do not realize the need for it; 3) they are too shy and timid about explaining such matters to their children; 4) they think the responsibility rests upon the pastor; 5) some parents think that the children receive this information in a general way in the school; 6) too many parents think that the children may be left to themselves to find out about such matters (O'Brien, 1953, p. 21).

Closely related to this problem of parental inadequacy is the attitude of many educators that the business of sex instruction should be turned over to other agencies, particularly the schools. Here again the statistical evidence is both startling and disturbing, especially to those who believe that the parents are primarily responsible for this type of instruction. For example, before a series of lectures on reproduction, sex development, physiology, and conduct were given to junior high school students in a midwestern city, the parents were asked to sign statements approving the attendance of their children at the lecture series. Although a local clergyman protested against letting the children attend, approval was received for 1249 girls out of 1253, and for all but one of 1094 boys (Kirkendall, 1950, pp. 44-45). In 1948 the Gallup poll reported that 57 percent of persons questioned about Kinsey's book, *Sexual Behavior in the Human Male,* favored making such information available and only 11 percent disapproved, the remainder having no opinion or a qualified one (Kirkendall, 1950, p. 45). In an article appearing in *Family Life* for September, 1946, "Parents Demand Sex Education in Schools," it was reported that 97 percent of parents questioned thought that the subject of sex education should be included in the senior high school program, and 75 percent thought it should enter into the elementary school as well. In another poll conducted by the magazine, *Successful Farming,* it was brought out that while Catholics and Protestants think differently on the subject of birth control, they think alike, together with non-Church members, on the problem of sex education. Sex education in the schools was favored by 63 percent of the Catholics, 63 percent of the Protestants, and 64 percent of the non-Church members. Finally, when the magazine, *The Nation's Schools,* polled school authorities concerning their opinion on sex education, it was found that 96 percent of all schoolmen responding favored inclusion of sex instruction in the school program, both in a generalized form and in a specific form for certain age groups (Kirkendall, 1950, pp. 45-47). Small wonder that one author, on the basis of personal experience in the teaching of sex education to children, concludes that: "School, not home, is the place for physiological sex instruction to be given because of the freedom from the emotional block . . ." (Kirkendall, 1950, p. 54).

These data are of tremendous significance to the problem of the parents' role in sex education because they indicate conclusively that a very large number of parents, regardless of religious denomination, are only too willing to abrogate their responsibility in the matter of educating their children in this important area of human behavior. This despite the exhortations of Popes and priests, ministers and educators, that sex instruction belongs in the home and should be a normal part of parental instruction of the children.

While there is some disagreement as to how the parents should handle their responsibility of sex instruction, there is widespread agreement among many different authorities that the home is the proper place for sex instruction. As one writer remarks in this connection:

There is too much passing of the buck. The parents look to the teacher, the teacher to the pastor, and finally all turn in desperation to the 'Y', the club, the 'Big Brother,' the scoutmaster, the biology expert, the juvenile judge,—to anybody and everybody for relief. The problem originated in the home, and it is there that the remedy must be found and applied. And unless we secure the effective and continuous cooperation of the parents, so many of whom have shown themselves to be indifferent and even criminally negligent, church and school, and, a fortiori, any other agency cannot succeed" (O'Brien, 1953, p. 17).

Even the United States Public Health Service which has published material on sex for the help of educators frankly acknowledges that the primary responsibility for sex education devolves upon the parents. Similarly, the National Educational Association urges upon all parents the obvious duty of parental care and instruction in such matters and directs attention to the mistake of leaving such problems exclusively to the school.

The Catholic attitude regarding the parental responsibility is well known, especially since the Popes have taken pains to define the responsibilities of parents where the education of children is concerned. The following is a typical example of such a papal exhortation, taken from Pius XII's allocution of Women of Catholic Action, October 26, 1941:

With the discretion of a mother and a teacher, and thanks to the open-hearted confidence with which you have been able to inspire your children, you will not fail to watch for and discern the moment in which certain unspoken questions have occurred to their minds and are troubling their senses. It will then be your duty to your daughters, the father's duty to your sons, carefully and delicately to unveil the truth as far as it appears necessary to give a prudent, true and Christian answer to those questions, and set their minds at rest. If imparted by the lips of Christian parents, at the proper time, in the proper measure, and with the proper precautions, the revelation of the mysterious and marvelous laws of life will enlighten their minds with far less danger than if they learn them haphazard from some unpleasant shock, from secret conversations, from information received from over-sophisticated companions, or from clandestine reading, the more dangerous and pernicious as secrecy inflames the imagination and troubles the senses. Your words, if they are wise and discreet, will prove a safeguard and a warning in the midst of the temptations and corruption which surround them "because foreseen, an arrow comes more slowly" (Pope Pius XII, 1941, pp. 141-142).

This basic idea has been echoed in many other places. For example, the Catholic Bishops of the United States made the following statement on November 15, 1950:

Fathers and mothers have a natural competence to instruct their children with regard to sex. False modesty should not deter them from doing their duty in this regard. Sex is one of God's endowments. It should not be ignored or treated as something bad. If sex instruction is properly carried on in the homes, a deep reverence will be developed in the child, and he will be spared the shameful inferences which he often makes when he is left to himself to find out about sex (Catholic Bishops of the U.S., 1950, p. 142).

Incidentally, the Bishops protested in the strongest possible terms against the introduction of sex instruction into the schools, arguing that such instruction must go much farther than the simple imparting of information and must be given individually. This attitude of the Bishops, it should be noted, should not be taken to mean that the schools should play no part whatever in sex education. The general viewpoint is that the primary responsibility is that of the parent but that the schools can be used as an important supplementary agent. This point we will leave for further discussion later on.

Despite the unmistakable attitude of the Church on parental responsibility for sex education, the majority of parents are quite willing to ignore the whole matter. When it comes to adequate sex adjustment or the future marital happiness of their children they are quick to abandon their responsibilities. Parents are willing to educate the child for college or for a career; they are eager to do everything in their power to foster the vocational adjustments of their children; they will go to great lengths to promote physical health; but when it comes to the crucial issue of sex adjustment, they seem almost totally incapable of meeting their responsibilities.

This unhappy situation is due to a number of causes as we have already noted. Some parents are deathly afraid of sex, especially in relation to children. Having been conditioned negatively to sex for so long they find it impossible to deal intelligently and objectively with the problems that arise in this area. Like the late George Apley they prefer to think of sex as a three-letter word. Then there are the parents who are ignorant of the content of sex instruction and its methodology. This ignorance makes them timid in working out their responsibility, and they much prefer to settle the issue by the use of literature or referring the children to the parish priest for instruction.

There are many parents who fail utterly to grasp the significance of proper orientation to sex experiences and practices. They wishfully believe that sex adjustment, like the variations in body temperature, will occur naturally in the course of events. They keep telling themselves that as long as Jane and Tommy go to church regularly, pray hard and receive the sacraments, the less they know about sex the better. The only thing right about this attitude is that the kids had better pray hard or something drastic is very likely to happen to them. These parents fail to realize that the various phases of human adjustment are inseparably linked together, and that human happiness in this life requires some adjustment in all areas of human conduct and human relationships. Finally, there are the parents who simply shirk their responsibilities. They are lazy, indolent, and unworthy of the trust that God has given to them. These parents are the most serious offenders and will profit the least from the admonitions of priests or of bishops.

ATTRIBUTES OF ADEQUATE SEX ADJUSTMENT AND EDUCATION

In order to define clearly and specifically the role of parents in sex education, it would be necessary to consider briefly the attributes of good sex adjustment as well as the attributes of good sex education. Here there are a number of factors to be considered. What, exactly, are the parents' responsibilities, and how should they go about working them out? Secondly, there is the factor of sex instruction itself. What is instruction as distinct from information? What knowledge should be imparted, to whom, how, when, by whom, under what circumstances? Thirdly, what are the requisite conditions for adequate sex instruction? How can these conditions be created? What conditions must be avoided if sex education is to achieve its aim?

Perhaps the best way to define parental responsibility in this area is to indicate the attributes of good sex adjustment toward which every parent should direct serious effort. There are several such attributes which can be easily distinguished: 1) An adequate understanding of the nature of sex. This attribute is confirmed by the fact that individuals making wholesome and socially acceptable adjustments to sex are almost always better informed about sex than those who are making poor adjustments. 2) An adequate heterosexual orientation. This rule applies particularly to the adolescent period, but it is an attribute that parents must consider very carefully in working out a program of sex education. An inadequate heterosexual attitude is a sure sign of sexual maladjustment. 3) Adequate concepts regarding marriage and family living. Sex is inextricably bound up with marriage and family life, and the person who approaches adulthood with immature or negatively conditioned attitudes regarding marriage and family living is not sexually well-adjusted. 4) The growth of a system of internal controls. Self-control, based on internal discipline, moral ideals, and religious practices is basic to good sex adjustment and parents should always aim toward the development of internal controls especially where sex behavior is concerned. 5) Integration of sex experiences and practices with moral, social, and religious attitudes and ideals. This sort of thing is necessary to wholesome sex adjustment and should be a primary aim in developing a program of sex education. It should be noted that these criteria of adequate sex adjustment could be used to govern *any* sex instruction whether undertaken by the parent, the school, the priest, or the counselor.

This brings us to the question of attributes of good sex education. The first important thing that comes to mind is the difference between sex information and sex instruction. The first of these may be nothing more than a passive assimilation of what can be dangerous and even disintegrating information. The well-known "gutter" approach to sex knowledge belongs in this category. Parents especially must be wary of merely informing their children regarding sex, which incidentally can be done in many subtle ways as well as by a method of direct communication. We should remind ourselves here that countless studies indicate that casual information often has damaging and sometimes lasting effects on adjustment and personality.

Sex instruction, on the other hand, is integrative as well as informative. Here the facts necessary to sex adjustment are brought into proper relationship with other facets of adjustment. They are integrated with attitudes, ideals, values, and goals. Sex information should be brought in line with the boy's and girl's attitudes and values regarding the opposite sex, religious practices, the responsibilities of matrimony, the virtues of purity and self-discipline, and the like. It is this approach that converts simple communication into wholesome, personal instruction.

Equally important to a worthwhile program of sex instruction are the conditions that determine its efficacy or failure. One of the most important of these conditions is the context of parent-child relationships and the home atmosphere within which any instruction takes place. In the home where there is emotional warmth, affection, mutual trust, and ego security, there exists a good groundwork for sex instruction. In this type of setting it is easy for father or mother to broach the problems of sex whenever the occasion demands. Mutual trust between parents and between parents and children encourages the children to turn to the parents for information, help, or counsel. It helps also to soften the reluctance of parents to tackle what may be a touchy problem for them. The love of parents for their children, and of children for parents is the surest guarantee that sex instruction will achieve its wholesome aims. As noted in a Pastoral Letter of the German Bishops assembled in conference at Fulda in 1913:

> The first natural and necessary element in this environment, as regards education, is the family, and this precisely because so ordained by the Creator Himself. Accordingly that education, as a rule, will be more effective and lasting which is received in a well-ordered and well-disciplined Christian family; and more efficacious in proportion to the clear and constant good example set, first by the parents, and then by the other members of the household (German Bishops, 1913, p. 124).

There are many factors that tend to undermine this type of setting. Jealousy between parents and children, or between the parents themselves, destroys adequate family relationships. Cross-identification, in which the boy aligns himself with the mother, or the girl with the father, is a situation conducive to bad relationships. Parental rejection, over-protection, perfectionism, immaturity, and a host of other conditions set immense barriers to the task of adequate sex instruction. In this kind of psychological environment it is extremely doubtful whether the aims of such instruction can ever be realized. Until these barriers are mitigated or removed, the task of parental sex instruction remains insuperable.

Another essential condition is a wholesome, objective attitude regarding sex and sex instruction on the part of the parents. There is nothing more damaging to adequate sex instruction than timidity, shame, embarrassment, or hyper-emotionalism regarding matters of sex. The attitude that sex is shameful, disgusting, and immoral, makes it impossible for anyone to deal adequately with the problem.

A third fundamental condition is a wholesome receptive attitude on the part of the children receiving such instructions. To the child or adolescent for whom anything relating to sex is tainted, sex instruction can be traumatic. From the earliest years of childhood the youngster must be gradually prepared for the facts and the developments relating to sex life. Extreme care should be taken to avoid the inculcation of negative, damaging, or restrictive attitudes, attitudes that are more often than not childish reflections of immature taboos in parents and teachers. Where such attitudes already exist every effort must be made to modify them in the direction of more wholesome viewpoints.

Finally, we come to the problem of method. Parental attitudes, parent-child relationships, and other factors referred to, are much more important than *how* such instruction is accomplished; but the relation between these factors and methods should be emphasized. The question is often raised, for example, as to which parent, the father or mother, should give the instruction. Usually the answer is that the father should instruct the boy and the mother the girl, but the problem isn't solved that easily. As some writers have pointed out, sex education of a child is properly the responsibility of both parents. Therefore, unless both share in it the child may get a one-sided, incomplete view of sex, and a feeling that this is a matter about which men and women cannot speak when in the presence of one another. Moreover, because of emotional immaturity, sexual maladjustment, or sex anxiety, the father or the mother may be completely unqualified to discuss the delicate questions of sex with the children. In any given instance it may be that the mother is better qualified to impart all of the sex knowledge to all of the children, and this is a procedure that must be adjusted to existing circumstances.

The information given children should be conveyed in a straightforward, matter-of-fact manner divested of emotion, and free of confusing analogy and circumlocution. This does not mean disturbing frankness, but it does mean that the necessary information is imparted in a manner that the child can understand without either him or the parent getting excited about it. If this process can be aided by literature, mutual discussion, or illustration, without damage to the relationship between parent and child or to the instruction, then such methods can certainly be used. The program of instruction should be an organized one beginning in the very earliest years of childhood where informal means may be used to acquaint the child with certain sex realities and continuing through later childhood and adolescence. Each phase of instruction should be tailored to the emotional needs of the child, to his questions, to his developmental level, and to the demands of the total situation. This tailoring requires considerable skill on the part of the parent, and a thorough knowledge of what the child is prepared to assimilate. In this connection it is always wise to follow the general principle that it is better to be a year early than an hour late. Sex instructions should be gradual and should be pointed toward the goal of imparting such information and forming such attitudes as will be necessary for the young adult to cope with the sexual problems and realities faced with in adult life.

Time does not permit me to reduce all these ideas to a set of principles, but I would like to refer the group to a recent statement of such principles in *Fundamental Marriage Counseling, A Catholic Viewpoint* (Cavanagh, 1957, pp. 133-134). There the author develops 16 basic principles for adequate sex instruction, particularly as they apply to parents. In my opinion these 16 principles are a very adequate statement of rules that parents should follow in developing a program of sex education.

REFERENCES

Catholic Bishops of the United States. The child: citizen of two worlds. Statement of November 15, 1950. *Cath. Mind,* 1951, *49,* 137-144.

Cavanagh, J. R. *Fundamental marriage counseling.* Milwaukee: Bruce, 1957.

Fleege, U. H. *Self-revelation of the adolescent boy.* Milwaukee: Bruce, 1945.

German Bishops, Pastoral Letter, Fulda, 1913. Quoted in J. R. Cavanagh. *Fundamental marriage counseling.* Milwaukee: Bruce, 1957. p. 124.

Kirkendall, L. A. *Sex education as human relations.* New York: Inor, 1950.

Kirsch, F. *Sex education and training in chastity.* New York: Benziger, 1930.

O'Brien, J. A. *Sex-character education.* New York: Macmillan, 1953.

Pope Pius XII. Guiding Christ's little ones. Allocution to Women of Catholic Action, October 26, 1941. Quoted in R. B. Fullam (S.J.) (Ed.) *The popes on youth.* New York: America, 1956. Pp. 141-142.

Sattler, H. V. (C.SS.R.) *Parents, children and the facts of life.* Paterson, N. J.: St. Anthony Guild, 1952.

Sex Education: Role of the School

J. FRANKLIN EWING, S.J.

*Father J. Franklin Ewing, S.J., holds the de-
grees of A.B. (1928), A.M. (1929), and S.T.L.
(1936), from Woodstock College. He received
his Ph.D. in Anthropology from Harvard University in 1947. Father Ewing has been on anthropological expeditions in Lebanon and in the
Philippines, and his anthropological studies
have taken him through much of the Near and
a considerable portion of the Far East. Father
Ewing was appointed to the Fordham University faculty in 1949 as an Assistant Professor
of Anthropology, and was designated Associate
Professor in 1954. In 1953 he founded the Institute of Mission Studies and has continued to
serve as its Director. This Institute is dedicated
to making cultural anthropology and missiology
available to prospective missionaries and to
persons concerned with the work of the mis-
sions. Father Ewing is the author of almost 200
publications in the fields of anthropology, missiology, and allied subjects.*

This paper is specifically oriented toward the role of the high school
in sex education. However, many of the general principles here enunciated may be applicable to earlier or later age groups.

SEX EDUCATION MUST BE KEPT IN PERSPECTIVE

We may start with the anthropological view of "education," that
does not draw such a sharp line of demarcation between formal and

informal education as we may do in our civilization, but considers the whole process one of enculturation, namely, the induction of the new human being into a culture. This process is sometimes called socialization. Of this important and complicated process, sex education is only a small part.

Enculturation involves the complicated task of inserting an immature human being into all the patterns, meanings, and values of a culture. Of this enculturation, a particular, if peculiar part is sex education. In our civilization, more than in some other cultures, sex education is beset with physiological and psychological difficulties. It would seem to the anthropologist that the sex education of the Catholic young person in our civilization presents peculiar difficulties. These difficulties derive from the fact of Catholic doctrine (which, e.g., demands premarital chastity), and from the milieu of *American* Catholic attitudes. This milieu may engender "Puritan" or "Jansenistic" difficulties with regard to sex, which may well be inimical to proper sexual adjustment in married life. Most marriage counselors have encountered the latter category of difficulties.

SPECIFIC CHARACTERISTICS OF SEX EDUCATION

The most vitiating lack in the questionnaire to be discussed below is the absence of a definition of sex education. Therefore we attempt here to give such a definition. Sex education is that portion of the enculturative process which deals with the preparation of the immature person for the ideals and practices of mature sexual life; it deals also with the immediate physical, psychological, and religious problems arising from sexual changes during puberty and adolescence.

Now let me list the specific characteristics of sex education, in the preparation of which I have found the following references particularly helpful (Fullam, 1956; King, 1947; Landis & Landis, 1954):

(a) Sex education should be kept in perspective as part of "enculturation," that is, total preparation for adult life in a culture.

(b) Sex education should be accurate, for the age group, and should frankly meet the natural curiosity of the child. Especially in early youth, the child is interested in immediate mechanics, and not in long discussions of process.

(c) Sex education should begin early. This goes beyond the scope of the present paper, which concerns only sex education in high schools.

However, we should here note that preparation for the training necessary at the time of puberty, should start in the elementary school. Obviously, this training should be adapted to the age group.

(d) Sex education should prepare for puberty particularly; this is a very difficult period for the young one. "Better one year too soon, than one hour too late."

(e) Sex education should be considered a gradual process, and not a matter of a one-shot lecture or conference.

(f) Sex education should always use a frank, scientific vocabulary, as far as possible. In other words, although "family words" may be used, it is better to employ the accurate words (such as "penis"), which will be favorably associated with the various phases of sex in later years.

(g) Sex education should emphasize the supernatural, as well as the natural virtues. It should emphasize the means for preserving chastity (sacraments, prayer, special devotions, awareness of occasions of sin, etc.), and the reasons for such preservation, particularly its integration with the present spiritual life and with the future married life.

Some of these principles overlap in our discussion with the same principles enunciated by other speakers. However, we reiterate them, because the same basic principles hold for parents as for any activity of the school which does the work of the parents.

THE ROLE OF THE SCHOOL

In general, the school should: (a) cooperate with the parents in the matter of sex education; and (b) function as the surrogate of the parents (in the present situation, which we have to face).

Catholic insistence on the fact that the parents are the primary educators in all matters, including sex education, it theoretically sound (Sattler, 1952). It is entirely consonant with anthropological data and principles of the functions of the family. These functions may be more or less numerous, but they usually include the economic, the religious, the psychological, the social, and the moral. The family in all cultures is the primary agent of enculturation, and, as we have pointed out, sex education is only a part of this process.

Specifically with regard to sex education, all observers agree that the parents are not fulfilling their obligations. Thus Fleege (1945) points out that father and mother ranked very low (sixth and seventh after: companions, the street, books, magazines, priests) as sources from which 2000 boys obtained their first information on sex. For later information, father and mother ranked ninth and tenth.

The family has become a very special thing in our civilization. It is reduced to its ultimate components, the father, the mother, the children, and usually a very limited number of other relatives. In general, the family has given over to surrogates in our civilization many of the functions which the extended family takes care of in other cultures. One of the surrogates in our civilization is the school.

In order to get some idea of what our Catholic high schools are actually doing in this regard, a questionnaire was sent out to "the Student Counselor" of Catholic high schools in the dioceses of New York and Brooklyn (now Brooklyn and Rockville Center) in New York State, the dioceses of the State of New Jersey, the Jesuit high schools of the New York Province (State of New York and Northern New Jersey), and one in the New England Province. However, with an emphasis on the Metropolitan area, a fair representation of smaller-community high schools was attempted. Unfortunately, we allowed for no accurate break-down by sex of students; however, the majority of high schools replying were concerned with male students.

A culture-bound element in the addressing of the questionnaire was the fact that it was sent to the Student Counselor. Perhaps some schools do not have such an official. This fact may have affected the percentage of returns. Replies to the 196 questionnaires sent out were returned by 66 institutions; therefore we had 33.7 percent of returns. The percentages listed in the right hand column after the following questions on the questionnaire, refer, naturally, to the 66 institutions replying.

The following were the questions asked and the replies received:

1. At present, what actual practices do you (or others in your institution) use to make sure that your students receive what may be called "necessary" sex information. (One of the defects of this questionnaire —and one always realizes defects of questionnaires after the answers are in!—was the fact that we did not draw attention to sex education as naturally integrated with other instruction.)

	Percent
(a) special course concerning sex	11.9
(b) series of lectures (not scheduled as a course)	30.0
(c) instructions during retreats	81.8

(d) private conferences: scheduled 16.6
        "   "   voluntary 65.1
(e) Confession (where confessor takes the initiative in sex instruction, regardless of presentation of a sexual problem by penitent) 24.2

(This was a "trick" question, and it is interesting that the high percentage represented ignored the fact that moral and pastoral theology dictate a very reserved attitude on the part of the Confessor with regard to initiating sex questions or instructions.)

(f) Others 48.5

In general, certain trends will be noticed. Apart from classroom instruction, which many respondents mention, instructions during retreats plus voluntary conferences seemed most favored; confession with or without some sort of special lectures often were mentioned as auxiliaries. No one of the respondents mentioned integration of sex education with other forms of education, with the exceptions that will be cited afterward.

2. In your opinion, which of the techniques or combination of techniques checked under (1) have been most effective in affording proper sex instruction? Which has been the least effective?

Answers to these two questions were scattered and the best that we can say at the moment is that the most effective method seemed to be a combination of several techniques; the least effective method was unrecognizable in trend.

Perhaps this, too, was a somewhat loaded question. It is our impression that educators are in general less able to give empirical answers than other would-be professionals.

3. If you were given complete freedom and full responsibility for developing a sex education program, what would be the essential elements of your program?

In general, this question was unsatisfactorily answered, in terms of anything like percentages or trends. Affirmative answers usually included answers to question 1. Individuals thought of bringing in medical people or priests for special instruction. However, existing means seemed adequate to most of the respondents.

4. Do you ever officially get together with the parents of your students as a group (not for individual problems) and discuss sex education?

To this question the following answers were recorded:

Yes .... 16.6 percent
No .... 83.3 percent

Although there were several notable exceptions to this overwhelming trend, it seems to us that the school has not faced up to the Catholic position that the parents should be the primary educators in this and other respects. Nevertheless, the general impression that we all have, that parents are inadequate for the purposes of sex instruction, is backed up by several respondents.

In the above connection, one respondent tells us that the guidance department of his school sponsors a series of panels for parents every school year, during which there is discussion of the spiritual guidance of teenage boys. Parents are encouraged to get in touch with the guidance department and are encouraged to send their sons to seek help from confessors or from teachers. However, at the end of the questionnaire, the respondent writes:

> In answering the above questions, I do not mean to imply that schools should assume parental obligations. However, since so many parents shirk their duties, I do believe that we should step in to give what help we can. As far as spiritual direction goes, the average parent is poorly equipped to deal with problems except in a very general way. Here, the school can help.

This was a male respondent.

We have the following from a female respondent.

> The ideal way for sex education is in the home, in my opinion. But since this is neglected in the majority of cases, the high schools should offer a special course. Young people have great problems and I think most of them are due to lack of knowledge. Some are too timid, either in confession or if private instruction is offered, to discuss their problems. But if these problems are discussed and explained in a class lesson followed by a discussion and question, the timid individuals are properly informed.

One respondent indicates a basic set of difficulties in child-parent relationships. This individual indicates that the child's parents are the symbols of authority. Speaking specifically of boys, he indicates that they do not easily confide in those who can punish. Also, they know that parents have a way of bringing things up, to their (the boys') embarrassment. This respondent too, does not think that parents in general do a good job of sex eduction. Specifically with regard to our question, he indicates that the one who talks to the parents should not be the one who talks to the boys. Otherwise, the boys will feel that possibly their secrets are violated; on the other hand, the student counselor can be so easily misquoted. This is a useful insight, we think.

At any rate, it is clear from our percentages that the schools are not actively helping the parents in regard to sex education.

5. Do you recommend the Christopher records to parents, in order to assist them in the proper sex instruction of their children?

To this question there was an even break of answers:

Yes .... 50 percent
No .... 50 percent

Individual reasons were given by a few respondents, indicating in some cases that they did not know about the records, in others that they thought they were useful but not too valuable, and in others that they were of no use particularly. Nevertheless, 50 percent affirmative answers should console the makers of the records!

6. Do you use any other means of instructing parents in their responsibility in the matter of sex instruction?

Yes .... 27.3 percent
No .... 69.7 percent

Here again, the overwhelming trend is not to help the parents out. From the answers, it is impossible for us to decide whether the educators thought that the parents were beyond help, or whether they simply had not been alerted to this problem.

7. What percentage of your students have regular confessors?

We did not really expect an accurate answer to this question. As in the case of several others included in this questionnaire, we had the sly aim of bringing the necessity for certain things to the attention of educators. On the other hand, we received answers which indicated difficulties in the achievement of this ideal of the spiritual life. One of these was the fact that the adolescent would not want to hold up the line, when many confessions were being heard at once!

8. In general, would you say that your students would present their sex problems to a regular confessor, if they had one?

Yes .... 85.0 percent

No .... 15.0 percent

We consider the answers to this question largely a matter of optimism and pious wishing. We make this comment with regard to the positive scientific basis for such an answer. Actually, it seems to us that the application to a confessor by a student is most likely, if the confessor is amenable. This viewpoint ties in with the fact that voluntary interviews are favored by so many, and also with the fact emphasized by many respondents that the problems are individual, and can never be wholly solved on a group basis.

9. Can group instruction by classes or retreat-groups take care of necessary sex education?

To this question, the following answers were given:

Yes .... 47.0 percent

No .... 53.0 percent

However, many of those who answered "yes" emphasized the fact that in addition to such general instruction, attention had to be paid to the individual.

Perhaps we may sum up the manner of imparting sex instruction in the words of one respondent, who replied to our plea for titles of good literature to be recommended to students, with the following:

> Sex instruction is best given when it is wanted. It is best given by one who has the confidence of the boy in all matters of concern to him. It is best given by one who is not in authority over him. It is best given by one who understands boys and theology. Curiosity should be present on the part of the counselee. A counselor who is not shock-proof is not adequate. Giving sex instruction in conference is not a difficult problem for a priest. Wanting it and saying so is a big problem for an adolescent, which he can face up to at some time or other but not every day of his adolescent life. Therefore, one who is interested in boys should not suppose that any given day by the calendar would do.

There are two points which we might mention by way of an appendix. One of them harks back to the statement that sex instruction should be continuous and gradual. In this connection, one wonders whether high school is not already too late. A comment, in connection with question three, strikes us as worthy of specific mention here:

> I think if a thorough and skillfully handled treatment of sex were given in Freshman High School year, only a little more need be given in later years as particular problems arise. In senior year, marriage should be handled.

> In general, we find that the freshmen know a great deal about the facts of life even before they come to school. Most are mixed-up and concerned about them, and their overwhelming problem is purity. Given an opportunity, freshmen will ask about 75 percent of their questions about the facts of life and about purity. In second and third year, their problems tend to repeat themselves. I would definitely stress more and improved sex education in first year.

Another point, worthy of consideration, is the use of the Mooney Problem Check List,* particularly as an introduction to scheduled interviews. In this test, sex problems are kept in perspective, we might almost say "buried," among the many other problems of the young person. One of our respondents tells us that he gives this check list to be filled out by all the boys in his school, and only after this, schedules interviews with the boys. These interviews are scheduled by alphabet, and, as he indicates, give the boy a chance to make up his mind about what problems he wishes to discuss with the counselor. These scheduled interviews by no means rule out voluntary interviews.

GENERAL CONCLUSION

The role of the school in sex education, it seems to us, is twofold:
(a) to supplement and/or
(b) to make up for deficiencies in sex education by the parents.
This role should be undertaken in the light of the total function of the school (intellectual and moral) by means of group and individual influence.

REFERENCES

Fleege, U. H. *Self-revelation of the adolescent boy*. Milwaukee: Bruce, 1945.

* Published by the Psychological Corporation, 304 East 45th Street, New York 17, N. Y.

Fullam, R. B. (S.J.) (Ed.) *The popes on youth.* New York: America, 1956.

King, J. L. (S.J.) *Sex enlightenment and the Catholic.* London: Burns, Oates, & Washbourne, 1947. This book is one of the very best Catholic statements on sex education.

Landis, J. T., & Landis, Mary G. *Building a successful marriage.* (2nd ed.) Englewood Cliffs, N. J.: Prentice-Hall, 1954.

Sattler, H. V. (C.SS.R.) *Parents, children, and the facts of life.* Paterson, N.J.: St. Anthony Guild, 1952. This book, which includes a good bibliography, may be recommended to parents.

Sex Education: Role of the Priest

JOHN J. McCARTHY, S.J.

Father John J. McCarthy, S.J., is Assistant Professor in the Department of Casework and Philosophy of Fordham University's School of Social Service. After completing his graduate studies as a psychiatric case worker at Boston College, Father McCarthy continued his studies for five years at New York's Catholic Charities Guidance Institute, an out-patient psychiatric clinic for children and adolescents. He is consultant to several agencies working with the Puerto Rican adolescent, including the Reiss Foundation in its leadership programs. He also serves as student advisor on the Fordham campus. A member of the Academy of Certified Social Workers, Father McCarthy has served several times on the Committee which has been responsible for the planning and structuring of Fordham's Institutes in Pastoral Psychology.

In considering the role of the priest in sex education a distinction may be made between his function as confessor, or dispenser of God's mercy in the Tribunal of Judgment, and his role as counselor outside of confession.

As confessor the priest is bound by his office to give the necessary sex education required by penitents for the fulfillment of the sixth and ninth commandments. This is *per se* his duty as priest when he is either asked for information or when he is required to give direction because of the nature of the confessional matter. In the fulfillment of this role the priest is, however, hampered by certain restrictions. One of these is the time limit, especially if the waiting line is long. Another is the limitation set by the question involved, which the priest strives to handle as directly and as prudently as possible. A third restriction comes from the sacredness of the tribunal itself, which necessarily eliminates the pointedness of a medical exposé or any approach which would be offensive and not consonant with the dignity of the sacrament.

Within these restrictions, however, sometimes a priest finds himself lashing out against a penitent either because of weariness or exasperation, or even because of his own feeling of uncertainty and anxiety. By the mere act of ordination the priest is not endowed with insight into the unconscious struggle which goes on within himself, yet sometimes he may almost come to feel that a continual barrage of penitents, confessing sexual difficulties, poses itself as a threat to his own impulses. This threat may be resolved in many ways. But if a polemic against sin or a strong castigation of the penitent is discovered to be a veil for his own inner discomfort, the priest must honestly take stock of the situation and attempt to restrain any such projection.

THE NEUROTIC PENITENT

The time of adolescence is often marked by a neurotic-like type of behavior which is symptomatic of the physiological and psychological upheaval of this period. Some authorities classify such behavior as normal for this time of life. Characterological disturbances are often the reactive echoes of earlier unresolved parent-child conflicts. It is well to understand that the sexual misbehavior of this period might often be a manifest symptom of some kind of deeper disturbance which may or may not be sexual in its genesis. This can be as equally true of the "normal" youngster as of the more severely disturbed. A priest who carefully distinguishes between the sin and the symptom of this period qualifies his direction and judgment in terms of this implied disturbance.

Teenagers in the confessional generally only present the sin-problem because they do not understand the deeper upheavals within themselves, but they react sharply and in a pattern damaging to themselves if their sexual symptoms are not properly understood and handled with some kind of insight. Priests who work with such people

on a professional basis outside the confessional often have to treat
first the terribly mixed-up feelings which these young people bring
with them from the confessional.

The priest is not a psychiatrist but yet needs to develop sufficient
understanding of these personality upheavals. We all bemoan the
priest who handles his penitents in assembly-line fashion. We must
admit that many young people favor this approach because of their
shame and fearfulness, but they can also respond to an attitude of
kindness which seeks to help them understand some of the deeper
dynamics of a bad habit or sinful pattern. They will reach out if you
give them half a chance. Thus the priest, who can transfer into the
confessional some of the principles of client-centered therapy, will
find penitents responding positively to such an approach. This does
not deny the function of the priest as judge, but only stresses the
additional fact that we could well learn to permit the penitent to
verbalize in a sharing way the plan for his rehabilitation or continued
spiritual growth.

THE PRIEST VS. PARENT

In the role of priest as counselor outside the confessional, some
preliminary distinctions must be set up. Sex education in itself is primarily the responsibility of the parent, but often the priest finds that
this responsibility has been transferred to him. This may happen because of the loss of a parent, or because some parents are too threatened consciously or unconsciously to talk about sex. Then too the
parents may be too shy or timid to fulfill this responsibility or simply
fail to appreciate how important it is for the child to learn about such
matters from those whom he loves and trusts. It would be well to
emphasize the necessity of educating parents to their duty in this regard, if indeed we judge in the individual case that the parents can
handle the situation and if the general response from their children
would be a healthy and natural one. The priest then before assuming
the responsibility of sex education should first determine whether the
parent could perform this duty more effectively. If so, it may be
necessary for the priest to educate the parents on the performance of
their obligation.

Opportunities for such parent education are provided in pre-Cana
and Cana conferences, in parent-teacher meetings, in informal study

clubs and the like. You will generally find that people want to do what is right, and this message can filter down eventually to those who "don't see it." Priests and fellow co-workers need to organize, stress and push for such a plan of education. There is a sharp distinction between complaining about a state of affairs and doing something about it. Before we complain about the lack of a sense of duty in parents, we should actively investigate what means are at our disposal to initiate a plan for educating parents. Perhaps we can even push the process a step further back and help parents really believe in the functional beauty and inner sacredness of God's reproductive plan and His means for attaining this end.

THE PRIEST AND THE GROUP IN SEX EDUCATION

When, even with the above-mentioned plan, parents refuse, are neglectful, or fulfill their duty only partially, the responsibility devolves on the priest or other good parent substitute. Restricting ourselves to the priest's role, it should be realized that the priest must look upon the task of sex education as his real duty. He must fight the materialistic infiltration of so many damaging lines of sex education presented to youth. If he is silent, his silence can be interpreted as tacit consent to this damaging flood of sexual material, and he can be well assured that if he does not perform his duty, there are those who are all too quick to promote the dissemination of sex information that could be harmful.

There are two general ways in which the priest can perform this duty: either in a group or individually. Group education, with large numbers involved, is generally in the outline style with particular approaches varying with the priest's personality. Not all priests have this gift. The priest understudy might be helped by listening to an experienced priest give such a talk. It will be noted that the experienced person leaves the way open for individual discussion, if the young person so chooses.

In any small group interaction the role of leader is of primary importance. As group leader the priest literally assumes a father role, and thus his presentation should be that of a benevolent, understanding father who sees sex in a positive, healthy light. The undertone of his own feelings can be picked up rather sharply, and so he himself should analyze carefully his true feelings toward marriage, children and love. If, for instance, his basic attitude is felt to be: "Well this is second best and you can save your soul—but it's too bad you can't be a celibate," he has truly blocked the important meaning God Himself has given to the proper use of sex.

If the priest in his discussion is concentrating on the moral and theological values of purity it would be helpful also to be mindful of the physiological and psychological structures involved and their interactions. Sometimes the above-mentioned tendency might take the form of conceiving sexual activity as part of the irrational order and not the rational order. Thus we seem to be treating organs and not the total personality directing these organs to their proper function. We identify sex organs as the locus of sin, when actually sin is in the will.

Group presentation can make use of physiological and medical terms, but it is felt that it is not the function of the priest to make such a presentation a full physiological exposé. Instead we have the essential task of bringing to the world the Christian interpretation of the meaning of sex. Interpreting it in the light of reason and natural law is the first step toward its supernaturalization. It is God's plan for man's total sanctification.

Another dynamic feature of group psychology is that the group can set up its own reaction which filters down in turn to the individual member. Often the group serves to educate itself by both verbal and non-verbal communications. For instance, it can give a sense of assurance to an individual in the group who discovers that all its members have come to learn the same thing as he himself has.

THE PRIEST IN INDIVIDUAL COUNSELING

In the case of individual counseling in a private interview more attention can be given to the educative needs of the individual person. Sometimes the interview may be initiated by the counselor, which should automatically mean a rather slow, general approach with a future interview planned if the young person so desires. If, on the other hand, the appoinment has been requested by the person himself, the counselor can pace himself in terms of the reason given for the interview and the stage of educative development he already finds present. Moving at the pace of the person is an important rule. On what level is the person operating? We should respect this fact and work from here and not from where we think the individual should be. In fact in this entire procedure it is strongly recommended that our priest-counselors receive some direction and instruction in interview dynamics. We must bemoan the fact that as our seminaries are set up we give the students no real help in the techniques of the person-to-person relationship of the interview.

A final point is this: professional competence in the interview process calls for a keen understanding of one's inner self, with its strengths and weaknesses. Therefore, some analysis of this inner self is needed in the training of a seminarian. The short monthly interview with a spiritual counselor, who is not psychologically trained, is not going to fulfill this need. The necessary emphasis on a seminarian's intellectual and spiritual growth can lead to a disregard of those unconscious drives and motives which shape and form so much of the individual's conscious feeling life. In helping a youngster secure the self-awareness and self-judgment his growth problems need, a priest must first be aware of his own inner resources and potential for helpful personal relationship. In this sense then we cannot neglect the personal resources and even the personal needs of the priest, because these enter so intimately into his work as guide and director in giving sex education.